The Poetry Center
of Chicago
www.poetrycenter.org

Hands on Stanzas [sm]

2004-2005 Anthology of Poetry

The Poetry Center
of Chicago
www.poetrycenter.org

37 South Wabash Avenue
Chicago IL 60603
312.899.1229
info@poetrycenter.org

Published by The Poetry Center, Chicago, Illinois, 60603

Copyright © 2005 by The Poetry Center
All Rights Reserved
Printed in the United States of America, June 2005
Manufactured by McNaughton & Gunn, Inc.
ISBN 0-9720751-5-1

Book Cover Design: Guy Villa. **Cover images:** "Lighthouse Sandwich", K.C. Clarke; Aaron Siskind image on the spine used courtesy of the Aaron Siskind Foundation.

Edited by:
Kenneth Clarke, Shirley Stephenson, & Michelle Taransky

The Poetry Center was founded in 1973 by a team of Chicago poets. The organization's charter established three guiding principles: to promote and develop the public's interest in poetry, motivate and encourage poets, and advance the careers of poets by offering them professional opportunities.

The Poetry Center operates two branches of programming: The *Hands on Stanzas* poets in residence program, and a 32 year-old Reading Series of monthly readings by emerging and nationally recognized poets, writers and musicians. The Poetry Center is in residence at The School of The Art Institute of Chicago.

Table of Contents

Introduction

Our world is ever changing. Inventive thinking, effective communication, cultural fluency and what The Poetry Center calls 'creative literacy' are increasingly critical skills for our youth to possess. Those involved with *Hands on Stanzas* see the program's positive results produced in these areas first-hand.

More and more research indicates that programs like *Hands on Stanzas* provide new challenges for successful students and often engage students who don't respond to traditional educational programming. Furthermore, lab-coated scientists who poke around in the human brain with gadgets that measure brainwaves are finding that reading and listening to poems improves the way youngsters and adults learn and remember.

The most important findings, however, remain those contained in this book — the poems and testimony from administrators, teachers and students alike.

Since 2001, more than 10,000 students and their teachers have had a *Hands on Stanzas* poet spend almost an entire school year in their classroom. Nearly 7,000 of these young writers have been published in anthologies like this one, and as many anthologies have been distributed free of charge.

Hands on Stanzas poets-in-residence share great poetry with their students and teach them to write and perform their own poems. In addition to the class work, poets, students and schools organize school-wide special projects, turning every school into a 'poetry center.' The poets themselves have the rare opportunity to work directly in the field of poetry.

As I've observed in years past, the range of insight and talent found in the poems is surprising and delightful. Some of the poems offer a glimpse at the everyday life of Chicago's young people. Some are the stuff of great poetry.

Kenneth Clarke
Executive Director

STUDENT TESTIMONIALS

Poetry
Poetry is running through light,
running through freedom,
running through light.
Tell me how you like your rhythm.
Rhyming, funny, sad or exciting,
you tell me 'cause I like them
all.
—Jasmine P., 8th

"I've learned a lot about poetry in this program. I didn't know there were so many forms of poetry, and I am amazed how you can get ideas from almost anything."
—David M.

"[Poetry] will help me be an actor, a script writer, and a poetry teacher."
—Herman A., 7th

"Poetry might help me write my own magazine."
—Eduardo V., 7th

"When I read poetry to my classmates I feel like I'm explaining my life through rhyming words and rhythm. "
—Alicia H., 7th

"When I grow up my goal is to be a famous poet, but if not I could be like Mrs. O'Toole or Mr. David: a poetry teacher."
—Shatrice M., 6th

"Poetry might help me with my writing and take me to a good college or high school."
—Marie B., 6th

"When I read my poetry to my classmates, I feel proud because I never thought I could write poetry."
—Elaine V., 6th

"Poetry will help me accomplish my long-term goals like being a better writer, reader and learner."
—Monica C., 6th

"Before this class I thought poetry was just rhyming and talking. But now I think poetry is feeling and voice."
–Clemente H., 4th

"If poetry was an animal, it would be a monkey because a monkey can do many different things."
–Stephanie H., 4th

"Poetry has its own sense of style. Poetry is like jazz, it flows."
–Erika S.

"Whenever I read poetry/ I know that everybody/ was made for a reason."
–Robert A.

"Writing poetry is like being a Liberty Bell."
–Gavin R.

"Poetry is a piece of music in my head, with ballerinas dancing."
–Nicole K., 4th

"Poetry is a big red house where the dances are held."
–Ashley S.

"Poetry is something beautiful through which we can learn more words."
–Cindy P.

"Poetry is like the universe, because it will never end."
–Brenda R.

"When I read my poetry to my classmates I feel like I am doing a play in front of millions and millions of people."
–Quamir M., 4th

"Poetry is magic because it's like another world."
–Jessica B., 4th

"When I read my poetry to my classmates I feel like I am on a stage and I'm a famous poet reading to the people that love my poetry."
–Julia M., 4th

"When I read poetry to my classmates, I feel strength."
—Eric W, 11th

"My long-term goal is to be a baseball or basketball player and I could use my celebrity to voice poetry."
—Abdul, 11th

"Poetry is different than other types of writing because you have to be more creative and more passionate with the words."
—Branick G., 11th

"Before this class I thought poetry was something to do in my spare time, but now I think poetry is elegant and classy, and expresses different levels of intellect."
—Ladroyan W., 11th

"When I read my poetry to my classmates I feel like a ray of sunshine or perhaps a butterfly breaking from the cocoon."
—L. W., 11th

"When I read my poetry to my classmates, I feel like I am reading special powers and I am making a difference."
—Levell A., 11th

"Poetry class teaches us to put thought into musical words. . . This class brings the sun up in your mind."
—Apu S.

"I feel that the poetry class that Mario teaches us is great. It helps me with my writing; he is a really amazing poet and teacher."
—Bianca S. C.

"Poetry has helped me with my fluency."
—Fernando G., 5th and James G., 5th

EDUCATOR AND OTHER TESTIMONIALS

"[Since *Hands on Stanzas*] many of my students pay much more attention to detail, which helps with interpretation and comprehension."
—Judith Diaz, Teacher, Casimir Pulaski Fine Arts Academy

"One of my students discovered he's a poet at heart, and has completed a twelve-page book for class."
—Stacy Ambler, Teacher, Cesar E. Chavez Academic Center

"Poetry increases students' vocabulary knowledge which will help on the language arts section of standardized tests."
—Jennifer Kenyon, Teacher, Cesar E. Chavez Academic Center

"*Hands on Stanzas* exposes students to another adult who is sharing his talents."
—Debra Liu, Teacher, Hannah G. Solomon Elementary

"A couple of students who had been unresponsive and reserved have taken to expression and writing in a serious way."
—Tim Bernier, Teacher, Joseph Jungman School

"[With *Hands on Stanzas*] there is more critical thinking; inference skills emerge and increase."
—Ms. Miller, Teacher, Stephen F. Gale Community Academy

"*Hands on Stanzas* has helped my students with their fluency."
—Lorenza Ramirez, Teacher, Joseph Jungman School

"I have a high percentage of students with learning disordered and I notice much more effort and even skill in many of their works with Pam . . . The program has improved my students reading for information, depth, accuracy and detail."
—Nicole Matti, Teacher, The School of Entrepreneurship at South Shore Campus

"I am delighted that so many of our students have the opportunity to explore the world around them through verse. Clearly students participating in The Poetry Center's programs are writing about things that matter in their lives. Poetry encourages a creative response to ordinary challenges…. Thank you for everything that you are doing on behalf of our students."
—Arne Duncan, Chief Executive Officer, Chicago Public Schools

"I'm so happy that our school was chosen to have a Poet in Residence. The students that are in the program have been writing some amazing stuff."
–Heidi O'Toole, Teacher, Cesar A. Chavez Academic Center

"Since *Hands on Stanzas*, my students get excited about sharing their poetry with their classmates . . . and my students check out and look for poetry books in their home and school libraries."
–Emma Garay, Teacher, Galileo Scholastic Academy

"We want to take a moment to share with you the positive effect you have had on our son…. He is so enthusiastic about poetry and he attributes it all to you. He went as far as to say that he 'loves' poetry and that you inspired him. When a child describes his feelings with this much conviction about any subject, you know you have accomplished your goal of awakening his desire to continue to learn…. Please keep up the excellent work you're doing."
–Letter to a *Hands on Stanzas* Poet in Residence from parents of a participating student

"Every time they write or read something through this program they're encountering certain vocabulary. Those words are going to stick. Those words are going to show up on tests. Those words are going to be known forever."
–Gary Moriello, Principal, Gladstone Elementary

"I think our children need to be exposed to whatever they can be. I think if the suburbs can provide their children with a lot of these activities, then why can't we as inner-city schools? There are certain intangibles, as well…. Like when the book is printed with the children seeing their poems in there, and the parents seeing that… This is exciting."
–Alfonso Valtierra, Principal, Galileo Scholastic Academy

Country Cooking
Lauren M.

in the kitchen
frying chicken
baking potatoes
smoking turkey necks

Country Cooking
mmm mmm
Country Cooking

good for the soul
good for the mind
good for the stomach

bad for the heart

Problems
Azrieal W.

go home to it being filled
with problems
too many to count
death dating wrong choices

too much
I feel buried under it all
anymore I might break
crying
does nothing
yelling
does nothing
it just keeps piling on

like a wave constantly crashing
on me
daring me
trying me
wanting to break me

how I wish that someone could free me
of this pain
everlasting pain
when will I be relieved
when will my angel come to my rescue

I will never know until that day comes

Parenting
Apu S.

watch your child grow
like a flower
blooming and blooming
like a bright day

watch them walk out of these doors
one summer's day
afraid that they might
never come back

being a parent they have to trust
that their child will grow
be beautiful
and come home

That's the Vibe
Jashaun T.

feel the beat
flowin' through my veins
right down to my heart
BOOM BOOM BOOM

that's what it is
the rhythm bumpin'
the people jumpin'
that's the vibe
people getting' down
to the nitty gritty
partying
havin' fun
now that's my vibe

Dedication
Maris I.

spring, summer, winter, fall
you're there through it all
I give you the praise

friends come and go but you're the
only one I count on
I give you praise
there for one another

thick and thin
best and worst
tops and bottoms
I give you the praise

sisters and friends together
forever
I give you praise

family we stick together and
we protect one another
love you sister to the very end
I give you praise

My Big Brother
Tai Jene F.

my brother - my friend
thinks he's "the man"
he talks his talk
he walks his walk and does his thing

he protects me from danger
like a man is supposed to do
so don't mess with me
or it will be him you have to go through

we argue and fight
but make up by night
he says I'm the coolest girl
I say he is my world

I love him to death
like a sister should
I'd do anything for him
anything I could

but the funny thing is
he's actually the brother
I always wanted

but we are family
he is my cousin

My Superman Star
Dalesha C.

when I think of you and what you are
I dream of you as my superman star
to come rescue me and save the day
to take me away from all the decay
to fly over buildings and trees
fly through the night
see all that we can see
get away from the world
just you and me
get away from the stress
relax and be free
the day you rescue me is the day within
I'll treasure as long as I live
the day will never end

I See Dead People (Message to Youth)
Lori H.

I like 'em like Poetic Justice
the ones that keep me blushin'

don't matter if I was in a wheelchair or on crutches
bust this one again

or bum rush this
I can flow without no pen
but you can't touch this

I'd run a marathon like Forrest Gump
I'd jump or dump you
in the trashcan like a punk

they're bums that live in a trashcan
looking for little girls
so they can harass them
duckin' so boys won't blast them

runnin', dyin' to live
I've gone past them

oh, they up and died
I outlast them

make them learn
watch them burn in ashes

32

8ᵗʰ Grade
Nana O.

Last year of elementary school
Classes to take 8 periods a day

Study study study
Test test test
ISAT then SPRING BREAK
Spring fling dance
The luncheons next
Then the IOWA test
Then school spirit week
Field trip (maybe out of town)

Then

GRADUATION DAY
We graduate
Then it's all over
We move on to our next assignment

HIGH SCHOOL

LUTHER BURBANK ELEMENTARY
Principal: Dr. Hiram Broyls
Teachers: Ms. Arce, 5th, Mr. LaCerba, 5th, Mr. Stasiak, 5th

Daniel Godston, Poet in Residence

Daniel Godston received his M.F.A. at Mills College and his B.A. at the University of Michigan. In addition to teaching through The Poetry Center's *Hands on Stanzas* program, he teaches composition and literature through Columbia College Chicago's English Department, and creative writing and other art forms through the Office of Community Arts Partnership's arts integration program. Daniel also plays the trumpet in a few local jazz ensembles.

When It Is My Birthday
Sarahi A.

When it is my birthday
the flowers grow. When I get
old the trees get old.

When the trees get old
you get old too.
The trees' leaves fall down
and the leaves get dry.

The flowers get old
when the flowers get yellow.
The leaves fall down, then they
grow new green leaves.

Ode to a Star
Kasandra A.

I have my own star.
When I look it is right there.
That's why it is my favorite star.

What Can I Fold?
Eveline G., Jaime C., and Tania V.

I fold a piece of paper to make an airplane because I want
to throw it, a piece of paper because the teacher told us to,
a pair of pants when I'm getting ready to go to sleep, plastic
when I recycle or want to save it. I fold a letter and a picture
because I want to mail it, a flag when people take it off the flagpole,
my clothes when my mom does the laundry.

I fold a box because I want to put it away, my folder before I put it away.
I fold the newspaper because I want to save it, my fingers around
the pen when I write, my folder after I get to school, a hat
so I can put it in my drawer.
I can fold a napkin so I can blow my nose, a piece of construction paper
so I can make projects with it, a pillow because we want to sleep better.
I can fold glasses so I can put them in their case, a shirt
so I can wear it later, a sweater so I can put it on later when it's cold.

Ode to a Lime or Lemon
Jonathan B.

A green apple
is like a green
lime. A green
lime tastes sour
like a lemon.

A lime grows
on a tree,
which is a
green plant.
A lemon
is yellow like
the sun.

Armando's Dream
Javier D.

A man is going somewhere and he is in his kayak
and there is a big rock and there's a cave
that looks so deep. He is paddling in the kayak
and the kayak is red. This man is alone
and his name is Amando. He is practicing
for the Olympics and he is going to win
a gold medal. He sees some dolphins and whales
and sharks. Then there is a storm and he surfs
into the storm and the storm takes him
to the Olympics and he is the winner.

Ode to Apples
Jonathan E. and Kevin F.

Apples are red, green, and yellow. We use apples
to eat. Some people use apples to play.
There are yellow ones too. Apples are sweet and juicy.
My family loves apples too. My cousin has an apple
tree. I always go to my cousin's house to grab apples.

There're different colors of apples. Apples are red, green,
and yellow. For me red apples taste better than green ones.
My favorite color is red. I wish my house was made of apples.
I wish I could eat apples all day. Apples are like a part of me.
If I don't get one I don't feel happy. Apples are so good.

Ode on Washing the Car
Federico G.

I like to wash the car
because if you're bored
you can waste time so you don't
stay bored all day long.
The other day I asked my dad
if I could wash the car again
because it got bird poo all over it.
I got used to washing the car
and I didn't get tired doing it
because I was so excited
at school that I told
all my friends that I know
how to wash my father's car.

Purple Horse
Iris H.

The purple horse turns into a beautiful flower
and the purple horse looks like a beautiful shirt.
I like my purple horse and all my friends
like my purple horse. It's a good horse
and my horse turns into purple grass
and my horse could turn into everything
purple and my horse likes purple.

The Park
Edwin O.

One must have a mind of summer
to regard the park
and to run and have fun.

Of the May sun, not to think,
to look at the sun
too much because it is too shiny.

For the listener, who listens in the summer,
the birds are singing,
children are yelling in the park.

Green Tiger
Karla R.

old green
green tiger you look
so green in the
green green forest

Shantell
Larisa R.

My name is Shantell. I am ten years old
and I like the color baby blue.
I'm from Chicago
but I love to go to the Wisconsin Dells
and back to Mexico.

My favorite song is Alacranes musical.
I like spaghetti and I like to play outside at night,
and I like to play in the summer too.

Blue Polar Bear
Shantell R.

Blue polar bear blue like the sky
Blue like the clouds blue like
the thunderstorm blue like blueberries

Ode to a Mango
Johann S.

Mangos, with you I get happy
but when I have to go somewhere
I would be unhappy without a mango.

Your taste is so delicious. My brain
goes, "Orange, orange, and orange."
When I take a bite of you I think of Mexico.

Stores have all kinds of mangos and fruit
but I always choose you
because you are the tastiest

thing I have ever tasted.
I'm the luckiest kid in the world
to have you, mangoes.

Ode to a Blueberry
Luis B.

A blueberry is a blue fruit.
I like blueberries because they are very blue
and they are cool. They taste very good to eat.
When you eat one you feel like eating more
and more because they are so good.
A blueberry looks like a grape fruit.

Ode on Walking Pudgy
Cynthia C.

Walking Pudgy is like pulling a ton of bricks!
Or getting dragged across the sidewalk.
Putting the leash on him or pulling him
away from garbage is like fighting a bull.
Telling him to stop is like telling a car
going full speed to come to a complete stop.
He eats everything in sight like a vacuum cleaner.
He runs around with twigs in his mouth.
I try to pull the twigs out but I get bit.

Waterfall
David F.

A waterfall is like a human,
A waterfall is like a girl's hair.

It looks beautiful,
It is bright.

I would compare both
And they are almost the same.

If I Were a Guitar
Hunter F.

If I were a guitar
I would be sold for a lot of money

I would be played by a nice person
I would be a new guitar

I would be played at concerts
They would play the music I like

Ode on Cleaning My Bird Cages
Karina G.

My family's birds are cute and adorable,
but I have to clean the bird cages.
It's a lot of hard work.
First I work on the pericos' cage.
Pericos are birds that like to speak.
I clean their cage and fill up their food dish.
Then I work on the canaries' cage.
Our canaries like to sing all morning.
I clean their cage, and finally
I work on the parakeets' cage.
I clean their cage and give them food.
Our birds are cool and beautiful.
Birds are like our soul.

Ode to Peaches
Yoselin G.

Peaches are round
They are red and brown
Open them and you will
                See their pit.

They taste delicioso
You can eat them anytime
You want. The peach
                Is as big as the world.

Ode to Watermelons
Mayra H.

Ode to watermelons are good. They are tasty and juicy.
A watermelon is red and green. I sometimes have it
on Christmas Eve. I eat it on my birthday,
especially in the summer. Summer is the best time
to eat watermelon. Watermelon is my favorite kind of fruit.
I eat it for breakfast. My family loves watermelon
too but not as much as me. I eat watermelon
with my friends. My friends enjoy eating
watermelon with me when it is my birthday.
Watermelon green is like grass green and watermelon red
is like a heart that is red. I love the colors red and green.
Red is my favorite color. Green is my second favorite color.
Watermelon is like if you're eating grass with a heart of love.
I think watermelon is like a heart and grass.

Winter Song
David J.

I am David the Red
Nosed Reindeer.

I brighten up the
night.

I like to fly through
the snow.

I feel happy when
I fly.

I always know what
to do.

I am always near
Santa.

I am always in the
right spot.

That is all for
my song.

Ode on Mopping the Floor
Adrian M.

The mop that you're mopping
with looks like hair. It's hard to clean
all of the house and we mop the stairs
and the first floor where I live.

My sister and I take turns mopping
the floor so we don't get too tired.
Every time we finish we get
really tired and I go to sleep.

Or sometimes if I'm not too sleepy
after mopping I go into my room
and watch TV or play my Nintendo
Game Cube or my other games.

Ode on Cleaning My Closet
Eliane M.

If I have to clean my closet
I start by throwing out the stuff
I don't use anymore.

I have so many shoes that they
don't fit in my closet. I have
five pairs of shoes that are
bigger than monsters.

I also have one thousand t-shirts
and magic socks. They are one
inch long but they fit me.

They fly around the closet. I have
so many things in my closet and
I need everything in my closet. I just
threw out one pair of socks that is not magic.

Ice Poem
Brisa R.

An ice cube has a
shape like a window.
When an ice cube melts
it looks like a lake.

Ice cream is good
for the summer,
especially on those days
that are very hot.

Ode on Cleaning My Room
Antiara T.

My room is very messy. Sometimes I get carried away
cleaning my room. It is the messiest room in the world.
Sometimes I think it is a messy jungle.
A jungle is probably cleaner than my room.
Sometimes when I go home from a friend's house
I get scared because of that messy room of mine.
I hate cleaning rooms but I love messing them up.
We have so many toys. I bet there are
a thousand toys in our house.

Ode on Washing the Dishes
Denise R.

I love to wash the dishes.
Sometimes I have to put the dishes
in the dishwasher. That's ok
because I can save a lot of time that way.

Some dishes do not fit
into the dishwasher so I have
to wash those by hand.

Then the dishwasher is done
and the dishes come out
hot like the sun.

Cannot
Veronica R.

Monkeys cannot talk, so why
do people say that monkeys are like us?

Cats cannot dance, so how come
there is a dance called the cat dance?

Papers are not like scissors, so how
come you can get a paper cut?

Romeo
Pedro G.

I have a turtle named Pizza,
and I have uncles and 3 sisters.
I live in Merimac. Once I had a
bad dream about the Grim Reaper.
I love my neighborhood,
and I love gummy bears.

Dear Watermelon,
Edgar S.

You are juicy, you are green,
and you taste good when I eat you.
You start off tasting good
and then you taste sugary
and you smell like pineapple.

Ivone
Darian S.

The old people say
that my grandma
          is an excellent
                    person.
My grandma might
                    be 62 but
          she still acts
like if she was young. She likes
                    kids. When it
          is my birthday
                    she gives me
          40 dollars
                    sometimes
                    60 dollars.
My grandma   She's like
helps poor people   a mom for
by giving them   everybody
money.   in the world.
She lives here in Chicago.

When
                    I was a little girl
                              I used to
                    look like your mom
                              and I
                    still do.
                              I used to be
                              the smartest
                              girl in my class.
                    I was always
                    in the honor roll and I
                    got straight A's.

I am not   and now
that smart   that I'm
but I say   kinda old.
that she is.

Poem
LaShirl S.

The deepest spirit comes
forward to the shadow of death
which moves, and the spirit
moves secretly.

44

Snowflakes
Alma T.

I am a snowflake.
I fall from the sky.

I am as white as an angel's wings
and as cool as winter's breeze.

I am as unique as a fingerprint.
There's no one like me in the world.

Ode on Washing Dishes
Romeo T.

The foam rising
is like the beauty of a
sunrise.

Water splashing in the
sink is
like waves splashing on the beach.

Soap creating foam
is like parents
creating life.

Washing a plate
is like removing the word dirty
from your vocabulary.

The Park
Tatyana T.

One must have a mind of summer
To regard the hot air that blows
Through the park and the wind.

In July I feel like the wind is in my hair.
For the listener, who listens in the park,
when I'm in the park I feel happy and warm.

Orange Frog
David G.

An orange frog is a streak of water,
then the ocean.
Relating to the difference between happiness
and the feeling of sorrow
that makes us sad. I can't tell
how the orange frog tips hungrily
toward land, then soaks
up the water of the pond,
of this uncontrollable need
for both water and land.
It is a weird thing, the life of an orange frog,
to be both afraid and happy
on water and land.
For each holds promise of life and death.
It's like the life of a soldier going into battle.

Snow
Jordan T.

Snow is like rain but colder
And when it snows you can play football.

You don't get hurt. You can slide
on it like pro skating.

Ode on Cleaning the Toys Out of My Closet
Antonio P.

Cleaning my closet
is very rough. I
clean up toy wrestlers
that are very tough.
There are dragons that
breathe fire and knights too
that slay the dragons.
I have cars that glow
in the dark and they go
as fast as a shark now.

Folding Poem
Edith V. and Giovanni V.

A bird's wing folds when the bird wants to stop flying,
a piece of paper because you could make a hat.
A card could fold so you could cheat easily,
a map because you can fold it and take it with you.
You could fold a piece of pizza so it could be easier and
tastier to eat, a tortilla so you could make a quesadilla.
A wallet folds so it's easier to fit into your pocket,
and money is folded so it is easier to fit into your wallet.
Suitcases fold so you could carry them wherever you're going.
Travel papers can fold so they can fit into your suitcase.
Homework folds so you can fit it into your book bag,
a book because you could read it, a leaf because you
could fold it, a dress so you could put it in your closet,
a flag so you can store it, glasses so you can put them
in a case, a chair so you can store it. Clothes also fold
so you can fit them into your closet.
Paper can fold into origami so it can entertain you.

Ode on Helping My Sister with Her Homework
Yaritza V.

Helping my sister is like helping myself.
She does homework, I do homework.
The only difference is that mine's harder.

We do math together. We do most
of our homework together. She bothers
me a lot with her homework
even when she knows what to do.

After she's done with her homework
I have to check it to make sure it's right.

Water, Air, and Wind
Deshajon D.

The wind blows through my hair. I can hear the breeze
in my ears saying that the rain is coming. Sometimes
my sister and I ride our bikes through puddles.

When it is foggy I can't see and I run into things.
The sound of a water fountain
makes me think of a kitchen fountain.

Unknown Mysterious Nature
Sergio A., Jose O., and Stephanie P.

When you hear the fury of thunder it says,
"Get an umbrella." You can learn that it feels
like eternity when an earthquake hits because
it is very scary. You can learn that the sky moves
in mysterious ways, it communicates with us
with shapes. By listening to the whistle of the wind
you know it's going to be a windy day indeed.

Nature is a beautiful thing, sounds like soft music.
The trees sound like the wind, the bushes sound
like robots moving. Squirrels sound like birds chirping.
Opossums sound like dogs barking, and pine trees
smell like Pine Sole. I hear willow trees sway
back and forth. Now I know the sound of how
the trees move. I could hear the birds sing
in a tree. Now I know how birds get attention.

I could hear the raindrops fall on the floor, drip, drip, drop,
drip, drop. Now I know when it rains. I could hear
the wind blow on my face. Now I know how it sounds
when the wind blows. I can hear an egg crack
by its nest. Now I know how it sounds when an egg cracks.
I can hear my friends call, "Come and play." Now
I know that my friends want to play with me.

A Whiteboard
Erik B.

A whiteboard in the class is an inspiration to me.
The color brown marker is like the color of my eyes.
The color red marker bursts out into flames.
I need to put them out so I need a blue marker—
blue is the color of water. Water makes me relax,
that's because blue is my favorite color.
Green is also my favorite color because it is the color
of fall green grass. So when I need a whiteboard
I look up in front of the classroom. My favorite
colors are also the colors of the rainbow.
I like the rainbow because it has many colors
and all of those colors can be used on the whiteboard.

Air
Angelica O.B. and Lisette M.

You can never touch the air, but you can feel it.
It is shy because it doesn't show up. Everywhere
you go, it follows you. Every time, everywhere,
it still follows you. You can never run away from it.
It is stuck with you forever. It will never show up.
The air is beautiful, like a nice cold breeze
in the summer. It feels great after running. It feels good
after I play outside. When it moves the leaves in a tree
it looks like the leaves are dancing. Air sounds
like a nice whistle, and it makes everything move.

The Black Eagle
Luis B.

The black eagle can only be seen in the day.
In the dark you can't see it by the bay.
The ocean waves like the black eagle sways.
When you dream you see the dark.
It is like you can feel its touch. When you praise
that's like you're rising from the ground
like the black eagle. The black eagle can be smart.
How do you know it knows art?

Music All the Time
Elena P., Itzayana M., and Jennifer H.

A joy I feel in my head, thinking, crying, singing.
The piano is a soft wind. A piano, all the time,
music all the time. Water blue, sky blue, all the time.
Clouds white, moons white, all the time.
A flute in the water playing beautiful music,
a trumpet loud in a desert all the time,
flowers blowing in the wind all the time.
You could hear new words you never
heard before. See, you could relax with music.
When I hear a piano I think about birds.
Every time I hear a harmonica, I feel like I'm on a train.
When I hear an accordion, I feel like I'm sleeping.
When I hear a flute I feel like I'm flying with the birds.
When I hear a drum I feel like I'm in the jungle
with the monkeys. A piano, all the time, music all the time.
Water blue, sky blue, all the time.

Movement
Jacklyn G.

A finger pushes the buttons on a flute.
An elephant stomping on a street
is it smacking on a drum.
A bird singing is a harp playing.
Piano keys going up and down
are curves on a mountain.
A guitar is a foot stomping.
A butterfly is a triangle.

The Silver Monkey
Marco E.

The silver monkey shines with the streak
lightning of the sun. The people will be amazed
at the silver monkey.

The silver monkey will help the state
like a hometown hero. It will help the earth
creating a better world.

It will turn into a statue
so everyone can see it.

Cards
Oscar E.

One card has shapes, another one has lines.
Cards have different colors like blue,
another card is yellow.
Cards have numbers like 5, others have an A.
One has a Queen, another has a King.
One has Hearts, another has a Diamond.
One is wide, another is thin.

Crazy Weather
Isabel M.

A tornado is like a big whirlwind running
around house by house. A hurricane is like a circle
going around and around. A water vapor is like
an invisible gas. A sundog is bright as a rainbow.
A breeze is calm. Some clouds are like cotton balls.

Pink Grasshopper
Edwin G.

A pink grasshopper sings at night.
                              The beautiful hopper
in the sky, resting in the daytime, singing at night,
                    with his friend, the deep blue sky,
the hopper hopping, the hopper hopping
                         with the blue sky.
A great thing in a small thing the ways
                    he lives and sings.
When he sings he could make people cry
                    and he does that at night.
Sometimes he could sing in the daytime
                    but that's not every day.
He could cry but sometimes
                    could get a little shy.
You can see pink grasshoppers in the park
                    but they're better in your house.
Singing in the day, singing at night,
                    pretty good rhymes.
He hops away, you go home,
                    you think of him in the sky.

The Purple Monkey
Irene G.

The purple monkey was happy all the time.
Everybody liked her. She was very funny,
but she died in 1965. Everybody was sad then.
But before she died she had a baby,
a little pink monkey.
The little pink monkey was cool.
You would like him if you met him.

What I Like About Folding
Lucy L. and Rodolfo M.

I like folding because it's fun. It doesn't take a lot of time.
You can make animals out of paper. It is entertaining,
a fast activity. I like folding my paper so I can make a paper plane.
Things could fold as well as my finger. The wallpaper could fold
as well as a blanket. Paper could fold, and cards, burritos,
and money. I fold a book. I fold jeans, I fold a lot of things.
I could fold napkins as well as quilts. I could fold a t-shirt
as well as a sock. I could fold glasses as well as a tie.
I could fold a notebook as well as wallpaper.

Running with a Silver Puma
Flemas R.

As the silver puma and I
                flash through the jungle
the sun's energy runs through me
                and shines on the silver puma
shedding light even to the
                darkest parts of this jungle.
As the silver puma and I run on
                the trees seem to close in on us.
Getting faster and faster
                I see a dash of light.
Going toward the light
                I start to feel free,
feeling the love and compassion
                of my family for me.
As the silver puma and I reach the light
                we gaze into each other's eyes.
The puma jumps into the air
                with sunrays hitting it,
coming down now, but
                having all the colors of the rainbow on it.

Dream Tower
Rafael P.

I see a tower, and it's about 30 stories tall.
It is in San Francisco, and it's gray,
and people go to that tower to see it,
and the tower was made in the 1900's,
and it is still there in San Francisco.
It is memory and people
take pictures for memories.

Air and Water Poem
Jesus S.

I am going to the store.
It is 2 minutes away from here.
A soft cool breeze is in the air
like someone blowing
into my face. Suddenly smoke
seems to come out of the store.
The smoke is polluted air, vehicles' cause.
I come out of the store and feel mist
on my face. It is me playing in a water park.

The Sun
Nathalia M.

One must have a mind of summer
To regard the long dry winds and whistles
Of the trees in the parks;

Of the July sun,
All the people in the parks and pools,
They're all having fun riding their bikes.

For the listener, who listens in the sun,
And all the pets playing outside with their masters,
Doing things they can't do any other time.

Listen Carefully
Israel T.

If you listen to a waterfall you learn to be calm and peaceful.
Listening to a tiger makes you learn to be tough.
Listening to a monkey makes you learn to be crazy.
If you listen to a bird tweet you learn to feel good inside.
If you listen really carefully to a robin it makes you feel
Like you're the happiest person in the world.

The Aqua Panther
Will T.

The aqua panther is my friend.
He is with me till the end.
His heart is surrounded with lightning,
The lightning that comes with his roar of thunder.
His eyes glow as bright as the sun.
His body flows with electricity when he runs.
You think the aqua panther is just
In my imagination. I tell you he's not.
I know I've seen him,
Whether you think so or not.
Those who think so follow me.
You will be able to see the aqua panther.

The Feelings You Hear
Bobby R.

A maraca is like feeling water on your face.
A trumpet is like the thunder you can hear
when it's raining. When you hear the thunder
it sounds like a beat going on and on. When
you're quiet you can hear a harp playing
as if a person was playing it. Sometimes
when I look through my window
I can see the stuff I hear, and what I hear
is the music of the Dark Blues.
When I go outside I hear the beat of
a piano being played over and over again.

My Dream of a Woman with Something Coming Out of Her Hand
Christine T.

I had a dream of a woman with something
Coming out of her hand, and it was all over
Her body. It looked like a snake. She had black hair
And was wearing a fur coat and sunglasses.
She was stepping on the grass and was by a building.
Her name is Jennifer and then she asked me
To take a picture of her. Then I remembered
She was just somebody that I knew. I used to help her.
She was very kind but my friend didn't like her.

Fire
Brandon T.

A forest fire is like thousands of stars
Being blown up into flames. A campfire
Is like sitting down by a house fire.
Fire crackers sound like thousands
Of guns being fired at the same time.
In the dark a candle flame looks like
A cigarette lighter. A spacecraft being launched
Into space is like a huge forest fire.

THOMAS CHALMERS SPECIALTY SCHOOL
Principal: Patricia Vaughn-Dossieau
Teachers: Ms. Mindeman, 4th, Ms. Williamson, 5th

Marvin Tate, Poet in Residence

A widely published poet and performer, Marvin Tate merges poetry with music. He has performed his work at the Wicker Park Poetry Fest, The Knitting Factory (New York City), Old Town School of Folk Music, Nuyorican Poet's Cafe (New York City), Lollapalooza concert, Iowa University, and others.

Nakisha
Nakisha

hi my name is nakisha
nakisha, nakisha wa sup
i got in trouble in school
nakisha, nakisha wa sup
i won't go back to school
nakisha, nakisha wa sup
mom made me wash the dishes
nakisha, nakisha wa sup

d.m
Dontrell

dontrell don't disappear
without fear or tear
dontrell don't love dip
he just loves the chips
dontrell did things
but he still wears the same ring

Black Is
Stephon J.

black is the color of your skin
your culture everything that you think
it is, it is if you ever take adventures
you will see that black ain't just being
a pimp   BLACKS are in every part
of the world we're like a big chalk board
the history of our ancestors that have past
go to church, you'll see and pray
you'll see

Drugs
Cortney A.

i hate thugs
some do drugs
do you know what love is
it don't help drugs
just give me a big hug
like a rug give me a big
hug

11/10/04
Desjwa R.

i want to live
in africa, china, chile
jamaica, nyc, paris
asia, g-unit, cashville
my momma, the bahamas
antartica, hawaii, brazil
st.louis, maine, utah
miami, los.angeles,
halle barry, kansas
wahington, boston
oregon, new jersey
mississippi, texas
denver I WANT TO LIVE

Carmel
Little J.

i was walking
and saw a pool of carmel
i jumped into the pool of carmel
i jumped into that pool of carmel
with my clothes on i was coming
from school my book bag was full
of yummy carmel my pockets too
i loved it, i'd never seen this house before
it was strange i took a big bite out of it
it was beautiful that carmel was good
i went home i was soaked in that
yummy carmel

The Letter J
Janae B.

january likes to jog
i jump into january
jog, jog, jog with me
you jog the same way
as january but come the end
of january bike riders jog
so get prepared my jogging people
by the time i get back
you better know how to jog
and to get you body heated

57

Lies
Charles W.

i lie
you lie
he lies
the world lies
parents lie
television lies
clothing lies
hair lies
shoes lie
books lie
clocks lie
boxes lie
a fox lies
history lies
WE ALL LIE
who else lies
friends and family
mysteries lie
science lies
doctors lie
people lie to get money
they try to be funny
the police lies
and diseases lie too
WE ALL LIE sometimes

Haiku
Monique C.

people in prison
are losers and are lonely
they can make changes

Light
Malcom W.

see me in the light
i will never ever fight
you cannot find me

Haiku
Shericka

i have a pretty
coat in the hall closet
it talks really slow

Birds
Tyvell A.

the birds are real noisy
we have two birds in classroom
such pretty colors

Haiku
Dwight L.

spring is fun i like
to run all day long i won't
stop even to sleep

Untitled
Joyce K.

jana jacked the kite store
to get a kite jackson avenue
is kind of quite i juggled juice
on Jupiter but the judge made
a judgment that i cannot jump
around her court

Too Much Darkness
Courvoisier E.

one dark lonely night
the darkness is just too much
i need sunlight now

Peaceful
Shamaa M.

look
at the city side
so beautiful on your eyes
good looking the city is so booking
like beautiful queens
look at he city grass so firm and green
this is life feeling the hype
awww cook those blows
but everything seen is peaceful
no police and sin doings
the people everything peaceful

Black Is
Charles W.

black is black
black is back
black is my heritage
black is my stack
black is love
black is the dove
black is my everything
black is above
black brings out colors
black is my brother
black is on my shoulders
black is this poem
black is a song
black is me
black is our crew
black is the beef in my stew
black begins with me
black is rap
black is strong congregation

Nature
Courvoisier E.

i like the big trees
they keep the sunlight off me
now i' am cool

Why?
Malcom W.

why am i sitting here
eating
why do i have four eyes
why am i so mean
why am i in this class
why am i sad
why am i a boy
why do people fight
why am i small
why is this window broken
why do i listen to mr. tate
why are some people famous
why do people make love
why do people have ten fingers

Can
Carnail A.

carnail come to america
and can 150
come and arrange a wedding
in america
carnail can act angry
in spanish can america
and africa come along
coming apart can also come ahead
carnail came to america to call
all the americans

Black
Carnail A.

black is being apart of your community
it is more than the color of your skin
if you are black it is not because some=
one made you that way you were born black
it's a good thing black is how you look and act
it's about more than saying you are black but
proving you are you hold what you hold
do what you are told you are black and proud
it's more than just being with the crowd

Believing
Desjwa R.

i believe
in myself
and my mom
pen rin sin
but i can't taste
the air my future
is old it used to be
a gorilla crying
but dude was dieing
i can fly got shot
by the FBI momma
hit me with a chicken wing
no more burger king

Super Model
Johnny L.

i want to live
in a mansion
next door to a super model
i can go there anytime
and stare at her
and love her
she'll look like a goddess
a trophy wife

Basket Ball
Shamond A.

basket ball is great
basket ball is my best sport
basket ball is truth

Valentine
Janae B.

i got a valentine from timmy
jimmy billie tillie nickey mickey
rickey dickey laura nora cora
flora donnie ronnie lonnie
connie and eva sent one too
but i didn't get one from you

62

Age
Charles W.

we age with the years
we develop as we should
i love the birthdays

Untitled
Leisa, Porche and Paris

big fros and big nose
pants flooding and missing tooth
head big teeth are too

Who Will Win
Anquimette H.

what goes down
in your hood
am i misunderstood
about what goes down
have a little fun
play a game
when i come around
show off what comes around
goes around now do your thang
play a little song
have some fun
you're the victorious one

My Poem
Laquita W.

my next door neighbor
went outside to get some
air she sat on a chair
she wore green and was very mean
she got cable it sat on a table
she is sometimes funny
and have lot's of money
she lives on the one hundredth floor
with a gun she shot her son
and started to run

My Blues
Bianca M.

my mom
gave away my cats
i wish i had
them back
there name
precious and figiro
i was their hero
i loved how they munched
on their food
they were always there for me
when i was sad
but now i' am mad
sad mad sad mad
singing the blues
under my breath
while on the couch weeping

Tree
Jakymia J.

tree
tree
you don't see me
i love me
am ontop of every tree
tree
tree do you love me
tree get off of me
let me seeeeeee
tree don't scare me
tree am sorry tree

Chicago Love
Jakymia J.

it don't matter
where i live
i just want to live
it does not matter
where i live i just want
TO LIVE it don't matter
it don't matter it don't matter
it don't ...i just want to live

F.W
Felisha W.

felisha walker eats fish
sandwiches and oranges
felisha walker plays games

Neighbor
Stephon J.

nest door neighbor
told me to get a perm
my next door neighbor hit me
with a comb
he fell off the steps
he the walked quietly
to put on his glasses
my next door neighbor
told me to go to church
sing to the pastor

Earth
Takeyall B.

we stay on the earth
fun to be on planet earth
sometimes it's boring

CESAR E. CHAVEZ ACADEMIC CENTER
Principal: Sandy Trabek
Teachers: Ms. Kenyon, 7th, Ms. Ambler, 6th/7th, Ms. Humphrey, 6th

David Rosenstock, Poet in Residence

David Rosenstock got his B.A. at The New School and is currently working towards his M.F.A. in writing at The School of the Art Institute of Chicago. He was the recipient of the Irwin Shaw award for a novella and the Ottilie Grebanier award for a short play chosen by Mac Wellman. His work has been published in *The Brooklyn Review* and *Dial Magazine.*

David says, "I recently saw a statistic that placed inner city kids above wounded combat veterans when it came to rates of Post-Traumatic Stress Disorder. This grim assessment plays out in a few of the following poems, but rarely does it faze the students. They refuse to let the gangbanging rob them of their voices. I can't thank my partners in this endeavor enough: Ms. O'Toole, Ms. Ambler, Ms. Kenyon, and Ms. Humphrey. Through their efforts, the kids are rewarded. However, the benefits of exposure to poetry at a young age cannot be gauged. It goes beyond preparation for standardized tests. Writing follows you home, sleeps in your bed; it's a guardian angel of sorts. The world can be a cruel place, especially for a kid. What better way to fend off peer pressure, hardship, and disappointment than with a pen? Poetry lets them know they're not alone, and that their words matter."

Never Ending
Shatrice M.

Something like food and someone like God
        is never ending.
For example, a man watching TV about a man
watching TV about that man watching TV.
        And it will never end.
"Oh my lord I think I lost my wedding
        ring," my mom said.
        And do you know what I said, "Keep
looking, it will never end."

What about
        the violence going on
around the world?
        When will it stop? That was
a stupid question
        because it will
never end.

Hard Rock
Denzel T.

I am at a hard rock concert with
people I know. I hear the music
of bass guitars, the strings tuned to
perfection, so loudly deep into my ear.
Fighting, so brutal, so deadly, fists
swinging left and right,
beer bottles crashing
to the floor.

Women dancing to
the music, to the beer and hard liquor.
The pleasant smell of food, enchiladas,
hot dogs, nachos. Just the smell makes me hungry.
Cigarettes burn my lungs.
I start to cough as smoke fills the air,
not like a scent from a candle.
I taste the air,
not only do I know that it's not
a sweet candle, now I fear

an intoxicated man following my footsteps
to my doorstep.

The Hammer is Hammering
Ignacio R.

The hammer is hammering
its way to the construction site
where they will use him
until he breaks apart. But
the hammer went
bad and left for
Neverland. He found Michael Jackson. The hammer killed
Michael and saved the kids. But the kids said, what have you done
to my daddy.

Be Prepared to Receive Something Special
Marie B.

My cat is special to me.
He loves to play in plastic bags.

Sometimes he bites my hands.
Each time he jumps onto a table, I point
to the floor and he gets off. He only goes
on the table if there is a bag.

He runs like he just saw a ghost. He
knocks on my bedroom door when he
wants to come in.

He likes to sleep in weird places
like suitcases, dressers and laundry baskets.

Cold
Maria G.

In winter people
With their jackets
Freezing in the
Street

When the ice cream
Is melting you put
It on the freezer so it
Could be cold

People with their
lips frozen in the
winter

Pressure
Aaron T.

All the pressure, the pain
people cause by calling others by dirty
nombres, mouths running in the backyard
like lions that haven't been tamed.

In my dreams something comes
from the light into the dark.
Its teeth are fangs.
Its mouth is calor. It is saying palabras.
What is it saying?

In the morning I sit on my camas
thinking about dreams, about
the dirty names and about the dog
that came from the light to
the dark with words on his hot mouth.

Train Coming
Gabriel R.

train coming
car in the highway
conductor blowing the whistle
attack
they are cutting wood
chicken runaway
they are biting nails in a door
airplane and sky
the train is coming
is in the highway
the train is coming   there is a
car coming   the conductor is
blowing the whistle
the train hits the conductor
the attack hits
where the conductor
fell many people are crying
the great conductor has fallen

The Smart Thing
Armando B.

The smart thing is to
Prepare for the unexpected.
What do traitors do?
They betray you.
What do back-
Stabbers do?
They stab you in the back.

What do you do
When a fire begins?
You put it out.

I fight fire with fire.
I get tired after a while.
But remember,
The Universe will tend
To unfold as it should.

Up Above
Martin M.

Glimmering high
up above,
the Aurora Borealis
full of green

Dear, mountain,
cats, bears.

All around,
looking up
at the light.

Souls of living
things playing
with the light.

I wish I could
see it
again.

Folks in the Neighborhood
Krystal N.

Around my block
folks are selling crack, standing on the corner.
I know where they are going to end up next.
All these folks are going to get shot or go to jail.
These folks are black. All these folks do is
sell drugs. They look so innocent, I think
it's a shame to be standing on a corner.
And there's a church right next to where
they're selling drugs.

Drowning
Ashley J.

I walk up to the diving board and look
at the water, which is twelve feet deep. All the kids
and parents are silent because I delete them out. I jump,
I came back up, then I go back down.
I start to panic and sink back down. I see nothing underwater
except for my drowning life. I float to the bottom.

Super School
Mike M. and Luis P.

There's this game called football and
their championship game is called the Super-
bowl   this argument I had with my
parents why do you go to school
even if we go to school we will end
up dying and forgetting everything we learned
Why did they call it the Superbowl?
It's torture for us kids   does it
take place in a bowl or a stadium?
We could be working in our house
instead of going to school   if they
won and they win a golden cereal bowl
Who invented school? How come
quarterbacks get blamed for everything
the guy who invented school must have been
the stupidest person in the world how come
they have to play in the snow
we would have been smarter alone
this is freaking dumb

Untitled
Marverth P. and Mrs. Heidi O'Toole

My dream is to have coffee every hour
OK my family   annoying loud family
if I can have coffee every hour I will be
a frightening scream If I don't
so happy life will be an amazing journey
when I have coffee I feel exciting
when I got out for a walk
all the world is coffee I will
explode
I will go to school
If I don't have coffee, drops
will run out of my nose
then I would spend time with
my family
come back for coffee I miss it
my mom starts to yell
where is my coffee?
I already drank it
my mom can be I don't
know
I make myself a cup of coffee
I don't have any brothers or sisters
I take my coffee to work

Dead Bones
Salvador J.

Bones are bones
they are filled
with pain, tricked
by life

Their life taken
away cruelly and
painfully, they lived
their purpose

Now parts
of them are here
forever
dead bones
always dead bones.

An Old Woman's House
Iliana V.

Living on the edge of an empty street
With the wind howling in the shadows
Trying to escape the darkness
Like a cat escapes a dog.
The doors creaking,
Screaming
To fall off and run away.
Windows
Broken
Of so much fear that they commit suicide
Darkness
Surrounds only that house
Inspecting it
Ready to capture
Anything
Anyone
That dares to confront
The house
Like a guard in a bank
Like a cat and her kittens
Like a canopy and its birds
Guarding
Daring
But dangerous.

Dear Prisoner
Jesus G.

      Scared out on the
      streets.   So scared   and
worried something is going to
happen. To be scared of night
outside.   A space of scare
in the night.   To always
feel somebody following you
or someone watching you. People
shooting out the night and thinking
the shot is coming towards you.
People hide in cars and count to ten,
wanting to strike out at you
and take you away

On the Air
Marverth P.

On the air there is such a flair
and maybe
I'm floating away
and maybe
I feel my strength rising
and maybe
I can feel myself sing
and maybe
You might think I'm lying
but the truth is
I can't take all the noise
it's driving me crazy
and now
I can't see the world
because
I am trapped inside my dreams
then I see that
I am just out of my mind
and then
maybe I'm lying
to everyone I care about
if I just had the chance
to get out of the four walls
that won't let me out
and maybe I am just flying
through the air
where there is such a flair
and I can feel myself floating away
and away...
la la la la la la la la la....

Dear Prisoner
Andres R.

I am a prisoner at school.
They won't let you paint
your hair. That is
pretty wacky. All of a sudden
blue is a gang color.
Mostly all the colors are gang colors.
Can't wear anything but red, white, or gold,
but girls, you can paint your nails.

Deep
Miguel M.

Put your foot in, not too deep,
go further, knee high, go further
until its waist high, go further,
maybe chest high, go further, then
you know it you're gasping for
air

Telephone
Iliana V.

Ringing, ringing, ringing
Seems to be eternal pain
Until someone stops the trembling of the mind
Keeps ringing
Ringing
Ringing
Ringing
Silence
No words
No sounds
Ringing.

A Space in the Sidewalk
Jocelin E.

      I was walking on the dusty road. My mouth felt tired and dry. I
had been chewing on gum for half an hour. It had lost its flavor. My
neighbor walked towards me asking me, "Why are you outside this
early, it's four a.m.?" I told him I couldn't sleep, so I decided to take a
walk. He left and said to be careful; it's not safe for a girl my age to be
outside. I kept walking until I noticed it was five a.m. I got tired and
noticed in the floor there was lots of gum and thought of all this juicy
gum running out of juice. All that gum being collected in the floor and I
had just added the gum I dropped. I wondered if it would still be there in
ten years. I decided to grab it and throw it in the garbage. I noticed that
if I dropped it, it would be somewhere nobody could get it stuck in their
shoes. I would be saving a space on the sidewalk for something more
important.

Mysterious and Alone
Alicia H.

As cold as ice,
Rolling in the snow,
I crept up to see
The mother and her
Kin sleeping in her
Arm in adaptation.
Below a steep hill.
I move close,
The mother watching
My every move,
Waking up, the cub
Runs to me and
Jumps in the snow,
Looks at me with its
Glassy eyes. Laughter,
Playfulness, creatures
Move gracefully, like
A ballerina dancing on
Stage. The mother and her
Cub run into the water,
They sail away on an
Iceberg. I watch them
Until their figures
Disappear. The clouds
Separate and change colors.

Dear Prisoner
Tadeo R.

Dear prisoner of pain
I have watched the sun go
down. I have been hearing the massive
screams of pain. Should I help
should I not
every night I think of your bloody
face bleeding and bleeding
as if it were a faucet on
all the way next day
I heard a gun shot
I saw an officer in critical condition
I saw trails of blood that led to a car
I looked at your cell
Nothing but trails of your
departure.

Dear Prisoner
Ramón G.

on Monday I didn't come because
somebody killed my uncle. And on Monday
I went to see him on his last
day of the world and I was crying.

And it was in the night, it was
like 12:00 and he got out of work
and he went to buy a coffee
and somebody killed him.

The worst thing is
that they never found who killed him
and never is he in jail.

Dancing
Maribel V.

I'm excellent at dancing.
I dance Mexican dances.
I go to many places like Springfield, California.
We dance with thirteen boys.
The dresses are beautiful.
I am an excellent dancer.

Every Day of Boring Life
Miguel M.

Every day of boring life I have to go to sleep
in the coldest room in the house.
My door won't close, and I'm scared the mice
might get in.
Every day I listen to the dripping
kitchen sink rusted
on the end of the faucet.

At night it is the worst walking
outside and somebody throws a gang sign
and everybody is on alert.
I got a new phone installed, and a man
with a deep voice calls looking for "Oscar."
It's always the wrong number.

Do Not Rush Through Life
Sandra C.

Do not rush through life,
Pause and enjoy it.
Don't lie about your age
When you're only fifteen

Stop getting into clubs
With a fake I.D.
When you should really be
in class.

You'll be wishing you
Were here again
Learning…
Instead of lying
Behind a dumpster.

Laundromat
Mike M.

I was in a car as my Mom drove down the street with the trunk loaded with dirty clothes, wondering, "Why do we have so much dirty clothes?" Then the answer hit me like if I was falling off the car and then a little kid hit me in the head with a baseball bat.

When we got there I was told to stay in the kids' section. It smelled like a baby's diaper being cooked in the hot sun.

One Afternoon
Lee G.

One afternoon I came home from school and I smelled coconut, marshmallows, and orange Jello and I said what's that smell she said salad I said original salad she said ya I was you know I don't like that nasty kind of salad what am I a veggie or something or man she makes me so mad.

So on that night I snuck into the kitchen and opened the refrigerator and saw some fluffy white and orange stuff but mostly white stuff I was so mad I screamed Nana what the heck is this she said Hawaiian salad I said what the hell is Hawaiian and she said just taste it I said OK when I taste it I felt so warm I just kept eating and eating and eating like a little pig.

78

The BBQ
Alicia H.

      The BBQ is being started up by my uncle Ivan. Blazing fire in the summer heat. My Mom is in the kitchen tenderizing meat, with a hint of garlic on the steak, hamburgers, and chicken, along with the hot dogs. Grandpa standing by the stove making rice and beans. Auntie Jenny coming into the house, I help her with the boys, while she carries the pop to the refrigerator. Then she starts on the guacamole dip. I step outside for some fresh air, playing with my friends, having a contest to see who can hula hoop the most, as my family brings the food, plates, and utensils. Behind the yellow house, the backyard is filled with grass and daffodils and roses. My uncle Xavier and my sisters, Kianna and Crystal, call me to come and eat. The table is lined with steak, enchiladas, rice, beans, chicken, soup, and hamburgers At last we sit down as a family and give thanks.

Spanish
Iliana V.

Palabras that have no meaning.
Cama, patio, calor
have no signifigance.
To me
persianas covering them
in a dark, gloomy, cold room.
Having no appreciation, except in sueños.

I confuse palabras,
cama, calor, obscured by persianas,
and me, in the patio, with sueños of Spanish not existing.

These words
so confusing
so useless
A river next to a water fountain
A heater in a desert
Spanish next to me

Dear Prisoner
Dimitri B.

River of sadness, there's no one to look up to
anymore. Just the other day, my grandfather
was alive, playing catch with the football.
Bad news, my grandfather is dead.

It's Round
Jesus L.

It's round. I'm walking towards it. My face is
in it, it's kind of wrinkled but it's me.
I'm in the center there like, kind of
like a big rock. There's snow around.
I get farther away. There isn't
snow anymore. It seems like it's
summer so fast it's a puddle.

There is a Train
David T.

There is a train, it's stopping in
Texas, then it's going, it looks
like it's going into a tunnel and it keeps
going. It sounds like it's stopping
and going and stopping and going.
Now it's going.

Now it sounds like a plane.
It's going to take off. It's preparing its
engines. It looks to see if the
tail is off the runway. It's in the air now.
It's been 3 hours since it's been there.
Another plane is taking off. It has
its engines on. It turned its engines
off now on. It sounds like it's going
to take off. It's taking off. It's in
the air. Now they are on air. They are
talking to other people.

Now I hear classical music.

Dear Prisoner
Victor L.

I too. Sad. Parents. Friends.
Be late for school.   I used to have trouble
on the streets, because my hair
was cut too short. I feel angry about me,
because I don't make something
to change. I feel coy about it.
But, a good thing is, I can get
out of this.

Dear Prisoner
Tamara M.

Sadness. Loneliness. Depression,
All because your mother passed away.
Slowness. Death.
I found in you.
The funeral. Cries. Silence.
I was in.
I got out.
You should too.
"I wish she were her!"
"I wish she were here!"
Sadness. Loneliness. Depression.
That is what you should leave.

Basketball
Group Poem, Div. 318

There are tears, and there are years,
The ice is melting.
Basketball.

I love the summertime the best.
The sky is blue.
Today is a rainy day.
Nothing, nothing, doing nothing?
Too loose out.
I care about people.
To run in the dark screaming.
I am sleepy.
Basketball.

They Hunt in Night
Group Poem, Div. 218

They hunt in night
It is hot and when it's hot I get mad

Cars are given tricked out new looks
Your feet stink
One day I was walking at night and it was dark
One day I was walking and I fell
My only friend is my misery

The Cold Bridge
Marco M.

I'm standing here on this cold bridge

It looks like it's never going to end

I keep on walking

It's getting colder

I can't feel my legs

It was this morning when I ate

Somebody help me

Before it's too late

My Neighborhood
Aaron T.

My house sits back
in the hood.
I seen it on the corner where
my mom said
don't stand. I was five, how was
I supposed to understand.
Mom praying to find a new land.
Homeless rooting through dumpsters,
looking for some cans,
just to get a few dollars.

Hoping he would get a little bite of
honey.
People getting shot everywhere
on the fourth of July. That my
neighborhood.

Love Doctor
Isaac M.

My hood is like a romance working
through valleys to my hood people only caring
about the money minute after minute

Dear Prisoner
Ruben C.

A monkey. Not lucky. Locked up
in a cage. Day and night. So bored.
Lives there forever. Taken away
from his family. So confused.
So hairy. So mad and sad.
So overheated by the hotness.

Dear Prisoner
Alex G.

Love disappearance
Looking for you
Can't find you
We miss you
Where are you
Your family is waiting
Have a new baby
Upset
Waiting for you
Your wife is going
To leave you
You got to get out
From that ugly cell
Not for the past three years
The prisoner is released
Now the wife is married
To another guy
I am so sorry prisoner

Dreams
Elaine V.

Sueños, these dreams are so real
I forget that I'm asleep.
I can almost feel the color of the sun.
I'm playing in el patio with my friends.
We are laughing.
And I am feliz.

The Wetlands
Luis C.

I hear the Caribou's hooves
crunching blades of grass.

Cold
Jose T.

Cold key not
warm. Like a cellar
or the cool side of
your pillow.

Like the Arctic
at night. Like
jumping into a pool
in the morning.

Jingle Bells I
Javier M.

jingle bells ring loud
the jingles were stolen
by Superman's wife

Jingle Bells II
the bells were stolen
when Wonderwoman got caught
Superman found her

Jingle Bells III
Superman is fat
Superman Wonderwoman
have one unibrow

Gangs
Kimberly C.

Where I live people always fight, mostly gangs
saying, red sucks and baby blue is true,
killing each other over a street.

The Phone
Erik Q.

The phone is ringing
we hear it but
we don't pick it up
let it keep on ringing

Hello Darkness
Group Poem, Div. 311

So dumb
WHAT
Moving salt in a wound

You never know what's next
You can do anything you want
Never let your guard down for a second
Never give up and keep going
Love is forever
You don't have much time

Today is boring, nothing ever happens
It is an old dog
It all started with a piece of gum
The undertaker, the man you go to before you die
Flowers in the air flying as if nothing's there
Hello
Darkness

CHRISTOPHER COLUMBUS ELEMENTARY SCHOOL
Principal: Joseph Edmonds
Teachers: Mr. Halicki, 6th, Mr. Martin, 4th, Mr. Zuderman, 3rd

Gene Tanta, Poet in Residence

Gene Tanta was born in Timisoara, Romania, in 1974 and arrived with his family in Chicago in 1984. He is a graduate of the Iowa Writers' Workshop and translates contemporary Romanian poetry. His poems, visual works, and translation have been published and exhibited nationally and internationally: *Epoch, Ploughshares, Circumference Magazine, Exquisite Corpse, Watchword, Columbia Poetry Review.* Two collaborative poems with Reginald Shepherd are forthcoming in *Indiana Review.*

About his experience as a Poet in Residence at Christopher Columbus Elementary School, the poet has been heard to proclaim: "When I enter a classroom, I feel like a ballerina inside a bullring vigorously flapping the purple cape of permission before my students' imaginations. They love it; I love it—Olé, Toro! Read the poems, and watch out.

The important foundation of self-confidence, love of knowledge, and inquisitive spirit of the 3rd, 4th, and 6th graders I worked with was laid down by the hard work and capable leadership of their teachers: Harry Zederman, Steve Martin, and Andrew Halicki.

Especially, I'd like to thank Principal Joseph W. Edmonds who always had to offer nothing but support for our poetry-related projects. Thank you all!"

Untitled
Manuel G.

One time I had asthma
and I inhale exhale
and life in the shadow
is kind of black and hard.

Untitled
Iatyana

the year of the snake.
the new years eve.
the lantern is burning low.

The Poem
Dariy K.

The sounds in the woods are strange.
You would be scared and snow is
cold. It feels like sunset but it's
not. Put the snow in a bucket it will
be only water. To drink you have to
lift the glass. Go. You drink from the
bucket.

poems for who
Paula N.

I have a poem for nobody
    to listen too.
I wrote a poem for some
body and on the way I lost
it. I wrote a poem to my
    friend and on the way
I lost it. I wonder
where might of it gone
did I drop it I wonder?
No I couldn't. But I
finally spot it. I found
it, I found it, now I found it.
    I wrote a poem to
    my friend and on
the way I found it.

Untitled
Jessica K.

The poor little girl that died on Lake street.

The poor little girl was lost all alone
crossing Lake street when a drunk
guy was riding a car didn't see
the little girl.

Then squash! He rode over the
little girl. I heard all the noise
from the ambulances and polices.

When they took her there was
blood on the street when I moved people
asked me why is the red stuff on the street
I explained it to them and I never forgot it
by the time I moved.

Untitled
Marzena

Life doesn't last long
it is never exciting so
much once they take you
and a minute later you
have to leave. It's much better
when you stay home.
    I want to read it.

The noise from up my attic.
Sara N.

We have an attic which has a
room. Someone lives there. I did
see her but not her face. She covers
her face with a mask. I heard a
scream a scream for help. She
screams help! So I go up to the
attic and she's dead. Someone went
up there and I think he is still
there.

Untitled
Kayla M.

Today is a happy night.
Tomorrow I am hoping it
is like today.
But if not then I have to
wait next time.

When I am mad or sad
Ulyana D.

I see trees all around me.
My own island I seek
over the ocean I seek a witch
on my ceiling saying I'll make you a chicken
a ghost in my closet say bloody fingers.
My parents said be quiet I'm working here.
I smell blood. And I hear the thunder out
side my window. My pencil is talking to
me he is saying take it easy on
my lead when I was doing my homework.
I become a tree with bugs on me.

It lives in a house a fish
Yeuhenya O.

It was swimming in an aquarium
It had bubbles from his mouth
It was swimming around the aquarium.

Untitled
Matthew

The bomb is
Inside of the airplane
Boom Boom the
airplane

Untitled
Chris M.

   White chickens peck at the rain.
The rain falls upon the white chickens.
So much depends on these chickens.

Untitled
Sabrina

When I am outside in fall
I would rake and rake
I like to rake
and the smell is
wonderful it would smell
like someone was
playing in a pile of leaves

Untitled
Katryna B.

I saw snow I was in
my house I was sitting
by my window. It was
snowing and snowing.

My brother and sister
were playing outside.
I didn't go because
I was sick.

The Picture I Drew
Amanda D.

I drew a picture of me hiding under my
blanket because bombs are dropping from
the air. My mom said just relax and don't
be scared and fight your fears. And I smell
smoke like burnt plastic while my mom
is talking to me and singing to me while cuddling
me. I try not to be scared and I feel like
a shivering piece of ice.

Untitled
Megan D.

(1) you know I'm good and way are
you bad. Maybe you are good sometimes.
(2) but I am bad too sometimes just like you.
and my family is good and bad too.
(3) and I hope you are good by-by

Untitled
Meira B.

Mrs. Green was covered
in fungus. She eats fish from the sky.
She likes to go to the Ocean
because she can see blue. So,
Mrs. Green let water go through
her eyes.

The Three Ways of Looking at a Turkey
Arsen O.

(1)
You go to camp,
in the forest
you hear something
in the bushes.

(2)
You look on it
until it comes out.
It comes out and you catch it.

(3)
It tells you don't eat me,
just look at me and let me go
you look at him forever
and you keep forgetting to let him go.

Untitled
Pavlo D.

My parrot got out of a cage it landed on
my shoulder.
I went outside with him.
And I was walking down the street.
I saw a car it was going fast and it stopped.
Some man got out of the car and said
"give me your parrot." And I said no and he
got in a car and went away. Then I had a good
time.

You Can Be
Lonnie W.

You can be, a tree even a bee
in a tree eating a key, you can be
a key eating a bee in the tree
you can be, a tree in a bee eating a key
you can be, a fly in a sky and die you can be,
a sky with a fly about to die with a tie.
You can be, a boy with a toy or girl with a curl,
you can be, a man with a can or a lady that's shady.

Free My Dog
Jessica B.

Free my dog from sitting in a cage
at night when she sleeps.
Try to free my dog from being old.
For my dog's light we put
on the light from the stove
so if she's thirsty she has a light to see.
My dog tries to get out of her
cage when her leg is bad she
won't get up. That means she has arthritis.
We have to carry her outside.
It is a cold winter,
she has snow on her back,
she is very cold,
she gets ice-salt on her paws
and she cries.

The Black Pencil
Josue B.

    it depends
on lead

glazed with black
    color

beside the clean
    paper.

Why Did You Want This War Iraq?
Tim S.

Why did you want this war Iraq?
You killed tons of people when you started it.
All these people were innocent.
This isn't fair!
We didn't do any harm to you
please tell me why you wanted
this war Iraq?

5 Icy Graves
Christina P.

(1)
Icy, spicy, dead, and read.
People call him handsome Ted.
Ted is dead of me and the ocean sea.
(2)
He hated Christmas Time. Ebenezer Strange.
Lift his spirit up from the dead.
To scare Christmas cheer.
(3)
Jhon Ron hated me for
killing his pet Bean. Hit him
crazy kill the Green bean seed.
Ha Ha Ha
(4)
Black and sack eat
his lack Jack be quick
Giant Ginger Bread Boy.
His name Bimbo crod.
(5)
The last Grave is
a class of 32 people gobbled
up. I'll get you too.

Untitled
Quamir M.

The Dark is a hermit that hides in the woods
it eats deer, rabbits, foxes. Dark drinks worm blood
and hides in the trees. Some people say you
can not see the unknown. People do not say his name.
The Dark really likes blood and poison stuff
he is really dangerous. If you are alone in the
woods watch out!

93

(I am somebody)
Yuliya M.

I am the dark of night.
Or am I the light of day.
I am somebody hear.
And I am here to stay.

I am a cat in the night.
I am a bird in the day.
I am somebody all the
time. All the time.

Outside on My Balcony
Stephanie H.

Outside on my balcony, I try to touch the snow
flakes while they try to touch the floor,
it's really windy snow with ice,
I close my door while I wonder
about how I became in this life,
it smelled like water the smell of nothing,
I shiver as I become to go in my
brain again talking to my moms brain
telling her how much I thank her,
then I jump off the balcony
in to the snow, my cousins catch me as I fall.
Now I'm outside in the snow.

Untitled
Trastasiya T.

Grandpa you go to war.
Don't go you're dying
don't please, come back
by, bye. I'll never see you
again. Why didn't you
listen to me.

Untitled
Martin T.

      [I'm a beat! What are you?]
I'm a beat! What are you?

My Bird and I
Solomiya S.

I was walking in the hot
desert with my bird on
my shoulder. We were struggling
so without water or food for days, months,
maybe even years. We thought we
saw a well. But it was just a cat.
It wanted to eat my precious bird.
But I refused. The cat was owned
by Indians. They took me and my
bird in a cage and no one seen us
again.

Returning From a Walk
Joseph F.

I was outside paused in the winter snow
with my dog because I had just walked
her and was returning home
when all of a sudden a really
huge dog came. We stood paused
as his master returned. While we walked
up the stairs he barked.

Untitled
Brandon V.

Mr. Cup gets drank from
everyday but when the family
goes on vacation he doesn't
get washed for a long time
he gets very, very lonely.

Two Ways of Looking at a Mountain Lion
Jonas M.

(1) Among twenty wet mountains
the only moving thing was the
body of the mountain lion.

(2) I was of two trees
like a house
in which there are three mountain
lions.

Stuck In My Brain
Clemente H.

I have no door
    to my brain
I can not find
    the entrance
    I have turned into
    circles
I'm in a box
with no lid
I'm in a road with
    a brick wall
I'm in a toilet
stuck in pee.

War
Steven T.

War is like a gushing wind
we are in need of a meal
we can't resist

people are hungry
we are able to knife.
People like to kill.

War is like a
bottle dropping.

Untitled
Serhiy N.

    Mr. Dog is a dog that likes to eat the moon,
but sometimes he is scared of heights.
Miss. Cat sometimes joins him. They eat
the moon with a cup of tea.

    In the winter the moon gets cold, so they eat
the sun. It's nice and warm there, they wish
they never have to leave, but they have to go
to bed, because if they don't they will turn
into fishes.

    Mr. Dog told Miss. Cat she is very pretty
like the sunset of the moon.

Four Ways of Catching a Lion
Vitaliy V.

I
Among the trees the lions
run free on the wilderness!
            Or do they run!
II
Put a trap hide in the
bushes. If you get bit don't
cry just take it easy.
III
Hunt them take it easy
with your rifle. Just don't
scare the fur out of
them.
IV
Just run they'll follow
you. Put a leash around
electric one. If it attacks
just zap 'em!

Four Ways to Avoid Weather
Jonathan F.

I
If it rains on
a gloomy day,
jump in between
the drops.

II
The heat
of the intense sun
can be cooled by
icicles.

III
A blizzard is just
a giant air conditioner.

IV
The lightning is an
angel calling you.

Will My Cousin Survive the War
Amber C.

My cousin name was Abraham Cerpa
he was a Marine. And he did a we'll
down he came back home and he has
to go back now. He has
to go to war in 20 days. He got scared
so he tried to escape from war and he
stopped in Kentucky and they got him
for escaping and put him in jail.
And my uncle and my parents
were trying to get him out of there
but it cost a lot of money so he is
still in there but I don't know he will
survive.

HENRY CLAY ELEMENTARY SCHOOL
Principal: Joseph Potocki
**Teachers: Ms. Barrett, 8th, Mr. Berdusis, 7th,
Mr. Laurincik, 7th, Ms. Preston, 8th**

Matthias Regan, Poet in Residence

Matthias Regan writes, teaches, edits and publishes poetry, American history and cheap art in Chicago. He is a Ph.D. candidate in English Literature at the University of Chicago. Recent works include *The Most of It* (1999), *Codebookcode* (2002), *Utility* (2003), and *Gulf War Decade* (forthcoming). "The disorderly, uncivil, farcical, artistic, desublimation of culture constitutes an essential element of radical politics" —Herbert Marcuse

Tension
Alaura D.

      I am fiery.
Just plain hatred.
Wanting to challenge and win.

      Sensing blood encrusted on my boots.
      Scars bandaged with filthy stanches.
      The person who sits, head tilted,
      Unconscious—reeking of bad breath.
      Showing nothing whatsoever.
      Facial features blank.
      As of out of the world.

Anticipation
Michael B.

The anticipation to have
fun. I walk up concrete
stairs, foot after foot

I hear the train the
metal wheels and the metal
rails clashing together
the horn warning it's near—

as we get off the train I fall
my feet hit the
concrete again as I did before
still the anticipation—

Normal
Sara C.

I used to be normal but never mind
And then I was hooked on horses
And now I am dead as day

I used to be bright but now I'm beautiful
And then I was bored so I found a boyfriend
And now I am lost in lust

I used to be dull but now I'm a diva
And then I was sitting but I went shopping
and now I am happy and humble

100

Las Mexicanas
Denise P.

Las mexicanas no
saben hablar inglés

pero cuando un hombre
americano les dice "KISS ME"
ellas dicen "YES"

Painful Heart
Alexandria Q.

The pain of a painful heart
Pitiful pain of a broken
battered, beaten up heart.
A heavy heart in a heap of
broken battered pieces in your chest
Its like having a dagger deep inside
the chambers of your heart
Having the dagger rip all the
rotting veins out of your body

My Purse
Sparkle O.

My pig-colored purse
blonde and smooth as baby's skin
holding accessories that will
never be shown to the world
beautiful roses on the purse

I slipped on it and fell
that's when I had to call
the nurse
Yes, that's my purse

Green Spiders
Casey G.

Spiders, live in my house:
my house is open
          I love your webs
green is my favorite too

I Used to Be
Roberto O.

I used to be crazy and stressed and
I wasn't happy with what you said
and then I was crazy but that
didn't work so now I am
gentle and peaceful
just like
a small
brown weasel

They Said
Brian C.

They said that you said that
I said that I said that my momma
said that your momma said that my
momma said that his momma said
that lil John said yeah what OK
yeah what OK

They Said No
Jonathan B.

They said no, they said yes
they said they grow, they said
they rest the people are
flowing the people are
wrestling the stars do not
come the people have fun.
We are in rows and in flows
of blood that glow the
people are cool the people
are fools.

He Tried
Nick E.

He tried Oh! he tried
to save many lives
he succeeded but
then again he
failed!

Martin Luther King, Jr.
David G.

Every time the Dr wakes
up he thinks Freedom

Every time he goes to sleep he
thinks leave them

Every time he dies we hear
his words

Just a Woman's World
Bianca G.

Dark browns like a mud mountain
Black hair like a crayon
I wonder
am I wanted
so I wait and wait and wait
tall as the sky
kind as a butterfly
sharp and nice looking
as an eagle

The M Poem
Caressa G.

I used to be mean but now I'm mistreated.

And then I was mad so I moved.

And now I am in Mississippi
and married to Mickey with
more and more green.

The green was unseen with
money unknown.

Money up to the ceiling, money
out of the world. Mickey
got mean and he cheated on me.

Now I moved to Missouri
with neither money nor enough
courage to be mean.

They Too, Will Be Ashamed
Kayla M. B.

They too, will be ashamed,
They laugh with a shrinking
voice every time my face appears,
they joke, and tease, and made me cry.
But tomorrow they will do
the same thing, but beside
they'll see how beautiful I
am and be ashamed!

They too, will be ashamed!

Martin Luther King, Jr.
Jameea B.

King, a very brave man.

Craving equal rights.
Making a path for others to follow.
"I have a dream," he would say,
"Blacks and whites and people of all
races will live together in harmony."

After being stabbed, ridiculed, and
threatened, he held his dream close.

After hearing King's powerful words
people of all races made his
dream into a reality.

The Civil War
Agustin C.

Blood and gore in the muddy wet battlefield.
Death comes for everyone in gray and blue uniforms.
Death marches in the dark cold mud with them.

Wounded, people shot in the arms, legs, and head.
Soldier's helmets have holes in them.
Their gray and blue uniforms are torn to pieces.
Their combat boots are worn out on their feet.
The soldiers lost to Death.

104

Nonsense
Maria B.

That is wrong but true. The cows
have spots but then they don't. Today
is Friday but Saturday. I am old but
young. My mind is full but blank.
We stand up for what's right even if
I'm standing alone. I ask everyone
"Today are you how?"

Martin Luther King, Jr.
Jacalyn J.

He stood out from the crowd
He was a beautiful dove
He spoke for his people

A tragic death
A change of life
A guitar with beautiful music

He saved some from hatred
He changed the way of living

He was peace
He was god sent
He was full of love

King Arrested
Michael M.

I could see the cop's four fingers
pressing on his chest.
The cop is looking down at King.
 Martin is wearing dark glasses.
The cop is looking down with hatred.
His hat is down but dark.

He is looking mad
there all in white
ready to fight but
at the end they're getting arrested

There's five police pressing back
but they're pushing forward but
at the end they're getting arrested.

The 54th
Mile M.

Dark skinned men, walking in light brown wet mud.
Getting wet dark dirt on their shoes.
Clanking of old rusted pots and pans.
Resting on their hard foldable beds.

Marching to go to a bloody war.
Marching through tall green trees,
Going up rocky and rugged hills.

Very honorable men in worn-out clothes
with holes in them and broken shoes.
Overlooking the bloody battle.

The War
Alex S.

They sit
They wait
They talk
Nobody can move them
They are on a strike
They demand food but the white waiter won't give it to them.
They sit
They wait
They talk
Nobody can move them
They want to move them but they can't
They sit
They wait
They talk
Nobody can move them
He has won the battle
He has won the war
Now everybody can
      sit
      eat
      talk

The Civil War
Emanuel C.

Northern soldiers
very tired and sick
walking and sleeping in deep muddy snow
every night tossing and turning and trying to find
a comfortable position on the rough ground
not knowing where to attack.

Southern soldiers
ready to fight
tense
clean and healthy
hiding in the green forest

Shot
Jamal J.

As the curtains close bringing darkness to the room
And the audience talks and laughs
not knowing death is in the room—

With a pull of a trigger
and a spark in the barrel
a silver bullet ready to kill
A sweaty palm holds the gun
like a cold glass of water

A silver shark flies through the barrel
It is released into the air
Slicing through the wind like a fish in water

The bullet splinters Lincoln's skull
Like a needle in the arm
Through the bone and into the brain
The bullet has accomplished its mission

Untitled
Ryan W.

1, 2
skip a
few
99, 100

The Monongahela
Juan S.

"A cloud of smoke hangs over it by day.
The glow of scores of furnaces
lights the river-banks by night.
It stands at the junction of two great rivers,
the Monongahela which
flows down today
in a [slow] yellow stream
and the Allegheny
which is blackish."
—*Charles Phillips Trevelyan*
letters from North America and the Pacific, April 15, 1898

What is Strange
Thomas S.

What is strange is this:
the death spoke to my heart
and took its soul. My body
burning up like a warm bath.
I hear music like a puffy cloud.
This is what is strange:
death spoke to the heart
and it took its soul. My body
like a warm bath burning
up like a puffy cloud. the music
floats like a death cloud.
Is this is what strange:
the death took it my heart like spooking a soul
the music burning up like a
warm bath with a puffy pillow.
Death spoke like music running
for hope and death.

The Narrow Path
Callie M.

A narrow path ran over the light-fingered pines
light-fingered, dark-fingered, light-fingered pines
over and under the dark-fingered pines
over and under the light-dark-fingered pines
through the forest of light-fingered pines
the wide path of dark-fingered pines
going in and out of the forest
over under in out, the light-dark-fingered pines

Masked
Yadira V.

The way her lips moved
Her surprised expression toward the man
His feathery glance
Them both in a hallway
Her masked eyes looking at his wide eyes
Him being so light on his feet

Her hand grasping a fan
A crystal ball sitting on the clear floor
The walls dark around them
Their shadows reflecting back at them
The crystal ball cracked in every direction

Dancing Lizards
Armando G.

Everyday when I go outside I have to be careful
Not to run into a cha-cha lizard.
They do not harm you.
They get on your head and dance
The dance of the Cha-cha.

They don't stop
Not until you dance the dance of the cha-cha.
You have to dance just like them.
You put your hands on your head.
Then you jump around in circles
Jump till you pass out.
They go off in search
In search of another victim.

The Armadillo
Michael H.

Two women are taking about clothes
ignoring the giant armadillo on the other's
face. The armadillo starts to claw
out one's eyes—

The armadillo wakes up
clawing into thin air
wondering what happened to the bloody eyes
The armadillo turns to a woman handing him tea
Then the armadillo realizes he was the woman

Man in a Kitchen
Issa H.

It's dark
with no light
outside.
Green cabinets
open
with brown rust.
Oven
Toaster
left untouched.
Towel on a chair
and a brown table
cleared off.
A nasty coffee maker,
black
liquid in a bottle.
I was confused
lying under
the table
half asleep
waiting
for the sun
to come up at
midnight.
Cracked
walls yellow all
over. A
clock is
missing
(I wonder where its gone.)

Trapped
Ryan K.

You can feel the tight ropes binding
　　the cold blue water rising
　　　　and rushing in
　　　　the driftwood is
　　　　crashing against him

The room looks fancy
the clothes are fancy
　　　　trapped
scared out of mind
　　the woman not awake

110

Not knowing what to do
    doomed to a watery death
    no hope no rescue
        all lost
            trapped

        No way out
        No escape
        fear rising
    a death by drowning
        a freezing prison

Straps closing hands and legs together
    can't move
the women unconscious
    the man not praying
            imminent pain

    It is an old age
    fancy but dreary
    a room with drapes
    a door
                    but trapped
    they are rich with tragedy

The Hollow Hallway
Jon K.

The planks creak as my feet fall upon
The flat surroundings covered with gravel
You can't walk without breaking your neck
The fountain is of no use to me
Pipes probably rusted

The railing wooden, ready to break
Although it felt like a rough scaly snake
The webs' silhouettes engraved in my mind
I opened the door and the bright light shined

The Mountains
Alex B.

The cool, foggy town. Almost as if
it were asleep.

Twisted trees and never-ending walls.
Broken fences and tattered window drapes.

But if you look beyond the dusty town

you may see tall mountains that
resemble ice-cream cones.

The tops glossed with smooth sheets
of ice and snow.

Drifting clouds pass by the very
tips of each slope.

It seems as if they are moving
ever so slowly. They almost seem to
bob, as if on a boat in the ocean.

Tiger
Charlene C.

A rustling in the greenery,
creeping through the leaves,
four padded paws
stepping on the soft ground.

A golden eye watching
a striped body
hiding in the shadows on the forest floor
hoping for something to come
through its path.

Waiting,
just waiting.

The Hunt
Casandra M.

Moving swiftly through the thick forest.
       Making sure my foot
       placement is perfect
       in between the trees
       and on the powdery
          snow.

With bow and arrows at hand I wait.
Steady movement trying to keep warm in my
       animal skin clothing.

Then,
out of nowhere a deer pops out of a bunch
of trees and bushes.

Young. The color of coffee with cream.

I put an arrow to
my bow.
Direct hit in the neck. It feel like bricks.
As I watch it dead in the snow I wonder about my death.
Will it be soon?

Hunter
Adan M.

The man looking ready
spots one

on the move passing past
ready to reload

miss one then target hit
down on the ground

blood everywhere on the hunter's
body

cutting skin off the
target washing dried blood
off the hunter

The Engineer
Juan R.

The engineer
tools in hand
the engineer
the engineer face sweating like a great water fall
the engineer heart pumping hard like an animals in a cage trying to
escape
the engineer
tools in hand
the engineer
the engineer's hands trembling
the smell of sweat
the engineer
tools in hand

the engineer
the engineer hard working
the engineer working day and night the heat of the engine melts him the
rusted tools covered in the engineer's   blood like a soldier's sword
covered with blood after battle
the engineer
tools in hand
the engineer

Happy Woman
Brittany W.

A woman in a factory,
happy because she received a raise

The picture on her shirt says she
probably works in a hot sweaty clothes
factory, standing over steamy irons

When she realized that her raise
only consists of two more dollars
an hour her happy grin slowly fades
away, like soap on a car getting
rinsed off with a hose.

Double Dutch
Lizvette M.

Girls and boys gather together
to play with two ropes that reminds
them of jumping when they were little.
They start turning the ropes as though
they were turning a wheel. One person
jumps in and then the next when
one person steps on the rope it is like
they stepped on a bug. It is over and
they start again.

No Fun
Mary C.

A dreary science fair project is certainly no fun.
Eating pancakes when you really want a cinnamon bun, that's no fun.
Green peas are quite lame compared to chocolate.
And going to bed early when you want to play a lot.
Your history homework is pretty bland, too

114

If you put in next to art class and then try to choose.
Swimming in a pool is boring next to a lake
and falling in leaves compared to picking up a rake.

Untitled
Alexis A.

Swat the snooze button
            It's morning again
homework on the mind

Untitled
Daniel C.

            Love is in the air
spring around the corner
            and now here comes rain

Untitled
Bobby G.

A green duck
            falls to the
ground. good dog!

Untitled
Javier G.

            The man sinking
getting smaller on the
            beach sand

            The man lying on
the ground, leaves falling
            around his body.

            The white snow
landing on the man
            as he walks.

Untitled
Jorge G.

        Ships, boats sail away
as he hears the humming sounds
        boats make. The less ships.

Untitled
Jesse H.

        A snail getting fried
by sun, brain wasting away
        nothing to do

Untitled
Matthew H.

        Lady in grader
dug continuously
        and was gone

Untitled
Cruz J.

        Someday there will
be something here;
        if not, than there

Untitled
Cody J.

        Books on five words start.
If lying was truth there's no life
        but five letters explain me.

Untitled
Max R.

        The black sky
not a white star in it
        no one looks up

Untitled
Kristy S.

Spiders are awesome
they're creepy, crawly, scary—
eight legs of fear!

A Day in Scotland
Amanda K.

The streets were dead.
Only a few parked cars in sight.
With a big church at the end.

Buildings lined the streets
With curtains covering the windows

In a house a man lies almost dead
No help in sight, just lying there.

In his kitchen he lay
Waiting for death to take him

Drums in the Deep
Christopher G.

One hundred million angels to the big kettle drum
And the whirlwind is in the thorn tree
The virgins are all trimming their wicks
The hairs on your arm will stand up
The terror in each sip and in each sup
I was walking and I came upon a
pale horse. And it's name was
death and hell followed with him.
They had taken the second hall
and the bridge.

Drums, drums in the deep.
Shadows move in the dark.

La Nieve
Ana M.

La Nieve es muy blanca
es como una estrella que cae
del cielo muy alta del cielo

Spring is Loud Like Music
Orlando C.

the loud, loud spring like loud
music, like loud, loud spring
like loud loud spring, with
music loud, loud like loud
loud spring, with loud, loud
spring with loud, loud music
with loud, loud spring, with
loud loud loud spring, with
spring loud loud like music
loud loud like spring

Henry Clay
Tim G.

Henry Clay is a man
big as two cars stacked up
He wears leather dark as
the night sky.

He is speaking his speech over
the noisy cars loud as
a car alarm. When he
was done he heard clapping
loud like a crowd
at a ball game.

MARY MAPES DODGE ACADEMY
Principal: Jarvis Sanford
Teachers: Ms. Bradford, 3rd, Ms. Brown, 3rd, Ms. Jackson, 3rd

Lisa Hemminger, Poet in Residence

Lisa Hemminger is the author of poetry collections *Complication Compilation* (Loki Graphics, 2002); *Colossus Taught Us (Once) & (Twice),* (Water of Life Press, 2000); and the short fiction work *Delivery* (GAD Publishing, 2000). She is studying for a Master's degree in creative writing at the University of Illinois at Chicago. Hemminger tutors, lectures and teaches poetry. Aiming at a goal of all-inclusive art, Hemminger has produced and hosted vaudevillian open-mic shows in Chicago since 1997. Her poetry and inimitable shows have been featured and reviewed by numerous Chicago-area print publications, websites, and radio programs.

A Change Of Plan
Group poem, Mahnlaye Boayue's fourth grade class

School is a place where children grow to be.
Go to the store jump in the pool I am am am am an angel.
My two eyes are sick. I wink and blink. Fat
red rats of our pharmacy have new doos. Look at your shirt trying to float!
I went to the park with an early start. We have new boots so
eat your crying peas. My friends wanted to
dance with a cute boy Lance, a lime they gave me a nickel. I took brand new
shoes and this clean school is ready.
We move hate because of this school I want to move like school with
dirty knees, me and my friends like bees we all like some payless shoes,
my new fleece and no bees people act like
fools we play all day and we just eat. Come to school to say hey-hey
school is a tool that's fixing my mind with knowledge is my brain
I think. Oh hey school back to school do you hear me dear, let me see you fear my today
Fall is here my heart in cheer I like to yell I hit the bell I like the blues I like to read the mail. I have
a mind that can make me think. I think all the girls in the world like pink. Forest and look at the bugs.
Fall is here hear my cheer make a move I started to talk, brand new shoe singing the blues. I wanted
 to have a dear chair to take another walk at 4 o'clock. My school is clan and so ready.

Poetry: A New Way to Look
Group poem, Mellodie Brown's fifth grade class

I looked out my peephole, saw ten clouds and two big bears coming out of them. I saw white; I saw snow,
the remains of air. I go outside and play in the snow. My tongue feels dry. I eat. Snow begins to melt in
my tummy. Oh well, I hope the clouds come back. I lick snow on my auntie's expensive car. I squished
snow really hard. I had a snowball fight, got hit in the face with a whole bunch of snowballs. I went to my
aunt's house on a wet cold day. The tasty food smells great. The tasty food makes me hungry. We all took
 pictures in front of the butterfly-filled tree. We all feel wonderfully grateful for the graceful bird in the tree
and we write a poem or story about it. Love poems because they are fun and fine. Love funny poems because

they are crazy. Go ahead; hate poems because they are dumb and boring! I hope you love haikus once
around the world, Chicago. I am OK for the day again and again as I find a new friend. I look out my
window, see five clouds one snow. Lions came out of them. The five clouds looked like a cat whose name
was Sue. The moon looks like pretty flowers, like la-la-land. Snow fell on my tongue so I went in the house
and taught. My mom came to me and my sister and said what is all this drama, this hard, white stuff? Snow
was fun to play in but half the time I couldn't. Why, I would like to play in snow angels with my friends. I
eat snow that tastes like grits. I eat snow that's clean, a snowman white as cotton, snow just as it is: a tissue
to cry on. It looks like foggy glow or a big T-shirt. Throw snowballs in connection, in different directions.
Snow comes, snow falls, go outside, and throw your snowballs. Does snow go back into the sky or run to
another forever country? Does snow keep coming or run away from the clouds or run away under my bed?

Spoiled Eggs
Group Poem, Zara Bradford's third grade class

Spoiled eggs at a zoo smell like perfume, turn and make a googly sound Like a fire bell dindindindin. Something smells like purple garbage bbrrrbbbrrrbbbrrr.
The dog Jamie Foxx twisted around his pole; he rolled on his back and fell in a hole,
which was a sewer that stank like his breath. His breath tastes like fire. Now he's climbing up a ladder
out from the sewer. A car asked him "How are you today?" then the car started to be a DJ who went
to the junk food store and bought pop rocks. The wizard of oz came to Dodge and saw a play called Crazy
and the Breath Factory. My friend dusted the factory in it. His Escalade (or was it a Hummer limo?) tastes
like wax and smells like gas. It shoots out bananas when you start it up. At the other store, Candy
said "Take me, take me!" His house smelled like bubbles. A bird tweet tweet smelled like spring and had
eggs that smelled like rotten candy. It was an owl in a cage looking with big eyes for an escape. His eyes
were like a swan's. Woke up went to my uncle's house, his CD sounded like hip-hop I think it was blue or
blues. I wish my desk was made of candy, that I could fly to Georgia to visit relatives, but I got tickled by
a water pistol of the FBI

Team Work
Passyun S. & Terriana W.

Go!!! Go!!! upstairs and clean your room. When you finish you can
watch the moon.
You are a Capricorn now, you can not eat cornbread in your pretty bed.
Tonight is a full
moon so you can play until 3 in the morning. It's noon now. Let's eat a
big raccoon before
we go home.

Dogs bark
Ericka F.

Dogs bark. I see pink dogs barking
Mirrors reflect. My family reflects me like a mirror.

The Verb
Daijah M.

My friend is playing rope.
We are playing with my braids.
I like soccer because you can kick it.
Red is the best color in the woods.

Untitled
Tyquon T.

I have a bell in my room. It smells
like perfume. My bell is golden.
Sometimes my dog plays with my bell and then lies down.
Some bells are beautiful like
my sister. My bell is always
there for me. Sometimes my bell gets dirty. My bell
Can spell anything. It makes me shine.

Snow Between Clouds
Verlean Y.

Between the clouds between the colors
of the book you've got to look between
clouds.

Snow
Rasheed C.

Snow is floating like a balloon. It's like rain that goes on a train.
Snow is like a crow.

Shoes and Glue
Bryanna F.

Snow is like shoes and glue. It flows
on top of your toes. I tell my sister
it's like paper and tornados. The sheep
and cows say meow and moo.
All day long stars stars stars paint Mars.

Untitled
Phil P.

Snow is like a flag in the open
but stings my skin like an angry bee.

Cow
Jeffrey C.

It is snowing like a cow.
It is black and white.
The First Snow
Destiny Bayman

The first snow
digesting her ice cream and cake.
The Pumpkin.

Untitled
Orlando S.

The rat is human...
The bear is crazy
in the forest.

Broken Heart
Tyriana O.

My heart is broken and hurts like somebody hit it.
My melody is broken into two parts.

The Wind
Shaquita W.

       I like to see the wind blow cool
Don't you see the leaves go?
       Makes a whisper by you.
Something is screaming in your ear.
       The wind says hush baby.

Untitled
Lorticia L.

Snow is spinning around the light
First it's day and then it's night. I spread a snow mat "We meet again."
I spread a snow mat "Please snow in." People didn't hesitate to
say, "Oh my it's night." WOW IT'S SNOWING. WOW I'M HAPPY.

Broke
Cherish L.

People always are broke.
My radio just broke, scattered on the floor
Had it for a year!
My memory just broke
Bam! there went my heart
Lonely in my house
Husband and kid gone for the weekend
My dog is hungry; he broke down
Ma, it was a dream, my child called me.

People Say
Mariah C.

People say school is cool
People say lock the door
People say story's good
People say pay me
People say do this, do that
People say don't talk

124

People say poems are lame
People say reading is a lot of words
People say running is a lot of pressure.

Untitled
Kevin W.

I broke her heart.
She broke my game. She slapped me 1,2,3
times in a row. She burst my bubble.
My behavior changed, my blood
sprayed, my legs felt like jelly.
I'm sad, I rode in my car, my tire broke.
Air went everywhere.
My memory has broken as well.

Untitled
Mia G.

I started to walk,

it sounds like a lot of people screaming.

They came over and hugged me and kissed me and
dragged me around and I saw door, clock, door, clock, door.

The Dream
Porsha M.

I heard the dream I remember the trees
The wind. I heard and I heard strong
I remember the trees the wind and the dream
I smell the rain and the color of the pain
I remember the dream as I cry like a dog I know
the smell of the rain and the color of the pain.

With the Weather
Candace S.

With the weather so windy whirling
around, crayons come from the clouds wet and
clap. People chewing candy. Classroom with
children Wild water floating Water coming

Dodge School
Robiane B.

Dodge School going through my head
I take a piece of paper and write with lead.
I'm getting an education so
I can go to graduation.
Now I'm going to college
To get some knowledge.

Poetry
Kaylin K.

School is very, very sad
All the times the teachers are mad

But they say it's not their fault
Then teachers say "That's what I thought."

But they talk during our class time
and then they ask can I have a dime?

Bell
Timothy H.

If I was a bell I would tell people there is a fire and I am a gold bell and a
big bell
And I am loud. Then the firefighters come and put out
the fire. I do it at night time that is my
job. boom! boom!
boom!

Clouds
Tatyana A.

Look like pillows in the snow
What do I know? I am 8 years old, I know
Snow melts into water, the air smells fresh.
I found gold money.

Untitled
Shenera T.

I was running sticking
Out my tongue fell

126

On my back wiggling
My hands jump up
and saw an angel. I thought it was my grand-dad.

Untitled
Angelo C.

It is cold out there
standing on the bus-stop.

I will not work
in the snowing.

I will drag my bag,
I will stay in the house

Thanksgiving is coming.

Untitled
Bianca P.

It hurt me so bad but in the same way it
helped me. When I was little I couldn't jump
I couldn't fly, but I tried so very hard.

Sweet Sweet Light
Jabree G.

The sweet sweet light I get from
the moon, the fog is so bright, the sun
needs fire so the moon, the fog mixes
together. The sky is blue but so so dark.

Untitled
Jamari B.

Snow is like a bear that hugs you all night.

Untitled
Raevaughn W.

Snow is like grandma's hair, soft and hard.
If you do your grandma's hair
you can cut yourself.

If your grandma's hair cuts you
Don't cry just call mom and she cuts your grandma's hair like Snow
White.

White and Snow
Taylor C.

Snow is like my dad's shaving cream. That white snow and
That white shaving cream.
That snow is like that white wall in my classroom.
White and snow look like brother and sister.
Snow is like what's good about ice cream.

Excerpt
Sydney M.

...Buildings get broken by tools
and mechanical things. When a tree breaks
you can see cracks in the broken bark or the branches
coming apart, leaves falling or ripping.
A stump starts to appear. The tree is no longer living the way it's
supposed to be....

Symbols
Kierra R.

Top of an Arc
A rainbow from rain. You can shout
so loud it calls your name.

Person Swimming
I play all day and
Say do you want
To play tomorrow?

Roller Coaster
I spin I spin
Ha ha ha it's fun
To play but not
To watch.

Zombie.
Let's play in a hat all day. But I
Have to say go away now.

I am Glad
Porshia W.

I am glad the sky is painted blue
and the earth is painted green with
All the people living in
the world as king and queen.
Why is the grass green
Why is the moon brown? Why are
the stars white and why do we have
clowns? Why is why? It seems
all of them are in between.

School
Demetrius J.

School is fun and nice
The homework is hard
and the funny thing is recess

Greatest Day
Crystal D.

Greatest day
Perfect snow angels
of grace

Elephant
Camille B.

The biggest animal
in the rain and the biggest
baby.

Snow
Angelica R.

Snow is like ice cream and white chalk and cotton
candy and white paper cut into little pieces and white milk.

The Snow
Dantrell S.

Like a book
Like a flag
Like soup
Is a goat.

Untitled
Sierra C.

People say love is hateful
People say love is not what we have inside
People say love is not you and me
People say happiness is not what we should have
People say happiness is not your breath.

Helping on Holidays
Keuna T.

On Halloween we saw a parade. A man fell off his float and we helped
him.
Me and my mom made a pink ham. Then we played hopscotch.

Untitled
Jodara B.

My name is Jodara and Jodara's me I'm talking
about my possibility and the friends and kin
and my neighborhood listen now and listen good
I can raprapraprap until your ears flap I can
talk my talk until you go for a walk I run it on down
until you are out of town.

Jack-O
Mariah H.

When I went outside jack-o-lantern
Dancing in my backyard with a jack-o-lantern
A vampire sucking a boy's blood
A witch eating eyeballs and tearing into a jack-o-
Lantern. I fainted and the boy was kissing
A jack-o-lantern.

130

Untitled
Denikko B.

Five little pumpkins sitting on the gate
One fell down and said No Way
Ten ghosts booing in the air
A third one said we don't care.
The fourth one said it's Halloween night
And the fifth one said we are blowing out of sight.

My Bell
Loyal W.

I have a bell for Christmas.
Here it is down here. The bell
Stops the bad guys.
My bell is a king.
My bell gives money.
Get your hands off that turkey
Until I eat a cake bell!

Cat
Christopher M.

I saw a cat walking down the street
slip and fall. It was looking in a tree.
It went to kiss me on my lips.

Untitled
Ariel A.

It takes a long, long time to hold you carefully in my heart.
It takes a long, long time to say I love you. It takes a long, long time to get used
To you. It takes a long, long time to say thank you. It takes
a long, long time until you are a master. It takes a long, long
time for you to be my sunshine. It takes a short time to say......the end.

Letter
Latia S.

Dear Tasha and Pat,

I miss my aunt, I miss my grandma
and the rest. I miss playing in her hair.

I miss making pizza, making friends
with Lisa. I miss walking and talking with you.

Letter
Deon H.

Dear brother, how are you? I've never met you. I might see you one
day, if dad goes and gets you. Or if dad tells my mom where you live we
can play with each other. We can probably play basketball, with my
Playstation 2. I haven't seen dad.

Have you seen him? I know I look different from you but it doesn't
matter. I might see you one day, my friend, one day.

Untitled
Jeffrey K.

Mirror, mirror on the wall
I'm asking you may I please
play ball. Oh dear mom if I
cannot come outside, I will run away and hide
I write this on the chalk board you
can see right here is what I want to be.

Immortal
Yumail B.

If I had power it would
rain banana pudding with lots of cookies
in it. Sometimes people could get hurt if
they have magical power. I know the steps to use
with magical power. If someone talks too much
I will turn them to orange, yellow, green, pink,
white or purple cheese! But I probably
would get hurt if I try to control some magical powers.

Untitled
Vernon H.

Jump the gates and hurry up
Before he turns into a punk.

Untitled
Aunray F.

We have eyes to blink tink tink tink
Your shoes ain't got no grip
You may fall and bust your hip
I move and love this school

Untitled
D.A.

Once upon a time a
boy was in danger.
There was a man that said
he is in danger
he was in danger because
he did something bad
he killed someone
The boy hid somewhere safe
he wasn't in danger again.

Untitled
Mack M.

The sky is blue I go to school
I see things that happen how about you?
You swing on the swing I feel the air.
I walk in school. We have pencil and paper but one person doesn't.
My teacher said share.

Untitled
Brianna L.

You shoes are doing the blues.
Your socks are full of rocks.
Look at your pants doing a dance.
Look at your nose full of holes.

Untitled
Kelly S.

I get hit in the face and ankle with a white ball. I
have a snowball fight with a bird. We all feel fantastica.

DAVID G. FARRAGUT CAREER ACADEMY
Principal: Edward Guerra
Teachers: Mr. Nunamaker, 9th, Mr. Patterson, 11th, Ms. Relken, 11th

Marvin Tate, Poet in Residence

A widely published poet and performer, Marvin Tate merges poetry with music. He has performed his work at the Wicker Park Poetry Fest, The Knitting Factory (New York City), Old Town School of Folk Music, Nuyorican Poet's Cafe (New York City), Lollapalooza concert, Iowa University, and others.

Untitled
Alberto M.

in the middle
of a burned down forest
a huge ring of fire
scorched trees
the middle of nowhere
a group of angels singing
in white gowns
unstained by the fire
i sit to listen
their voices drown
the surrounding hell
turning into paradise
flawless fire touches me
but i can't feel it
time has stopped
reverting back to normal
i'am still sitting

Dreams
Selestina R.

thinking you're dieing
knowing it's a lie
wake up sweating
out of breath heart repeatedly
beating faster like the knight
who rides his horse to battle
stuck in a herd of cattle
rain rising from the floor
sky feels like grass the kind
that's on my dog's ass
rainbows and shadows
trees one minute it's bright
and then dark like life
smile's hide your true feelings
heart slowly darkens
it's hard to beleive that you
were ever happy at one time

Dream
Alejandra C.

it's raining
get the buckets
catch the money
cars are snoring
people walking on the road
go to the edge of the ocean
mermaids swimming
singing the breeze running
through your hair like prey
from it's predator
a dog sits on a chair reading
the news tips it's hat
sings hello to whomever
listens to whomever walks by

Untiltled
Noemi M.

school is boring
like watching water boiling
i'm not saying it's useless
we all need our education
instead of ending up in a
police station just because
a teacher has a pen don't mean
he/she has the power to rule
with an iron fist it's like prison
full of people being judged
by a jury when teacher judge you
remember the only person who
can judge you is god

An Old Man
Elizabeth C.

walking down the street
late night passing by
a boy cries for his mother
children leaving school
street klights turn on
cows knocking on your door
asking for milk hot night
humid air blowing towards you
white snow flakes falling down

136

neighbors takeing buckets
collecting money babies preparing
breakfast moms crying for books
to be read roses smell like fresh oranges
dark blue sky clock ticking dogs on bicycles
cars floating in the air purple trees cover houses
curved roads guys search for females
soccer balls rolling down the street
young girls crying for light god teaching people
how to live life

Untitled
David M.

my garden
is like a cementary
full of gravestones
my garden is like a prarie
my grass is long and unorganized
my garden is a toilet
smelly and full of it

Untiltled
Henry V.

the ocean
is like a cup
of water in your hands
you drink the water
life moves on
the cup is like the world
and the water is life
if you drink the water fast
your life goes by fast too

Dream
Francisco C.

walking on railroad tracks
watching everything move
at the same pace i start to run
everything is moving faster
suddenly a train pops up
from behind me it chases me
until i hit a brick wall and i stop

Untiltled
Maria C.

UNBELIEVABLE BLACK BOOMERS DETECTED
FREE HOLIDAY SALES SIX HOURS ONLY
INCREDIBLE WORLD RUNNING FREE
HALF BURBERRY REPEAT ONLY SIX
BLACK DOOR WISCONSIN
my eyes open the train isn't there
i see nothing nothing is there

Shadow
Migael G.

try to escape
fear becoming reality
inside my head
shadows chasing me
i run fast as i can
but can't escape
it's always on my back
the end of the road
no where to go
look ahead
no where to go
the ground caves in
but i'am still standing
in the air shadow catches me
i fly to a place neverland
can't reach the shadow
get's tired i 'am weak
like a tooth pick ready
to brake

START
Jose C., Flores F., Camacho, and Margarita S.

death of house wife
oceans face off
celebrity shows how
to play change your life
friday night running
out when midnight arrives
you'll be ready for visit
art school education
the books always better
further artist year Chicago

138

behavior support professional
rent it sunday school
web california
HEY!

Open
Victoria, Ebony, Brandy and Katarina

bubba from chicago
accused attacker
start to kill local
grand rapids until he finished
the arts entertainment museums
to run off free playing
rock at shop
you
january 3, 2005
award play repeated
oh what fun it is to drive
house glow engines
and entertainment clearance
theater pop!

Untitled
Basty, Maritza, Nancy and Gustavo

time turning right
pass 50-60%
interest unfortunate
love you? friday
two way weekend
land fast
plan nice guy
releieved twelve
cover beat new
fast bulls

SCROOGE SINGS
Rocia, Vanessa, Noemi, Jessica, Abel and Franscisco

all bad highschool students
help shop inside a new saturday
market place three free family pics
with friends give claustrophobics
off world with a free car in chicago
you're loosing new city shops

A Normal Day (in class)
Amar M.

my body comes to school too early

that's why my mind is still asleep

my teachers are getting angry
my mind arrives to school running
advisory at noon with mr. bacon
then off to gym to play soccer
gym is over next is lunch
i'm thirsty i buy gatorade
put it in my pocket
this is why i cut this class
and go to the bakery

Untitled
Naveli A.

nigeria never agrees
alabama nearly attacks
neveda navigates alone

I Don't Know
Javier O.

i don't know why
people get hurt
they cry it makes you
want to hurl and let time
pass by life is unpredictable
at one point you're high as a kite
then you're slow as mud
life is so unpredictable
makes you think
life is just a dud
life is so hard, complicated
so unpredictable
people die you ask yourself
why they invented jail
just so people can bail
one thing's sure we're all
going to die
i don't know why
i just don't know

Waiting
Martinez E.

who's waiting you
who's waiting you
no more excuses
no more excuses
no need cash no stuffed
no more your next pay day
excuses red zone no more
this is the place
yearly this the place
redzone bears this is the place
yearly games bears no more
red zone no more cash

Expectation Boundaries
Ebony B.

exceeding boundaries
beyond exploration
being equal beyond equality
expressing eternity boyness
enter beyond being enterconnected
everlasting beautiful everlasting
exceed everyone exploring
everyone everywhere

Scary
Sandra A.

scary animals
scare american society
almost subsequently

Untitled
Migael G.

many girls gone
mad magnificent
more bathered more money
gold medals making gay models

141

Boredom
Edgar F.

school is like going
to work yo work
and then you go home
and do more work
you sleep and then you
get up and do the same thing
over and over and over and over
again

Lost
Vanessa G.

i'm lost
i get lost every hour
i'm lost in the house
i'm lost at school
i even get lost at the mall
when i find myself in love
i find myself until i get lost again

Bike
Timothy D.

what do i have to do
to have the best bike
to have it presented
on the news then ride it
a long way to school
i take my bike it beats
a cold walk anyday
it's like freedom

No More Excuses
Elizabeth R.

hey
no more excuses DANCE
get $20 the next pay day
this is the new dance
yearly the redzone is waiting
for you this is the place
excuses off
cash is waiting for you

NO MORE EXCUSES
DANCE RIGHT NOW
no more excuses

Falling
Sandra A.

people falling
as if falling into a pool
full of snakes biting
like getting shots from
the doctor looking out
the window chunky fat birds
singing soothing melodies
people running chased
by angry sharks

Everyone Thinks
Martinez E.

everyone thinks
a person is like it looks
everyone trys to dictate
what i do EVERONE
hates to be told what to do
to be judged unfairly
everone get's tired
at some point when they can't
go on anymore they dig a hole
and cave right in EVERYONE
thinks differently some like clouds
some like dogs

Friendship
Silvia G.

friendship is like a baby
you have to feed it
you need to keep on feeding
your friendship to keep going
friendship is like a day at the arcade
you have to make it fun

Life
Brandie H.

life is like time
it's always running out
like a rose beautiful when grown
like the amazing when it's full
like friendship hard to last
like a dream full of thoughts
and fantasy life is like a whisper
soft and secretive

Together
Maritza E.

my roses are red
my tulips are yellow
i see one growing every day
by the meadow i pick roses
and tu;ips i put them together
to see what i can create
my roses and tulips are dieing
what can i do to create another
two together

Monday
L. M.

last monday
late midnight
last moon
last meal
long meter
less meaner
liquid milk
little meal

Untitled
Rosendolf

rejection feels really foolish
for romantics roses ready
for failing relationships

144

Mashed Potatoes
Miguel P.

midnight parrots munch
munstrously on potatoes
mashed potatoes make people
look pathetic

Should I
Victoria O.

should i write
a book about a dog
that looks like a fish
or should i write about
a fish in a dish i don't know
what to write about nothing to say
just sitting here like stupid like
i got all day should i write about
my mom they say i look just like her

Playing
Alondra L.

i play with playdough
she plays with grass
i listen to the radio
she fishes for bass
we're both having fun

STEPHEN F. GALE COMMUNITY ACADEMY
Principal: Rudy Lubov
Teachers: Ms. Dyse, 8th, Ms. Hayes, 8th, Ms. Miller, 8th

Anne Holub, Poet in Residence

Anne Holub received an M.F.A. in creative writing from the University of Montana and an M.A. in English and Creative Writing from Hollins University in Virginia. She most recently edited the literary journal, *CutBank*, in Missoula, Montana. Her work has been published in the *Asheville Poetry Review, Phoebe: A Journal of Literature and Art*, the *Beacon Street Review*, and *The Hollins Critic,* among others. She is currently a contributing writer and editor for Gapersblock.com.

Anne has to say, "I was truly blessed in my first year as a Poet in Residence to work with a great group of 8th graders at Stephen F. Gale Community Academy. From the first assignment, I was often surprised at the risks my students were willing to take with their poetry. I regret that more of them could not have poems in the anthology, but I will always remember the powerful words that they shared with me each week through their writing. We were able to study poets such as Rita Dove, Elizabeth Bishop, Pablo Neruda, William Carlos Williams, Robert Hayden, Richard Wright, Nikki Giovanni, Raymond Carver, Walt Whitman, as well as a host of others."

146

What We Think, by Room 450
Michael A., Alex S., Princess H., Demarcus F., Sharon W., Joyonta H., Chris H., Edilberto G., Vantner C., Althea A., James N., Reggie G., Kristi L., Shannon R., Ashley D., and Christopher D.

I like the way you talk.
I like the way you listen.
I like working when the class is working together.
I like pizza.
I believe I can get all A's.
I believe I can graduate.
I believe in me.
I feel alive.
I feel dramatic.
I can do my work and write.
I can't do my work and write and eat.
I can graduate in June.
I can dream of something that I would like to do.
I can draw a masterpiece.
I can dream of hot weather.
I dream about the future.
I dream of a better world.
I dislike what I might become.
I think about it all the time.
I think of the soft clouds being my pillow.
I think I'm hungry.
I hear my stomach growling.
I don't like broccoli.
I don't believe in failure.
I am somebody.
I am a person.
I am a person with a heart.
I am sad about leaving you.
I am whoever I say I am.
I know what's right and wrong.
I know the rules.
I know I'm going to the WNBA.
I will finish high school.
I will go to college.
I trust in myself.
I feel lucky.
I feel good.
I hate what I do.
I love to play basketball.
I hope I make it to the NBA.
I hope to be successful.
I hear thoughts and expectations.
I dream about the future.
I do.

I, by Room 451

Elizabeth L., Ronnell A., Jevon O., Omar H., Chanel J., Tanisha A., Lamar M., Nicholas S., Walter H., Mark Y., Bruce H., Michelle H., Shaundel W., Elwina D., Kimberly G., Migdolena S., Leroy A., and Montrel W..

I know I can do better in school.
I know I am not a good reader, but I am improving.
I know I'm silly.
I hear my mother and brother saying to do the best.
I hear people weeping.
I hear fire trucks every day all day.
I hear success.
I hear people arguing on the street.
I hear my mother's voice when I'm alone.
I want to be a football player and an actor.
I want to be a rapper.
I wanted to show him my new poem.
I try to keep everything together.
I try many things.
I could do more.
I could help the world.
I could ask you for some advice.
I could eat a whole pizza by myself.
I could be nice.
I see myself as a leader.
I am talented in some way.
I am a teenager.
I am a young man about to graduate.
I believe in faith.
I would like to finish school.
I would like to be heard.
I would like to have a very fat nose.
I smell the fresh air outside.
I smell spring.
I smell lunch already.
I lack self-confidence, but I always keep my head up.
I care about my sister's education.
I care about everybody.
I shouldn't let anyone discourage me.
I shouldn't be sad.
I have a lot of support.
I have a lot of dreams.
I like to express myself through poetry.
I should be responsible.
I should come to school every day.
I should vote.
I feel exhausted.
I hide in the dark.

I think what would my life be like ten years from now.
I think the world could be greater if people had better jobs.
I think we are going to be good friends.
I would help.
I wouldn't hurt.
I speak different languages.
I will always worry about your concerns.
I will never ever speak with bad words.
I won't be in jail when I get older.
I speak with a voice of pride.
I hate when people talk down on others.
I can be little, and still make a big impact.
I can behave, but sometimes I choose not to.
I can beg all day for a brand new bike.
I can help with the house.
I can make a change in our community.
I can make a frown, but I like my face.
I say I am somebody!

Class Poem, by Room 452
**Sharhonda C., Sandra R., Jose M., Jasmine G., Kemara M., Marco
S., Gary H., Cornelius M., Adarrylreo B., Russell H., Ashley B.,
Deneen H., Daniel O., Nyasia R., and Michael H.**

I will be the best I can be.
I will have an affect on something.
I will never forget you.
I don't know how to tell you how I feel about you.
I don't think that you are ready for me.
I am changing my mind.
I am an intelligent person that believes dreams will come true.
I am a black man.
I am a strong young lady.
I am a powerful voice.
I am somebody.
I am an American.
I am African American.
I like to read and write.
I saw you cry for the first time.
I saw the other side of my teacher.
I was going to your house.
I was feeling sad at the same time.
I remember when I broke my foot.
I remember when I was down, you helped me.
I remember when the apartment caught on fire.
I remember when I first talked to you.
I understand how you feel.
I understand that if you believe in yourself that God will bless.

I understand how you feel.
I understand my responsibilities.
I understand how you feel.
I think I understand.
I want to see you again.
I want to be loved.
I want to make it through high school.
I want freedom.
I think I'm headed down the right path.
I think unity is the key to friendship.
I think about my grandmothers who died.
I used to play football and baseball and basketball.
I used to think monsters were real.
I used to be really bad.
I believe I will be the greatest at whatever I do.
I believe in myself, family, and friends.
I believe everything will be ok.
I could be the first woman president.
I will do my homework every day.
I will try my best to graduate.
I will go to college.
I must become a stronger person.
I need to be closer with my family.
I can't wait to be an adult, to have a chance to make a difference in this country.
I understand what I have to do.

When My Little Brother First Came into the World
Michelle H.

When my little brother first
came in the world all I smelled
was dirty diapers, and a smelly baby.
I could taste the baby food
in my mouth.
I had no doubt that
one day this baby
would be my age.
He will come to a phase where
he will have lots of
girls calling and
falling to his needs.

Camp
Chanel J.

I remember it was like yesterday. Stepping off
the yellow bus into the fresh pine air
and looking around at the hard wood
cabins and the row boats rowing in the
green starchy lake. Kids being tenacious while
playing water games, the smell of new
tents being opened, fires being started.
Camp songs being sung while the birds were chirping
along while the crickets and frogs hopped away from
all the loud ruckus, feeling the leaves crunching
in my hands and mosquitoes biting, making me
smack myself. That day was a wonderful day.

Football with the Field School Bulldogs
Bruce H.

The harder I try, the harder I trained.
The better I got, the worse the pain.
I remember shattered bones, I remember
cheering fans. I remember going home eating
dinner from a can. Every night, every day
I would dream about hits, big hits, like
slaves slammed into a pit. Getting tackled, finding
myself eating dirt, every Sunday at the
laundromat washing white shirts. So when
ever someone cries I'll feel their pain
and that leads me to why I try, and the
harder I train.

Poem
Michael H.

It rained, and rained, and rained
day after day after day, only
if it would stop. Just one day
it wouldn't rain. I haven't
seen the sun or even the moon
just rain that can wash us all
away. Sometimes my house
just feels like a cave. Thunderstorms
that bring you a scare and hail
falls like rocks from the sky.
Finally, it has stopped. After
one whole week it has stopped
and I am free.

The Strange Man
Ricardo V.

When I went outside the rain sounded
like a lion. When I was walking I bumped
into a strange man. The color of his eyes
was like a blue sky. He was a skyscraper. That's
how the strange man looked and the last time
I saw him.

The Man Named George
Joyanita H.

He was black like night.
His beard was fuzzy like a
fresh cover out of a dryer.
George's eyes were brown like
a bear's fur. His legs were like a
skyscraper. Now he is as stiff
as a board. If you believe me
then go see for yourself.
Now he is as skinny as a stick.
To tell the truth, he was my grandpa.

Riply, Tennessee
Ashley B.

I like the hot summer days
and the warm summer nights.
I like the way there are just
roads and roads to get to the
places I need to go.
I don't like the bugs every
where. In your house, in the
air, and probably in your hair.
I don't like the boring afternoons.
But I do like the hot summer
days and the warm summer nights.

Untitled
Reggie G.

I'm sorry
Bo,
don't die,
live,

live forever.
My dog.
You're mine,
so live,
live forever.
No more.
No killing.
I didn't
mean to,
I didn't
mean to
put cat food
in your
water.
I'm very
very very
sorry.

Sorry Again
Kristi L.

Sorry I
wasn't the
person you
want:

a doctor,
a lawyer,
a teacher,
another.

I'm not
making a
lot of
money today.

I'm not
sorry for
what I
came to
be but
I'm sorry
that you
couldn't be
proud of
me.

The Girl
Chanel J.

The girl with the wavy hair.
The girl with blue and black Nikes.
The girl with the wide hips.
The girl in love with Spongebob.
The girl sometimes into her schoolwork.
The girl who makes more enemies than friends.
The girl with three older brothers.
The girl with the eye problem.
The girl with the caramel skin.
The girl that was 5'2".
The girl that likes to eat.
The girl that loves green extra gum.
The girl that liked to dance.
The girl that liked short boys.
The girl that liked adventures.
The girl that liked Christmas.
The girl whose birthday was in February.
The girl that wanted to be a pediatrician.
The girl that loved her family.
The girl was gorgeous.
The girl was me.

Untitled
Aaron S.

My bike with a popping chain.
My bike that is orange.
My bike that is big.
My bike with scratches on it.
My bike I left outside.
My bike that squeaks every time you turn.
My bike that is rusty.
My bike that was shiny.
My bike that I fall on.
My bike that fell from two stories high.
My bike that has flat tires.
My bike the bike I hate.
My bike that has ripped seats.
My bike that's mine.

Poetry
Christopher D.

It's fall now and I'm
walking on the leaves.
As I step on one
I can feel the nature
breeze.
Smoke comes out my mouth
like smoke out a chimney.
As I dress warm the
cold is my enemy.

My Day at Work
Mark Y.

My Dad was thinking about getting the job done.
Marcello was hungry after all his lifting.
Steve was thinking about beer like he always does.
Chet was thinking about his dog Harley.
Juan was thinking about tamales.
B.J. was sniffing and sneezing.
And I was wanting help with a heavy box.

2004 in Chi-Town
Montrel W.

The police stay on patrol on the street.
The fireman risks his life putting out fire.
The garbage man dumps the disgusting
garbage everyday.
The teacher stands for 6 hours, 5 days a week.
The lawyer solves cases, getting evidence.
Scientists explores new things, finding material
that's very old.
Mothers downtown working very hard, to
make a good living.

Something I Hope To Give You Soon
Bobby R.

Here is the
new car I
wanted to
give you for
your b-day.

I hope you
enjoy riding
around with
the new rims.
This is just a
thank you for
teaching and
helping me through
life, now you can
give that
black car to someone
less fortunate. As you
ride around in the new
Mercury don't forget to
drop me off home
after school, Ms. Dyse.

Navea Come Back To Me
Gary M.

I would give life to my niece Navea. I miss
her and wish she was still here. She would be three
years old now. I wish I could bring her
back to laugh and life. I miss when she
giggled and smiled. My niece was like a sister
to me and that I will always have her in
my heart and if I could get the chance to bring
her back I would just to bring her. I was happy
and see her and ReRe together playing
like sisters. Navea come back to me and
come home. I
                miss you
                        and
                            love you
                                    and
                                        that's
                                            4
                                                ever.

Happiness is All I Want, Happiness is All I Need
Brittny L.

As I walk through
the mall, my feet feel sore.
I'm so tired and overwhelmed
with gifts I bought for others.
I look at my list

and see there's one other.
How can I forget
this person? It's the most
important one. What can
I get this person? I
thought the shopping was
done. I look around,
scour the mall up and
down. There's nothing for this person.
I stop, sit, and think.
Then all of a sudden something
comes to me. I know what
they want, I know what
they need. I found out
happiness is all they want,
happiness is all they need.

The Snow
Jose M.

The snow is like birds
coming down from the sky.
It is like popcorn going through
your mouth. When it is snowing
it is freezing outside. It is like people
throwing small pieces of
paper and they fall on the
ground making a beautiful place.

Snow
Ashley D.

Snow is the opposite of hot.
Snow is the opposite of dry.
Snow is the furthest color from black.
Snow is the opposite of solid.
Snow is like crystal frost.
Trying to move through snow is like trying to
wade through water.

Untitled
Tanisha A.

I went by this building, brown
mostly gray, like all the city's smoke and noise
got ground into those bricks. The window

glass, so black it looked like tar. I thought
nobody lived there. Too quiet, too dark,
too gray. When I looked up I saw a
window open, the curtains blowing.

Car Lights
Ronnell A.

Telling left from right
all through the night.

I try to keep strong
because if I am wrong

it can cost people their lives.
That's why I am an important light.

I sleep outside when not used
and no need to go to the restroom.

I travel a lot sometimes state to state
and I never wake

from a dream.
Man, I can't even scream.

Untitled
Omar H.

I'm sorry to say
that I
gave that
homeless guy
your food.

I just wanted
to feel
good. But
to make
this up
I'll give
my meal
so you
could have
a meal
and feel
how a

homeless guy
feels.

Untitled
Jasmine G.

I imagine giving you a gift
but I thought you were really
there. Imagine when
my hand is out giving you
a gift, but there's a sweet
sound going around and around.
Imagine when there's a time
to share you won't always be there.
I wanted to say I love you but
you weren't there. Now
you are dead gone. I don't
have nothing to spare.

What Could be Going on Deep Down in the Sea
Sandra R.

I could see all the fishes
swimming away
and I didn't know why.
Why are they swimming away?
Is it because I was there,
or was it because a shark was
in back of them?
But still now all those different
fishes swimming away,
and all different plants at the bottom
of the sea.
What could be going on
deep down at the sea?
Are these species just swimming
to find some food?
Just swim around and find
something new.
What could be going on deep
down in the sea?

The Mistake I Made
Princess H.

I'm sorry
for
hitting my
sister but
it
felt great
because
after
a while
she
shut up
and
got over
it.

2004, New Year
Michael A.

I'm sorry
for doing
bad in
school but
I am not
going to
mess up
no more.

The Flowers That Caught My Attention
Edwrinna K.

I watch them as I walk
by. Pretty, yellow, they look
like the sun.

The way they swing side to
side when the wind blows,

the way their roots are trapped,
they look as if they were imprisoned.

I sing a tune as I stand and
watch.

I hurry home before it gets
dark. While I run off, I say in my
head, we'll someday meet again.

That One Book
Sandra R.

Touch it and it takes you.
All of the words that take you
and put you in it. You get scared
of thinking it could be you. What
could it be?

Untitled
Nyasia R.

I am hard and silver and sometimes
black. A lot of people have me. Most
people on crack. I have a hole in
the center. It has a very nice figure
but you can do years if you
pull the trigger. It's used for bad,
it's used for good. A lot of people
have them, especially in the 'hood.
Police carry me everywhere they go
so they can be safe, just so
they know. What am I?

So the Bike Speaks
Walter H.

I like what I do.
As I ride through and through
the wind and air flows.
Someone kicks the pedals.
I shoot like a rocket in
the sky. As I ride faster
and faster mile after mile
as far as my limits are.
It feels like I'm flying
through the great winds.
I think this is what a
bird feels when it flies.

Moving Star in the Sky
Jevon O.

The ground shakes
rocks are moving
the countdown
begins.

The countdown
ends. Higher and
higher it goes
a trail of smoke
stays behind.

Now leaving the Earth
with a red glare
like a moving star
in the sky.

Looking From My Point of View
Kemara M.

I'm looking,
seeing a group of boys in training.
They look so focused.
Hope no one gets hurt.
Keep your eye on the target.
That's what I'm thinking.
He punches with force.
Two boxing rings on the side of him.
He looks eagerly at the
rings wanting to fight
with all his might.

Untitled
Michael H.

I am here to see the annual
event. The horse racing marathon.
I saw the months of them training
and speculating about this event.
I have taken many pictures of people
training and I saw what they wanted
so badly, to have those split moments
of being worshipped, of being praised.
The first time I heard of this marathon,
I didn't think much of it, however now

I see how much the kids, teenagers,
and even adults how wish in there
wildest dreams to win, and even if
they don't the experience of being there.
I look around and I see the horses
being gathered. The kids getting numbers
on their backs. So many people, so many horses.
I saw the people getting upon the
horses all of them getting ready to race. They started
slowly to the start line. I just realized how dangerous
this could be, there lives could be
at risk, but they still raced.
And then I heard the shotgun shot
and the race began and I took the picture
that to me was beautiful and great.

City Boy Bruce
Bruce H.

City Boy Bruce, born and raised in Chicago
(2515 W. Jackson Blvd. in Rockwell gardens on the
west side to be exact). City Boy Bruce always
wanted to experience something new. They told
City Boy Bruce that he was going to Niagara Falls, Canada.
City Boy Bruce was so excited. He went to the
airport and heard that a plane to Niger was boarding.
City Boy Bruce thought the intercom said Niagara with some static.
City Boy Bruce boarded the plane to Niger, which is located
in Africa. When City Boy Bruce arrived in Niger, he was overwhelmed
with excitement. He wanted to experience all Niger
could offer. One day, City Boy Bruce went to a river
full of hippos to swim with them. City Boy Bruce
saw a giant mouth with a long tongue and four teeth,
little eyes, rough wrinkled skin, with a full-grown moustache.
This experience for City Boy Bruce was great.

Untitled
Kimberly G.

I am taking a picture.
I just arrived here just
the same as that boy
named Amed.

He was asking me
questions. He told
me he thought that
since he was from
Israel, no one would
talk to him.

I decided to take
a picture of the
kids, laughing and
playing with their
new friend Amed.

I am leaving this town
now. I am going
back home now
and I hope to find more
Interesting people.

Untitled
Christopher H.

Guns
war
hate,
rising above peace.
Oil
money
greed,
overpriced and overdone.
Peace
love
joy
gone and non-existing.

Feeling
Tanisha A.

Different things that I see that may
interest me. Maybe I should try to imagine myself
as the bird, to find out how he actually feels
about this weather. As the snow falls I try to fly
without it letting it hurt my wings. I need to fly
South, but the wind is blowing so hard
the only way I can fly is East. I just wish
I wasn't so cold, I could walk or fly
if I chose, so weak too much snow

for one bird to handle on its own.
So much snow I can't hardly see
where I'm going. I should just find
shelter for the night, but the way that
this snow is falling I don't think
I can make it.

Poem
Shea C.

The huge waves
washing up on shore as
if trying to get away.

While I was coming
ashore I spotted something
in the sand while pulling my boat
out of the water.

The buildings and surroundings
are different from what I usually
see. Where am I? The broken pieces
of wood and scattered rocks are weird.

Untitled Haiku
Ashley B.

The children will play
like the fussy dog outside
never quieting.

Ode to Myself
Deneen H.

Ode to myself, ode to my face, ode to my
hands, ode to my feet, ode to my eyes,
ode to my ears, ode to my arms, ode to
my toes, ode to my fingers, ode to my
lips, ode to my navel, ode to my stomach,
ode to my wrist, ode to my hips, ode
to my elbows, ode to my knees, ode to
my thighs, ode to my hair, ode to my head,
ode to my shoulders, ode to my eyebrows,
and most of all ode to the color of my skin.

GALILEO SCHOLASTIC ACADEMY
Principal: Alfonso Valtierra
Teachers: Ms. Garay, 4th, Ms. Lewis, 4th, Ms. Otero, 4th

Eric Elshtain, Poet in Residence

Eric Elshtain, the editor of Chicago's on-line Beard of Bees Press (www.beardofbees.com), is finishing his Ph.D. in the University of Chicago's Committee on the History of Culture.

His work can be found in journals such as *McSweeney's, Skanky Possum, Notre Dame Review, Ploughshares, Interim, Salt Hill, GutCult* and others. His latest chapbook, *The Cheaper the Crook, the Gaudier the Patter*, appeared last year from Transparent Tiger Press.

War After War
Joshua V.

Mars is a badge of blood in the sky. This planet is a symbol for gods of war. The shield and spear represent the symbols of Mars. The only thing that will never change is that outer space is wearing the badge.

Acrostic
Kendall W.

Grass,
Rat
Is a bear meal.
Zoo animal that
Zig-zags.
Lives by a lake
Year to the day.

Acrostic
Jose A.

Jamming is cool
Oh so cool
'Sike' it out and play
Electric drums.

Animals oh so many animals.
Motorcycles are me
And sting like a bee.
Yams are good.
Anthony was born two days from me.

Acrostic
Juan N.

Delightful boy
A person who likes bread
Kody is his nickname
Obeys pizza
Tater tots are his Kody snack
A weird kid

Acrostic
Violet S.

Christ's birth.
Holy Mary is his mother.
Really our leader
Is our
Survivor.
Trying to protect us
Mass of presents on this day
All is always
Silent.

Panda Baby
Maya R.

Pretty is what Maya is
Apples are what she likes
Noodles are my favorite sick food
Darts my favorite sport
And leave it there

Baby blue is my favorite color
Africa is where she wants to go
Baby sister is what she is
You don't know?

What is a Clock?
Nicole B.

A clock is a time machine
you can go back in time;
the hands are the years
and the numbers are the
animals that lived in that time;
the second hands are the
days that go by; the clock is
a time time machine and I don't
know why.

Acrostic
Tralisa W.

A big fat fish
No time for this
Is not my problem
Mommy help me Hurry!
Angels keep me safe
Long through the night
       Amen

Acrostic
Daniel D.

Mom
On
The
Hay

Acrostic
Kiera C.

Very silly sometimes
Is not going to ever get a dollar from me
Clear as glass no lies in that
Turn of your fire roaring too loud
Outstanding work never D+
Reading is what you should do
I think your needs are in your innerself
A good friend while I'm in need

Outerspace
Leyah W.

The stars are diamonds shining like crazy.
The planets are big, round, bouncing balls.
The meteors are flying pieces of gold.
The rings of Saturn are a floating race track.
The moons of Jupiter are huge pieces of round cheese.
The sun is a huge dandelion.

Sky
John Joseph M.

Skating angles on the rink
Kit blue blanket covering
You see it every where from day to day and night to night

My Dollar Bills
Sydnie B.

My dollar bills are presidents trapped
in dollar bills for many many years. They
are trapped when their days of being
presidents are over. They are trapped
so people everywhere can learn
their history and learn how they
got trapped.

Acrostics
Joseph I.

Dig a very big hole
Outside in the dark attacking a mole
Going to a pound after killing a mole.

Murdered by a dog
Outside in the dark
Lying on the ground
Eating nothing for Christmas

Acrostic
Jennifer R.

Must monkeys hang
On the tree hanging like they're crazy
No doubt that it looks like Jesus
Keeps jumping around like a kangaroo
Eats like a pig
Yawns and they're sleepy.

Acrostic
Coleman S.

Crazy person that eats
Other unusual things

170

Like mail and whale sushi.
Energized all the time
Man that likes soccer a lot
And so I am really fast and
Never stop until dinner.

Black
Laura Z.

Black as chocolate chips.
My hair is black.
The snow is black.
The blood is black.
Gatorade is black.
Arkansas is black.
Spanish is black.
The sun is black.

Green
Luis Z.

Green it is
so green today

why can't I
just say no

green is my
favorite color

that is why
I can't say

go away away
it is so green

today I got
to say no

but, I just
can't say no

I wish I
could say no

Sky
Paul Z.

The bright, bright moon at night
lights the street and you feel no fright
Gray, gray the sky is gray
and the evening goes in to late day
Red, bright red the sky is red
in the morning as you get out of bed
Blue, blue the sky is blues
as the hands on the clock strike two
Yellow, yellow the sky is yellow
in the evening when my mom makes Jell-O.
Colors, colors in the sky
from when I'm born and when I die.

Red and Blue
Kalyn K.

Blue the color of ink that goes across a paper
    you just want to keep writing and play later.
Red is the color of fire
it makes you want to go higher.

Green
Genevieve B.

The color of grass and trees
with green trunks and green leaves.
The color of a dyed poodle.
I sometimes find this color in my sutan noodle!
Green eyes and green plants, green balloons
and green pants.
The color of a sour lime
the color of an envious mime.

Blue
Cesar E.

blue is the color of sadness
red is the color of madness
blue is the color drowning water
green is the color of my fly swatter
blue is the color of ink
and I hate pink.

172

Compound Words
Francisco C.

basesea beansaw cookbread
ballflag soxbook bedclock
readhunter lakehomes middlelook
Ericbran firepage rulestink
gamesrock gradeschool sadname
kingkong icefork snowfly
pitchmilk cornmill hillcrop
wellsick oldcow bullkick
windfall firehair doggod
ragtag rapdog cakebrush

School
Nicole B.

chalkperson windowclock classpaper flagflock
folderpost pencilpen deskchair flycan

sparybelt seatboard hairpaint pizzatest
floorears tilenose rulerbook makerprint

treenorth erasersouth heartparty glasslegs
booksweater teacherdot clocklunch sciencerug

calculatorhoney butterraisin westeast pantgym
factorshoe clouddog book-it racedark

gradecheese spelling-bee maplead hairblack
redgreen blueyellow orangeorang sweaterjanuary

Loco, Amazing, Funny, Tubular Story
Mrs. Emma Garay's class, room 305: Angel A., Nicole B., Erika B., Caress B., Victoria B., Kiera C., Claire D., Daniel D., Daisy F., Nicholas G., Jose H., Jasmine J., Elijah M., John M., Juan N., Alexis R., Maya R., Morgan R., Violeta S., Erik S., Yolanda W., Tralisa W., Dakota Z.

Sometimes I can be really loco;
this is amazing.
It happens when I eat chocolate
and I feel funky.
It's really tubular,
dude. Then I start to run
so you'd better run
before I go loco.

That wave was so tubular,
dude, which was amazing.
Then you get funky
with creamy chocolate.
I wish I were made of chocolate;
I would run
to the 70s when it was funky.
Cocoa is loco
and sugar is amazing
and then it is tubular.
You are tubular
eating chocolate
with amazing
sugar. In gym we run
a lot which is, like, loco.
You smell funky.
George Washington's hair is funky;
Abraham Lincoln's hair is tubular—
the presidents are loco
with chocolate
on their faces. They run
like a monkey and sound amazing.
The sky is amazing,
the school is funky.
Then I run
away to a tubular
factory of chocolate.
Kids are loco.

This world is amazing—that's tubular.
The funky people eat chocolate;
they will run and go loco.

Mother Nature's Crazy Stanzas
**Mrs. Christina Lewis' class, room 303: Jorge A., Jose A., Heneisha
B., Francisco C., Mark C., Darla D., Anthony D., Michael D., Taylor
G., Vanedra H., Tia J., Cherokee M., Dina P., Nicholas R., Chelesi
S., Thalia T., Anel V., Joshua V., Temoatzin V., Deandre W., Kendall
W., Laura Z., Luis Z.**

But not again!
A cloudy sky—
I don't think it's great;
how does it create?
It's such a challenge,
Mother Nature is powerful.
When are you powerful?
I will be powerful again

174

when I have a challenge
with the sky
to create
something great.
How great
is it to be powerful?
I can create
a cloudy sky again,
even though I live in the sky
it is still a challenge.
There is a challenge
but it is great
to live in the sky.
I feel so powerful.
try doing it again—
to create
an illusion. I create
such a big challenge
to try to do homework again.
It is not great
to be powerful
in the sky.
The sky
is blue to create
a powerful
and big challenge
to do great
things all over again.

The sky is a challenge
because it can create something great.
It is so powerful to do its worst again.

Dreams
Anel V.

In my dreams
I fly higher than
a bird
        I have control of
the world
In my dreams the shortest
building is 10 inches high
and I go back in time
In my dreams Martin Luther
King talks to me saying
"Go on and explore the world"
In my dreams I'm the tallest

one in the family and I'm the richest
girl in the world
In my dreams I tease my
brothers
          In my dreams I appear in a
different country and wake
up talking in another language

Such a Dream
Angela W.

In my dream my
favorite pet snake grew
eight times the average
basketball player.
I was wrapped in him as
if I had a ten foot long
sheet wrapped around me in winter.

My dog grew as big as a
prehistoric T-rex running and
drooling her way through the
big, crowded city.

I painted the
dream with what
my eyes had seen.

I painted like Van
Gogh and then I
let go of the paint brush
and rushed. I was living
in the caveman's time.

Haiku
Alexis R.

Winter is sweet but
it is cold as frozen meat
but never like treats.

Haiku
Nick G.

It's fun in the sun
It's no fun without your son
It's fun with the son.

Simile Poem
Angel A.

A book is like a turkey.

An apple is as round as a world.

A door is like a human.

A horse can be like a dragon.

My brother can look like me.

My dogs run as fast as me.

Cats and Dogs
Victoria B.

Oh no, it's raining cats and dogs
They're all in the air
Should I call the authorities
or should I fix my hair?

Comparisons
Claire D.

1. A mole rat is like the American flag.
2. Windows are like eyeglasses.
3. A person is as big as the Sears Tower.
4. I'm as mad as a tiger.
5. I'm as cool as Alaska.
6. I'm as cute as Hello Kitty.
7. A chair is like a shoe.
8. A tie is as colorful as a rainbow.
9. A mask is as deadly as a lion.
10. A pencil is as yellow as a giraffe.
11. Eric is like a parrot.
12. Claire is like a bee.

Comparison
Nicholas R.

A computer is like water.
A cat is like a dog.
A gold fish is like a turtle.
A farm is like a house.
An airplane is like an eagle.
A boat is like a cheetah.

Comparisons
Anthony D.

A ring is as big as a body of water.
A key is as big as the world.
A car is as big as the solar system.
A letter is like the sun.
The globe is like the world.
A piece of paper is like a dinosaur.
A stray is like grass.
A piece of string is like grass.
A computer monitor is like the overhead.

Collaborative Poem
Mrs. Reina Otero's Class, room 304: Nelson A., Genevieve B., Maria B., Sydnie B., Jasmine C., Cesar E., Joseph I., Kalyn K., John M., Ariel M., Alyssa O., Evelyn P., Jennifer R., Brianna R., Bonifacio S., Lakendra S., Isaac S., Coleman S., Eric T., Angela W., Leyah W., Jesus Z., Paul Z.

I wish I could go to Las Vegas and see Snoopy and
            his life cycle I wish I was in Honolulu to see
Garfield run away from a huge tidal wave
            I wish I could go to New Port Richey to see Odie discover
chemical waste on Mars
            I wish I went to Honduras to see Charlie Brown's
            lava; I wish I went to El Salvador to see
            Batman and volcanoes; I wish I went to New
Mexico to see Catwoman and fish; I wish I went to
            Hawaii to see Fat Albert's long behavior
I wish Los Angeles had Fat Albert and electricity
            I wish I lived in Mississippi so I could see
Spiderman fall with the forces of gravity
            I wish I was in California to see Superman get
thrown off the ground by an earthquake
            I wish I was in Las Vegas reading a Garfield comic
riding cartilaginous fish

I wish I was in Wisconsin studying arachnids with
Snoopy I wish to go to California to meet Fat
Albert in a convex lens; I wish to go to Illinois to
meet Sponge Bob Squarepants in a concave lens
I wish to be in Mexico where Garfield studies stuff
like volcanoes I wish I went to Hawaii to see
Garfield study cartilaginous fish
I wish I was in Texas studying zoology with Garfield
I wish to go to New York to see Wonder Woman
study geography I wish I can go to New York City to see
Spiderman do biology
I wish upon a star to go to New York and visit the fat
cat Garfield to teach him about an
anemometer I wish I could live in New York City
where Batman collects rocks and minerals
I wish I could visit Texas to see the Care Bears float
in the air with gravity I wish I lived in New York
City where Venom works with gravity
I wish I lived in Missouri where Rhino studies
volcanoes and mountain ranges I wish I can go to
New York to meet Garfield who likes the human
body I wish I could go to Las Vegas to see
Snoopy and his life cycle I wish Boston was a
better place, a Spiderman comic-book

My Third Eye Can See
Dakota Z.

The ants getting ready to take over the
world. I can see the world's demise in 2027.
I saw the T-rex in the Jurassic Period. I can see
the gods shooting lightning bolts at me. I can
see when mythology come to life. The aliens
will join forces with the United States government.
Area 51 will explode releasing 1,000,000
species of aliens. I can see a baker making
a house of pizza. I can see the aliens
turning the world into Pee Wee's Playhouse #2
"da-da-da." I can see the rulers "or leaders" of
tomorrow "a.k.a. the future."

FRANK L. GILLESPIE ELEMENTARY
Principal: Beverly Slater
Teachers: Ms. Collins, 8th, Ms. Gabrecki, 5th, Ms. Lewis, 6th

Kazembe, Poet in Residence

Author, publisher, and spoken word artist Kazembe has appeared with
Haki Madhubuti, Sonia Sanchez, Amiri Baraka, Nikki Finney, and other
literary masters. Kazembe is the founding member of Vibe-n-Verse, a
professional entourage of spoken word artists and musicians. Vibe-n-
Verse has performed at numerous colleges and universities throughout
the country. For over seven years, Vibe-n-Verse has imparted their
dynamic mix of culture and consciousness (i.e., edutainment) via the
spoken word. He is currently working on additional volumes of poetry
and a long novel.

Haiku
Latoya R.

At first I did not
Know what to do for Haiku
Until this came up

Snow is falling to
The ground without a sound to
Hear but winter's near

Summer
Latoya R.

block
parties
and get togethers
new
t.v.
series
and better
things to
eat
tempting
parties
and great views
of life
that's how
summer is

Haiku
Passhun S.

the cold wind's blowing
through my hair. the snow falling
on my nose and melts

gray skies and black grass
people crying cold black tears
waiting for that day

Mississippi
Kendall S.

I always like
summer best
you can play
with your
games
you can
eat barbeque
and ride
horses
and eat
corn
and cabbage
and spray
people with
water guns
and play
dominoes
and go
to sleep

My Thanksgiving Haiku
Adrian H.

When I come from school
I smell turkey in the air
I smell food outside

We hear birds chirping
that's music to my ears
They are on a tree

I seek happiness
I see joy all around town
everyone is happy

I like to eat food
the turkey is very great
I like to have fun

My Cousins
Mark A.

My cousins are a real pain
they make me want to rattle my brain
my cousins really get on my nerves
they make my teeth want to curl
Sometimes I wish they would go away
And sometimes I wish they would stay
Other times I wish I could put them out
And sometimes they make me want to pout
I love my cousins with all my heart
I just hope they don't rip me apart

Summer Down in Mississippi
Brittnay W.

It's summer down
in Mississippi
it's hot
the hot air
is blowing dust
everywhere
I hear snakes
rattling
I see dogs
running
I smell momma's
cooking from
the side window
I feel the dust
blowing across my
feet
I'm sitting on
the porch
braiding my
sister's hair
the sun
beaming down
on us
the sky is
orange with a
little red
it's summer down
in Mississippi

WILLIAM E. GLADSTONE ELEMENTARY SCHOOL
Principal: Gary M. Moriello
Teachers: Ms. Quiles, 5th/6th, Ms. Sarauw, 6th, Ms. Wojdyla, 6th

Gary Copeland Lilley, Poet in Residence

Poet and teaching artist originally from Sandy Cross, North Carolina and now living in Chicago, Gary Lilley was a long-time resident of Washington DC, where he received the DC Commission on the Arts Fellowship for Poetry in 2000 and 1996. *The Subsequent Blues*, from Four Way Books in 2004, is his first collection of poems. His stories and poems have been published in many journals and anthologies. He earned an M.F.A. from Warren Wilson College in 2002.

I Go Copying Mountains Rivers and Clouds
Salvador I.

I go copying mountains rivers and clouds,
I pack my pen in my pocket. I cannot see
one bird flying upward or one spider
alive in his factory of silk,
with no thought, nothing, I am air,
limitless air which circulates the wheat,
and am moved by an impulse to fly
the insecure direction of one leaf,
the round eye of the motionless fish in
the river, the statues that soar, that
soar through the clouds,
the multiplications of the rains.

El •rbol Como Escoba
Jayleen B.

El árbol como escoba
Siempre barre como escoba
Cuando hay viento se alista para correr
Cuando hay sol se alista para taparse
Cuando hay frio se alista para el frio
Cuando esta lloviendo se alista para mojarse
Cuando esta mojado se alista para secarse
El árbol como escoba
Siempre barre como escoba.

The Tree is Like a Broom (translation)

The tree is like a broom
always sweeps like a broom
when there is wind it gets ready to run
where there is sunlight it gets ready to cover
itself
when it's cold it gets ready for the cold
when it's raining it gets ready to get wet
and when it's wet it gets ready to dry off
the tree is like a broom
always sweeps like a broom.

Yo Veo Dos Arboles Secos Moviendose
Salvador I.

Yo veo dos arboles secos moviendose
por el aire y por la lluvia tambien veo

que de tanta lluvia que cae se hira
un charco de agua los arboles se miran
tristes y a la vez contentos por que
tenian sed y en agua les quito la sed
me imajino que los arboles les don
las gracias al agua por que el
agua es buena para los arboles.

I See Two Dry Trees Moving
Salvador I

I see two dry trees moving
by the wind and by the rain and I see
ponds of water, the trees look sad
and at the same time they look happy
because they were thirsty. I imagine that
the trees give thanks to the water
because the water is good for trees.

La Danza de las Gitanas
Stephanie E.

Las dos
gitanas en
medio de
la noche

bailalando sin
parar pues la
luna en su
guia

La luna las
guiaba en medio
de la noche

A bailar su danza
alrredor del fuego
moviendo las manos
como pequeñas olas
y aplaudiendo a la
luna por iluminarlas
en esa noche tan
especial.

**The Dance of the Gypsies
Stephanie E.**

The two
gypsy women
in the middle
of the night

dancing without
stopping
the moon is their
guide

The moon
guiding in
middle of the
night

To dance
around the
fire moving
their hands
like little
waves and
applauding the
moon for
giving light
in that
special night.

**Otoño Fatal
Esli Z.**

El sol en las hojas de mi huerta hace
ardiente copos y monedas de oro.
Abetos y arboles grandes hacen paredes verdes
que van al cielo más azul que el mar.
El aire todavia esta quieto como aquel primer
intente despues de la muerte.
No hay susurros de un respirar de las hojas
que se mueven y el valle a mis
pies puede ser el perdido Eden
que veo atraves de mis lagrimas.
translation of Fatal Autumn by John Beecher

Otoño Fatal
Indalecio G.

El sol en las hojas de mi arbol
se hacen como copos ardientes
y monedas de oro. El abeto y el
secoya levantan unas paredes
verdes hasta el cielo mas azul
que el mar. El aire se detiene
como en el primer momento de la
muerte. No hay rumor de un soplo
de aire que mueva ni una hoja y
el valle a mis pies parece ser
un paisaje perdido del Eden
que veo atraves de mis lagrimas.
translation of Fatal Autumn by John Beecher

Otoño Fatal
Ivan S.

El sol en las hojas de mi huerto
hacen copos ardientes y monedas
de oro.
Abetos y secoyas se levantan como
un enorme muro verde para el cielo
que es mas azul que el mar.
El viento esta quieto como en el primer
instante despues de la muerte.
No hay susurro de un aliento que
mueva una hoja ni el valle a mis pies.
Parece ser el paisaje del paraiso
perdido del Eden, visto atraves
de mis lagrimas.
translation of Fatal Autumn by John Beecher

La Nieve
Jayleen B.

Una mañana me levante de mi cama y
mire por la ventana y vi algo que cai del
cielo y entonces me di cuenta que eso
que estaba cayendo era la felicidad y alegria
para todos. Los niños salian a jugar
a fuera con lo que estaba cayendo y
hasta la noche no se entraban por que ere
muy difertido hacer un muñeco de nieve.

188

The Snow (translation)

One morning I got out of my bed and looked
through my window and saw what came from
the sky. Then I noticed that it was falling,
it was the joy and happiness for all. The children
came outside to play with what was falling. They
played until night, it was fun because they were
making a snow man.

La Danza en el Pueblo
Ivan S.

Esta noche esta de fiesta
todos bailan alegremente
con sus largos vestidos de
algodon ligero, con un toque de
Luz brillante.

Los bailes son hermosos con
la musica del arpa, y el sonido
de la guitarra.

Que toquen los tambores,
que la noche esta de fiesta
todos bailan alegremente
la rica Danza del pueblo.

The Dance in the Town
Ivan S.

This night is to party
everyone dancing joyful
with their weightless dress
of cotton light with touch
of brilliance.

The dancers are beautiful with
the music of the harp, and the
sound of the guitar.

What touch the drum,
the night is to party
everyone dancing joyful
the rich Dance of town.

Ella siempre es bonita
Lourdes C.

Ella siempre es
bonita y cuando
ella cae del
cielo sonrio
y la veo como
todos los dias.

She is always wonderful
Lourdes C.

She is always
wonderful and
when she gets
down from the
sky I smile
and see her
every day.

Lo que cae del cielo
Luisa

Lo que cae
del cielo es
muy hermoso
en el invierno

la veo y siento
que me relajo

es lindo como
los angeles del
cielo.

The Look of the Sky
Luisa

The look of the sky
is beautiful in winter.

I feel relaxed when I see it

like the angels of the sky.

190

Nieve
Ivan S.

Es la purera mas sagrada
que cae en el invierno.

Unos la adoran por ser tan
inmensamente bella.

Es como una jolla preciosa
regalada por el cielo.

Snow
Ivan S.

Is the most sacred purity
that falls in the winter.

Some people adore it because of
its immeasurable beauty.

It is the most precious gem
given as a gift from the sky.

La Nieve
Gabriela

Un dia mire ala ventana y vi caer del
cielo algo ala tierra formaba montañas
pequeñas de ella y esperando que todos
disfrutaian de ella.

The Snow
Gabriela

One day I looked outside the window and
saw fall something from the sky to the
ground. It formed small mountains
and was waiting for everyone to enjoy.

My neighborhood
Steven H.

Where I live is
my neighborhood
on the west
side you see
people playing
basketball and you
see people gambling
and you smell dead
people in the air and
you smell bullets in the
air and you can smell fresh
chicken being made and you see
homeless people begging for money,
and trying to steal from stores,
and trying to break into someone's
car to sleep in there for warmth
and make a living.

In a Toy Store
Omar E.

There are people and kids,
they talk to each other.
Saying, Dad, I want that toy,
Mom, I want that toy, until
they buy them the toy. You
can hear the cashier saying
how much it costs.

Then in the night
all you see is a security guard
taking care of the store. You
can hear the security camera
getting everything on tape.

Untitled
Marquetta

When night falls the little stars
at night twinkle in the sky, the
police come and everyone hides
because it's past 11:05 pm. We play hide
& go seek then we have dance contests.
People would say I'm the best

out there, it looks like a cat
getting ready to pounce on us
then we all start to run, all of
a sudden I hear my mom call.

Las Vegas
Lavelle G.

The light shining, I feel as if I am in paradise.
A very nice place, look at all the gleaming lights.
It is so beautiful I cannot believe it.
The casino is open and clubs are too
the best thing about it that it's
something new.

My poem
Ashley

I am in a place where water does
not run and where cars don't stop
a place to the east where piles
of hail cover the houses on each block

I Am Writing About a Place You Have Never Been
Antoine A.

You have never been to the White Sox
Stadium, it's big, has thousands of
people, it's large and the White Sox
would bet you their stadium will
have you cheering for the whole game
when they win the screaming stays
the same, they're throwing the best
strikes, hit a home run, that's
the baseball rights, there's nothing
like that, a love, the swing of their bats.

Snow
Roshanda W.

Can you guess what I'm thinking of
and it's not above.

It's something you walk on in the
winter and it makes a blizzard,

it's very cold and it makes your
hands and feet freeze,

sometimes it's very deep and sometimes
very steep,

sometimes it gets cold and forms
into ice which is sometimes very
nice

so if you did guess already
what I'm thinking of, you're very smart,
and if you didn't, just restart.

Snow Days
Kevin M.

I can hardly see through the
plain bland color in front of me. I play
in the splendor of the substance. People
are shoveling and plows are out, everyone
is running about. Now that everyone is out the
substance that once had splendor is now dingy,
now no one can play but we can still have a happy
day.

Riding the Bus
Takaila C.

Riding the bus I see a lady wearing
too much make up like a clown. There's
a man sleeping as if he had a long
night.

Riding the bus I see a cute boy talking
as if he was talking to me. The bus
driver is looking sad as if she just
broke up with her boyfriend.

Riding the bus I see a fat person
looking like a big old bus. I see two
people kissing as if they were really in
love.

When I Get on the Bus
Kevin M.

When I get on the bus I hear many things. Something like a wailing sound as the bus brakes. People talk, it sounds like crows cawing in the morning. I see my surroundings out the bus's window and they are blurred like the colors of a rainbow. People stand there looking angry and shoving and pushing each other like a school of fish. Finally I reach my destination and get off the bus.

I Don't Like Chicago Because
Jermaine W.

I don't like Chicago because
they shoot people, killing each other
like a can of beans, and they got a
bad basketball team. I know because that
bald-headed man left and things cost
too much money like money grows on trees,
and people sniff drugs like it's candy,
and people dying like old green eggs
in ham, and that old president is stingy
with the money.

Past the Window Pane
Victor F.

Past the window pane
that abandoned house
a soft wind at dawn
in gray winter.

Out in the cold weather,
you could hardly hear
the wolves howl.

And people indoors
drinking hot cocoa.

Who Is the God Who Is High?
Robert C.

Who is the god who is high?
Who is the god who rules heaven and the sky?
Who is the god who watches me go by?
Who is the god that I love?
Who is the god who welcomes me above?

Grand Master Hyun's Hapkido School
Luis A. G.

It is peaceful there,
The sound of stick hitting stick is lovely,
I hear kids bowing and saying sumo to me,
The kids and masters like me practicing hitting bags,
We help our class and school,
We sweep, mop, and protect the school.
We care.
Thank you.

What I See in Nature
James B.

The things I see in nature are people selling and smoking weed. I see people doing drugs, going to jail, and people getting killed. I think people should not do all this bad stuff because bad is wrong and when you do bad you will get caught eventually so that is why you should not do bad. In the Bible it says if you do good in the world and get good grades, good will always follow you.

Untitled
LaVelle G.

A beautiful spring day filled with compassion,
bright red rose petals as soft as clouds,
flowers blooming,
birds singing,
a spectacular sight.

The sunshine lights up
and makes a beautiful day
nice and lovely,
the sun shines through my window,
I think about nature,
lovely,
beautiful, very soulful.

Spring has
culture,
grace,
style,
and soul.

Gone with the Wind
Natalia M.

I am not dead
I did not die
In the winter
Under all the snow
Is my grave
I am not dead
I did not die
The calm breeze
Touches your face
I am the spring
I am the calm water
In the brook
In the fall
Under all the leaves
There lies my grave
I am not there
I did not die
In the summer
Do not come to my
Grave and weep
I am not there
I did not die
I am gone with the wind

Alabama Old Times While Doing Slavery
Lonnie L.

People drinking, smoking, doing drugs, and most of them always talking about let's go get some Bud. Baby's crying, Mama's lying telling court people she'll soon be dying. Papa's gone, no one's at home. People cheating while their wife is at home eating. Our ancestors once were always beaten, raped, but some of them were smart, they tried to escape.

The pain they had to take just to give us African Americans a break. But some people just don't care going around beating up people and snatching their hair. If Martin Luther King were here, he would try to give these people some holiday cheer.

Ever Green Plaza Mall
Christian R.

Dust of the feet
Dust on the clothes
Clothes and shoes going
All day, all night

Now
Only stars and mist
And lonely clothes
Two cabaret dancers dying to
Try on the clothes

Voices of dollars
And sounds of cash registers

Voices of people jumping
Voices singing
Softer than the shoes
Softer than the clothes

Down! Down! We Go
Lonnie L.

Once there was a man who stood at his door sticking out his hand, he took in money, but gave out beers. Then all the people went out back and began to do cheers. The man said, "This is my porch! Now it is time to light the torch!" After they lit the torch all the party people began to jump up and down on the porch. The porch collapsed and the people that didn't fall bounced. 13 people died and all their mothers and fathers cried. The man that took the money lied and was acting funny. He knows that he jumped on the porch, because he was the main one saying light the torch! So people died, the man went to court and lied. 13 people gone, the man at home alone, crying because he just found out that his brother is also dying.

Pilsen
Brenda A.

The sun so shiny and very hot.
Everybody is
in the pools, going
to the park playing on the swings and on the slides.

Lots of cars passing by
making marks on the

ground. People crashing
in accidents.

Stars so nice you could see
the moon so bright.
Some people sleeping
dreaming good.

Gangs are still outside
looking for trouble, hearing
the people shooting all over
the place. Scaring people
at night.

Love
Fatima R.

Love is a sweet
thing.
Some people think
it's a joke.
Some people think
it's a formula
that really, really works.
Love is a great thing.
Some people hear
love whistling in their
ear.
Love is just something
that you feel.

The Weather on My Block
Mayra C.

In the sky at night I
can see the stars and the big
moon that is very bright.

Now I see a big orange
sun in the pretty sky, I can hear
the cars beeping, people talking,
I see a lot of kids going to school
and adults going to work.

I can see drops of water
falling from the sky, then I go
to school and start to write.

Untitled
Derrick J.

The fierce anger in fright like the teardrops of the stars in a lonely night and the names that she calls are so clear like the glance of a smiling peer, like the east and west game, it lives with cheer. No one can understand her, but what she expresses to me is so clear.

Places I Love
Erika B.

1. Magic Waters
Magic Waters is a magic place
Everywhere you go
You will see a different face
All day you see wet feet
Nobody will even stop to eat
There you will stop
In the pool you will drop.

2. House of Kix
The House of Kix
Has a lot of tricks
All the rides
Are like big ole tides
I get on the rides
On the rides I go
The kids are crowing
Like a black crow
In there it is funny
Also outside it is very sunny.

3. Galewood Park
Galewood Park is like an art
Every day I shall go
When I'm there.
People should know
And that's the way it goes.

On a Summer Day!
Shunda B.

I woke up on a summer morning,
went outside but it was boring,
went up to the candy store,
wind was whistling, and blowing through,
went out on Heath Street

200

no one don't know where that's
at because Heath Street is located
west, out to K-town –
that's the west side of Chi-town.
Girls playin' jump rope,
boys playin' basketball
sayin, man, that's a foul.
Went to the next block,
boys taking off their
shirts, cause they think
they hot.
Went to Comiskey, cluckers
begging for a penny.
Then a girl hollered and said,
ain't that Shunda. Then I
saw Mikassa, she said, where's
my dollar. I said, I'm about to
go home to eat some collard greens!

Why
Sakeria Y.

Why is there killing on the street?
Why does the killing try to happen
to me? Why is there fear here?
We have people who hustle
on the street, we have homeless
people struggling to sleep and eat.
Why are we falling apart? Why are
we supposed to be rich and why
are you sitting in the dust? Why
are we killing on the street? Why
is the killing happening around me?

Bag Lady
Christian R.

Bag lady carrying food, clothes,
                    and
                    chips.

Arms, legs, and thighs hurting from
                    the food, clothes,
                    and chips,
                    but the Bag
                    Lady can't
        help it.

Everyone knows
her
passing her by.

This person is my mom
and all
those bags make me
wanna cry.

She's dragging her bags
walking past the cabs,
she's sweating so much
she has to use a dish rag.

The Bag Lady is tired.
She goes home to take a
nap.
When she wakes up she
puts on her
lucky cap.

So now the Bag Lady's through
It seems like she's crazy
But if she is
I will always remember her
as my mom the
Bag Lady.

My Grandfather
Tiffany T.

My grandfather is very old.
He is eighty years old.
He lives with my uncle.
He has been blind for nine years.
He has gray hair.
He wears striped shirts.

He also wears blue pants.
Has long nails.
He combs his hair every day.
He wears Oxford shoes.
He is five feet tall.
He drinks a lot of coffee.
He lives in a basement.

He used to live in a house but he moved.
He is very kind to people.

He sings a lot but no one complains.
He is very good at singing.
It sounds like he is a professional.

Grandma's House
Lakia W.

Babies are crying 'cause diapers
need to be changed. The street is
wet and cloudy 'cause of all the rain.

The babies are still crying 'cause
of the rain, it seems like they will
never stop crying and they are in
such pain.

Now it's noon, the babies
want to eat. We give them some
crackers until we heat the meat.

The food is done but the babies
are fast asleep. I hate these
kinds of days when the babies confuse
me.

Friend
Tierra B.

A friend will not leave you hanging.
A friend will have your back.
A friend will not talk about you behind your
back. A friend will help you do things. A
friend will give you support. A friend will let
you know if you are hurting their feelings. A
friend will not let you get in trouble.
You know what? I have one of those friends.
And my friend doesn't leave you hanging.

Untitled
Derrick J.

A place that you have never been,
where screams drift away through the night
like baby animals crying and like watching Babe,
your eyes sparkle of sorrow
when something is shown, always wanted, like

people on the corners of my block, afterward
all silence, except for gunshots and ambulance
sirens.

Untitled
Yeritsa C.
after Mark Strand's "I am writing from a place you have never been"

I am writing from a place
you have never been.
It's where the days pass
like a flowing waterfall,
where the lives never
touch the ground, where
there's always music, happiness,
and cheer. There is a baby
and his eyes are like the sky.

JORDAN COMMUNITY SCHOOL
Principal: Dr. Maurice Harvey
Teachers: Ms. Laslkov, 5th, Ms. Lovell, 8th, Ms. Halicki, 6th/7th/8th, Ms. Topp, 4th

Cecilia Pinto, Poet in Residence

Cecilia Pinto received her B.A. in creative writing from Knox College and her M.F.A. in writing from the School of the Art Institute. Her poetry and prose have appeared in various journals including *Quarter After Eight, Fence* and *Rhino*. She was awarded first prize in Permafrost's 2002 haiku contest and was the winner of the *Esquire Magazine* prize in short fiction in 2000.

Cecilia says, "I very much enjoyed my first year at Jordan. It was a pleasure to be a part of a school community where learning is valued and students are given the opportunity to express themselves creatively. Jordan is home to many smiling faces and thoughtful students, what a wonderful combination."

Who and Where
Jaquitta J.

I am tall with small feet and fingers. I look like my sister and my mom.
When my shoes get wet I just want to go home and be home in my bed.
People told me that my mom looks like my sister.
All my life people have told me I will be a teenager in four years.
I am nine. People have told me that I am special.
I live where everybody lives, in Chicago, like you, and you and you.

When I Take My Pencil
Louis D.

It is like my pencil knows what I am going to draw on a Saturday
morning
Like a shark or a horse. It makes it come alive and the pencil rides the
horse
and the shark eats the pencil.

Red Roses
Yolanda C.

Down my aunt's house
beautiful, brilliant roses grew
with their fresh fragrance.
Blooming in the sun, ripe red.
Down my aunt's house, I saw roses
grow.

This is Just to Say
Destiny S.

I'm sorry that I ate your strawberries
without asking you, Mom.
Do not be mad at me just because I ate your
strawberries. I'm sorry, Mom.

What is Pluto Doing?
Feneish H.

What is Pluto doing?
It's resting and singing Pluto songs.
It's spinning around.
It's looking at the other planets.
And singing its Pluto songs again.

Pluto, Pluto up so high
make you jump up to the sky.
Say bye bye, Pluto's gone.

Who I am
Jennifer G.

Who I am is a person with short fingers and feet. I look like my aunt. We
have the same hair.
I like the snow but when I touch it, it feels cold. I see people huge but I
get smaller yet.
I like to play soccer. When I play soccer, I play well. I have a sister but I
don't want to be like her.
I'm not smart. I am helpful. My head is full of neat ideas.

The Dog
Luis M.

A dog is white black
winter the dog is cold
frozen the dog barks.

The Letter I
Pedro R.

Imagine the island
ignore the ice inside
an igloo you will freeze.
Indoors you will turn
into an invisible person.
An Indian city is icy
indicating it's cold.
I'm impatient walking home
to feel the heat.

Untitled
Virginia G.

I was a black clawfish trying to get away from
the store today because they want to sell me
and cook me and eat me.

Untitled
Delano W.

I look like my dad and have little feet, hands
and a big head.
When I'm outside it looks
old and rusty.
When I'm in the house, it looks clean and new.

Untitled
Deborah T,

The moon hangs over the forest, a lamp. As the sky becomes dark and
the stars are shinning bright. As if there is a group of stars ready to form
a wall to protect the moon from shattering everywhere as the craters
zig-zag through the dark sky. The moon is beautiful, so bright, lights up
the whole forest. The moon is big like a delicious sugar cookie
decorated with many stars!

2 Haiku
Kiayanna M.

When it's cold outside
the white snow falls on the ground
and the birds go south.

When it's hot outside
the yellow sun shines a lot
and the birds come back.

The Letter L
Roberto G.

Lake Lincoln is filled
with Lock Ness Sea monsters.
Some are little, some are large.
They are long. If you fell in there
you better pray to the Lord.
If you lift their upper jaw
It looks like a chainsaw.

I Am Sorry
Daniel B.

Sorry I went outside
when I was not supposed to. I hope
you forgive me. I went out
because it was hot
and I wanted to be with my friends.

Who and Where
Joseph G.

Who I am- basketball player.
Where I am- at the gym.
Who I am- smart person.
Where I am- spelling bee.

The Letter T
Devon H.

I take off running when I get a taco. I will run
and tackle some trash today.
I found a treasure that played a tune.
Today I made a tall tally mark
when I was talking.
My dog can wag its tail, that's a talent.

Who and Where
Rhode S.

Who am I?
I know I look like my mom
but do I really
or should I look like my dad
on an island far away?
Who would I look like?
I'm there and I look in the mirror
and ask who am I?
Where did I come from?
Why am I here?
I wonder and wonder
every second of the day.
I'm short yet might grow.
I'm smart, might not be long.
Who am I on this island today?

The Letter E
Shabnum A.

My mom is special to me because
sometimes she helps me, explains my homework to me.
She knows English better than me.
And sometimes it is easy for me to do it.
But everything is easy for my mom to do.

Untitled
Julio C.

I went outside.
You told me not to
although
I did go outside.
And which you
probably are going to
get really mad about.
Forgive me
There were kids outside
playing with each other
and having so much fun.

Crazy
Arelis G.

You'd have to be
crazy
to live in Rogers Park
It is always dirty.
You see many
gangs
You'd have to be
crazy
to live in the same
area where
I live.
You'd have to be crazy
to live next door to
me.
You'd have to be crazy
not to live in
Rogers Park
where it is multicultural,
where there are
always

good schools and good stores.
You'd have to be
Crazy.

Untitled
Jiselle L.

It's sacred and safe. Something that's not told.
The world is full of crimes but I can always find a solution.
So, there Wonder Woman, is on her way to rescue the world.
There's secrets involved throughout the whole world.
Help is always the magic word.
I'm a busy woman and have a lot of responsibilities.
I'm the same as everyone else, the only difference is
I have powers. No danger is near once you see Wonder Woman.

Untitled
Audrey W.

You have to be crazy
to want to live on
Damen and Jarvis
because they sell
drugs and get locked up.

You have to be crazy
to wear shorts when
it's cold. This is Chicago
not Alabama.

You have to be crazy
to not finish high school
before having a baby. You
must be crazy.

The Last Day
Megan G.

Today is the last day
in this season

Today is the last day
to breath this air.

Today is the last day
we play outside.

Today is the last day
of the summer.

Untitled
Cynthia M.

I remember the first
time we met. It was
a rainy day.

I was on a bench
crying. You came and
talked to me.

My world turned
bright when you
finished talking
to me.

Untitled
Christian P.

The woods are lovely dark and deep.
The woods are filled with eyes
that lie within the endless maze.
The moon is shiny as a light bulb
gleaming in the sky. Creatures
of the night come out, into the dark.

Untitled
Luis A.

You have to sleep to have energy.
You have to be happy to feel good and to feel relief.
You need to eat to be healthy.
You need to play to have fun.
You need to breathe.
You need to ride a horse to feel the air.

Love isn't Seen
Karen M.

This world you can
see the sky, the water
but not the breeze.

212

The breeze that keeps
you cool, that blows in
your hair. It's the same
with love. You can't see it
but you can feel it because
even thought you can't
see it doesn't mean
it isn't there.

I remember my grandmother...
Patricia P.

My grandmother is in Mexico.
I remember her by a picture and
sometimes I hear like
she is talking too me.
I remember the last
time when she hugged me.
I was sad and glad.
I was glad because I know
that she loves me and I feel sad
because that was the last time
I saw my grandmother. And my
grandmother is special.
Because there isn't another
person like her. I miss my grandmother.

Nervous
Joana G.

Squirrels are nervous because if they stand on the side
and a car is coming they return the way they came.
And that's the way some squirrels die.
They need to control themselves, and another idea,
they move less and shake their tails too much.

Ode to my Bike
Jesus P.

Oh how I love my bike.
My bike is black
with a little blue.
   It's a little
hard to ride.
Sometimes I
dream with my bike

that someone
is stealing it.
   I wake up
thinking that somebody
stole it.
When I ride my
bike I feel like
I am flying in
the sky.

Untitled
Ramiro R.

I remember in Mexico where I go to the rivers with my cousins to swim.
Erick was 9 years old and Omar was 7 years old. We go to get some fruit
like bananas and oranges. When I was going to get one orange,
I saw one snake.

Ode to my Car Collection
Cristian M.

I love my car collection because I've had them
since I was 5 years old. I am 12 years old.
I have 10 cars. 3 cars are colored red. I dream
I have my cars for real. When I wake up
I go look at them but they don't change.

JOSEPH JUNGMAN ELEMENTARY SCHOOL
Principal: Mary Ellen Garcia-Humphries
Teachers: Mr. Bernier, 8th, Ms. Cuadrado, 6th,
Ms. Ramirez, 6th

David Rosenstock, Poet in Residence

David Rosenstock got his B.A. at The New School and is currently working towards his M.F.A. in writing at The School of the Art Institute of Chicago. He was the recipient of the Irwin Shaw award for a novella and the Ottilie Grebanier award for a short play chosen by Mac Wellman. His work has been published in *The Brooklyn Review* and *Dial Magazine.*

David says, "At Jungman we examined works by poets, writers, and Hiphop artists, such as Pablo Neruda, Julio Cortázar, Tom Phillips, C.D. Wright, The Roots, Billy Collins, and De La Soul. Influenced by their unique forms, the exercises involved letters to prisoners, instruction manuals, odes, lyrics, and smells trapped in film canisters. Together the kids and I traversed a slippery slope that started all the way back at what a line was, and in the process we've gotten to the bottom of some of poetry's greatest mysteries. The experience has been without equal in my life. I've learned that for all the education in the world, if you can't define what a metaphor is in a simple way, it's all been for nought. The kids at Jungman continually pushed me to improve my communication skills and amplify my creativity. I can only hope I did the same for them."

Ode to Life
Luis C.

Life is a rock
so hard if you have it.

So hard if you try to
break it.

You try and try,
no success.

Life...is...a rock.

Ode to Sports
Alejandro G.

Sports are my life
soccer ball like
a clock working for
hours
football is shoes
on a cable going
on air
Tennis ball is
a yo-yo doing
tricks on the floor
Ping Pong balls is
a ball in the
casino
A basketball is
my head spinning
thinking about sports.

Dear Prisoner,
Martha G.

I too feel lonely sometimes
like no one is there. Or you
just think of settling for a girl
that is just there until
your looks fade away   she'll fade
away from you. But I   just don't
get the way you ignore mom
and find girls
and they're cheating on you.
I guess you're just a fish

216

in a bowl, going around to each girl,
each problem, over and over
again.

Your loneliness is like a bowl
with nothing in it
maybe just one drop.
I pray for you to be refilled.
It is like a death
never to be revived.

In My Apartment
Rafael

In my apartment I see white
walls everywhere.
There's a black couch in my
living room.
I hear a little person saying
where's my money.
I see the wood tiles that make
my floor.
Bulbs in the ceiling that make
my light.
My apartment is empty and
dull.
Fish stare at me from their
glass home.

Poem
Yvonne M.

My apartment is white
like a ghost.
The streets are filled with
people walking in all directions.
Birds fly and what they find, who knows.
At night you can't sleep because
you hear noises from all directions.
The people next door play
music loud.

People in the Hood
Cesar G.

I see gangbangers slanging
and kids tagging

Cars running through the streets like wildcats
and in the alleys I see big old rats

Through the night
I see gangs fight

I see crews fight against each other
All they do is talk about their mothers

Mothers and fathers
Screaming and fighting
Their kids are just hiding

Rap Poem
Damian T.

My name is Damian Tellez
I go to school to make myself better and show
people who I am
I ain't no kid
in the streets I want to be someone
in the future I ain't going to be someone dead
I am Damian Tellez you hear

My Hood is Scary and Dangerous
Lorena S.

My hood is like a junkyard
    It's very dirty
My hood is like cheetahs on the loose
    It's very dangerous
Around the corner is a bullet
    to the head.
Just walking out my door
    is like going to a new place
you never been before

When I say it's like a junkyard
    I mean it's very dirty not clean
When I say my hood is like cheetahs
    on the loose I mean it's dangerous
        gangs, drugs, and violence

When I say around the corner is
    like a bullet to the head
I mean all you see on the corners
    are gangs and violence

When I say just walking out my door
   is like a new place you've never been before
I mean everyday there's
new news that something
happened or it looks different

My Neighborhood
Martha G.

My neighborhood is full of
shootings, gangsters, and hoes,
with drugs changing hands
every 10 minutes. Viewing a
shooting every time I go
out, so my house is like
a jail I can't leave.
People doing drugs in a big
red building in front of my
house. 13, 14, 15, 16 and 17 year
olds doing drugs, selling drugs,
and making drugs. Walking
through the big gates taking
a shortcut, then gangsters
chasing me. I don't care.

Dangerous
Jasmine F.

My neighborhood is dangerous
like a poisonous snake
Cops swarming like bees on honey
Gangs are shooting one another
Car windows broken and houses
shuttered down the streets
Stop signs tagged with a spray can

Lyrics
Gabriela P.

Pilsen a neighborhood with kids
Gangs being careful in the park
like a prey watches its predator
Cars coming with a screeching sound
like a herd of elephants: Houses
yellow, blue, and red, bricks and wood
build them up. Gangs all over

the place with the police
after them, many colors that
they wear, like a rainbow, red, orange,
yellow, green, blue, indigo, violet. Boys
and girls in basketball while
others sharing what they have
with the less fortunate, like a bird
feeds its babies.

Surprise Woman
Christopher B.

tense not loose, tense, surprised
loud scream and screeching while
suprised, while gasping and
grasping and deep breaths

tense, not loose, tense
surprised, loud scream and screeching, surprise
gasping and grasping and deep breaths

Saturn
Mario Q.

A planet with a ring, little rocks
orange ball, no oxygen, little breath,
little breath, dried up lungs.

Can we fall off if we're on the bottom?
I know it's big, but it's too big for all of us.
Is the ring an illusion or is it alive?
Why, why, is this in the sky
Why, why, is this in the sky

Waves
Fatima C.

In Puerto Rico there are huge waves
with seaweed all over my waves.
I told my friend wait because the
waves aren't here yet.

They are as blue
as my friend's shirt. They go
wild when they party.

Waves have
beautiful voices.

Shallow
Nevin B.

I stepped into the lake
Smelled the nature in the air
Heard the birds in the sky
And saw the bottom of the shallow water
Along with the wind blowing in my face
        and pieces of moss
        coming from the wind

Anger and Hate
Martha G.

I hate the government
when they make their mistakes.
I feel anger inside of me
when the government makes
their mistakes.
And when they raise the
taxes. Or when they wrongfully
accuse a person of a crime
they did not commit. Or
get sued and make
civilians pay the price.
I feel hate and anger for the
government and there is one word
I have for them, Anarchy.

Love
Paige H.

For Valentine's Day me and my boyfriend
went into McDonalds. We could smell fries
in the air. As I tasted the burger
my eyes filled with love. I see people
ordering food and I hear them
smacking on it. As I
touch my fries my heart is pounding.
This is my day of love. I'm lovin it.

Deep Love
Steven O.

I just saw this beautiful girl,
with her gorgeous blonde hair
and glittering blue eyes,
walking past my house.

You could really hear her deepness
and likings she had of me

You could smell the fresh aroma,
inside, preparing for a first date

I could taste the creamy sensation
of her favorite fettuccini pasta
melting in her mouth

I could feel the tenderness and power
she had kissing my lips

and that's when I fell
in love

Love
Mayra R.

The taste of your
lips are like the strawberries
with sugar on summer

The smell of your
color is like
the smell of the
pancakes that your
mom makes

The touch of your
sense calls the attention
of me and the girls

I see the sun
shine when
you're close
to me.

Love is a Wolf Spider
Group Poem

My heart breaks the web,
my heart is a web.
Love is full of spiders,
heart shaped spiders.

The red spider bit my hand
and made me bleed.
Her hand is bleeding into the river.

Love is like a creepy spider
coming up to bite you in spite of you.

Love is a different animal.
Believe me sweety I got enough to feed the needy.
I don't care,
but I love you.

It matters what we feel.
No, it doesn't, it's how they are.

Hello,
Bye
Hi
Bye
Bye-Bye

I know where you are.
Don't try to hide.
I will find you.

What I Remember
Miriam A.

I remember my mom
putting on lotion
my uncle using cologne
my mom's perfume

my sister sick
drinking cough medicine
my mom putting alcohol
on my sister
my mom cooking
with onions

my uncle smoking
mom and dad drinking coffee
dad cooking
with spices
my mom
drinking coffee

Smoking
Gabriela R.

I remember when my grandpa
smoked, he said it was
bad for your lungs
and gives you cancer,
but he said it was good
for the nerves and always
calms him down. He always
smoked in front of me.

He said it tasted like wood burning and
smelled like burning food.
He said his brain was not healthy
because of smoking
too much. He said it was
soft like a pillow in a bed
lying down like
roses in
a bed.

He said that the edge of it
looked like houses burning and leaving
it like sand. He said the fire
was as yellow as a crayon.

Laundry
Gabriela P.

I remember when my mom washed my clothes
In the basement,
Red, blue, yellow clothes.
Separating them,
In goes the clothes,
She pours the Snuggle and
Sure enough the clothes are soft and cuddly,
The scent is so pretty and
It smells like sweet plumeria.

224

When I put my clothes on
I smell the plumeria scent and
Different kinds of scents like
Mountain Fresh, Plumeria, Lemon Breeze

One of My Favorite Scents
Yair H.

One of my favorite scents is #2.
It smells like my dad's
cologne. I smell it
when my dad hugs me or carries me
or when he leaves his clothes in the
hamper, in his room. I see $2
cologne.

Midnight Scents
Elizabeth H.

The perfume smell reminds me of my mom
when she is going out, her perfume
fills the air with an enchanting
smell of inexplicably mixed
scents. When I get close to her
to ask her what is the name of it.
I have to hold my breath
because I feel like I'm suffocating
in a deep pool of strong scent.

Her perfume reminds me of a lot of things
like a beautiful night on the beach with a big
moon, or a rainforest, a breeze of fresh air
and smells of different flowers
and plants surrounding me
and before she can answer me
I say midnights scents.
She smiles and leaves towards the car,
and I wonder if I'm correct.

Dear Prisoner,
Bertoldo V.

You got locked up. Also bit up
By the police. When they told
You get on your knees, you
Were damaged, hurt, but

The police didn't care, ever
Since you had nightmares.

Now you wish to get out,
But you can't.   Won't.   Until
You pay for what you did.
You killed a gangmember. Don't you
Remember, it was November 17, 2000.
What you did was dumb. Just
Because the person you killed
Hit you in the thumb with a bat.

Dear Prisoner,
Lara A.

My Mom
She's funny and smart
She's sometimes sad because
She wants to stay home one day
With us but she can't
She has to work a lot because
It's only her right now. My Dad
He's in jail. My Mom works very hard
I love my Mom
She's so pretty

Dear Prisoner,
Gabriela P.

The desk of hate   is looking awkward.
The days pass and the desk
changes place and form
I was in a cell,
a cell of nature captured
in a picture. As the days pass

I see a new point of view.
The picture captured and day-by-day
fading away
nature changes
from plants to houses

Dear Prisoner,
Jocelyn I.

I do hate cleaning   washing the
dirtiness of cleaning   I confess to doing
nothing   that's dirty   I found dirty clothes
their smelly   sticky   stained   I hate
the mystery of the clean   will never
be done.   We can change   by not getting
dirty

Dirty is sticky   smelly I hope
you're not dirty sticky smelly   I thought
you were clean but I hate dirty
The hate of smell   that's dirty
I hate dirty but I hate cleaning

Dear Prisoner,
Steven O.

I know people love   Tapping on the glass.
Banging on the glass. You just eat   and sleep.
I know you're bored. I wish I could free you.
Rescue you.   Save you.   Isn't it weird at night
when the lights are off. No one's watching you.
Then every day is the same. How
do you deal with it? I wouldn't last
a day in there.

Dear Prisoner,
Alex H.

I roar at you   You
Roar at me
walking back and forth

Dear Prisoner,
Melissa L.

I don't know if you can hear me.
It's so dark and cruel in there,
trapped in your room,
waiting for the punishment to end.

I've been grounded before.
I'd look out the window.

I'd see kids playing outside.
I'd beg my mother to let me go outside,
but every time I begged
her words crushed me.

Dear Prisoner,
Vanessa A.

Food, bread of sadness   hungry.
      starving.   Really miserable.
bed of coldness.   cold.   freezing.
love   the smell of freedom.
      can't wait to be released.   eager.
willing.   The spider of misery trapped me.

Instructions on How to Write
Fatima C.

Begin by scribble scramble
on the house walls. Let your arms go
wild. Forget your parents. Have Fun.
Write your name. Take it from the inside.
Hear the spaghetti in the kitchen.
Touch your mom's plate while you write.

How to Play Football
Oscar T.

Hearing the spiral tossed across the field,
the sacked quarterback on the whistling
grass, the pressure when it's fourth down,
tasting the grass before you're tackled,
the glory of a touchdown, and then,
you on the line, and bang, just like that,
it's over, you lose.

Instructions on How to Draw Gerbils
Conrado M.

First you feel the head of the gerbil.
Then taste the two dots for eyes.
Smell two rectangle noses.
See the fat circle of its body.
Hear the tail go long.
Taste one circle in half

228

each side for a touch of ears.
At the end you hear four sticks
for legs and arms.
That's how you draw a gerbil.

Instructions on How to Read
Felipe G.

First go to a place that's not that bright or dark.
Then sit down in that place.
You start putting the letters together
like ingredients in a stew. You can smell
the words burning in your ears.
Then you will start to taste the words
on your tongue.

How to Flirt
Stephanie H.

I taste my step when I walk
up to the boy. I smell the boy laughing
at me
when I tell a joke.
I always hear the boy writing
with a pencil when we talk and
when I walk away from him,
I can see his feelings
hurting inside his chest. I touch
his sad, soft voice.

Instructions on How to Love
Mayra R.

You have to feel the right boy.
Then taste his first name and last name.
Touch his reactions.
And see if he's taking you seriously
Smell if he's taken

Instructions on How to Rule the World
Yvonne

First I would make everyone fear me,
make them taste the anger of my words.
I would give people joy.

Make babies feel like queens/kings.
I would change the weather.
People would taste the sunrise.

How to Walk on the Streets of Chicago
Cesar G.

once you come out of your house
don't come out with your hat sideways
or roll up one side of your pants
fourthly, don't walk like you're all cool
or that you know something
don't stay staring at the gangmembers
just walk normal and don't wear the following colors—white and blue,
white, red and green, black and yellow, blue and red, gray and blue, and
black and white.
Then you will be safe on the streets of Chicago.

Instructions on How to Turn on Your Computer
Rafael

Begin by preparing your fingers.
Touch soap and water then rub.
Dry and walk to your computer.
Press the on button.
Smell the static while it's active.
See the mouse and put your hand on it.
Make the mouse taste your files.
Press start to find your path
and see your future.

Instructions on How to Write Your First Name
Steven O.

Introduction:
thank you for buying my book. You're probably the first to read it.

Grab a pen or pencil and a piece of paper. Then smell the life
of the paper and pen into your mind.
Think of the letters in your first name
and forget the rest of the alphabet.

There are two successful ways to write.
The first is to sit in a quiet room and try to tell
your pen to write for you by threatening
to take it apart.

The second way, the way I learned, is to listen
to your writing material for the steps of spelling.

After achieving one of these steps,
taste your pen and hope some of its greatness
rubs off on you.

You should have learned how to spell
and write your name by now.
Let's do your last name.

Instructions on How to Do Nothing
Martha G.

Begin by staring at a wall
blank mind, it's all black
no colors, no shape, no reason
yet I stand there doing nothing
that black place gets boring
yet I do nothing
same shape
but I do nothing

I taste the scarcity of chocolate
of different flavors
swiss, dark, and nothing
I smell a smell of nothing

Instructions on How to Sing
Miriam A.

You begin by standing up in your living room.
Then take a deep breath and listen for quiet.
Hear the chicken roasting.
Now let your arms go.
Then you act like you can hear the landscape.
Then you start singing and shake yourself out.

How to Bike Ride
Gabriela P.

Get on the bike.
Move and listen to the peddles whir.
Sometimes squeaky, sometimes fast.
Let the breeze through.
Each day everything is coming to an end.
The pedals tire as more pollution approaches.

Instructions on How to Play Basketball
Alejandro D.

Inside of the gym I bounce a ball on the wooden floor.
The ball floats in the air. When I shoot
from the three point line, the ball swishes
through the rim.
I do crazy tricks, like cross it over, pass it
behind my back, spin it on my finger,
and trip up the people guarding me.

Instructions on How to Serve Cereal
Virginia T.

Smell the bowl dancing on the table.
See the freshness of the milk.
Listen to the taste of artificially flavored cereal.

ANNIE KELLER REGIONALGIFTED CENTER
Principal: Adrian Willis
Teachers: Ms. Cap, 8th, Mr. Tesinsky, 6th, Ms. Wess, 7th

Gary Copeland Lilley, Poet in Residence

Poet and teaching artist originally from Sandy Cross, North Carolina and now living in Chicago, Gary Lilley was a long-time resident of Washington DC, where he received the DC Commission on the Arts Fellowship for Poetry in 2000 and 1996. *The Subsequent Blues*, from Four Way Books in 2004, is his first collection of poems. His stories and poems have been published in many journals and anthologies. He earned an M.F.A. from Warren Wilson College in 2002.

Sonnet of a 7th Grade Class
Nadia G.

The "punk" to the "preppy" and in between,
A wide variety: very diverse,
A better class in my days I've not seen,
Still so much alike as I'll show in verse.

You say, "Look at those weirdo kids up there,"
And then the teachers flip their teacher lids,
And wherever we go people will stare,
Sorry we're still a bunch of goofy kids!
Stare as you please, we really do not care!

And here the class makes so many wisecracks,
The "smart" kids who hate being called just that,
Some people will still be stabbing in backs,
There's crazy Livi callin' us all "fat"!
Still, love is one thing this class does not lack!

Undiscovered Love (a sonnet)
Taelor D.

Unknown emotions coming out at once,
Feelings so intense they pang throbbingly,
So meaningful, so important, life changing.
How can something so sad change me so quick?
Why do people change so much so fast?
Unknown problems come up in a blink of an eye,
But show my appreciation for them for I
Would be considered a fool, uncouth if
I didn't. Would it be okay? No, for
I am her love, we were intimate with our
Thoughts and our feelings of this mean world.
How could she depart? No, the question is,
Why, how, when could we ever try to depart?
She never will, for she is in my heart.

Baseball (a sonnet)
Michael G.

Baseball running, hitting, catching, batting
throwing, and pitching. Fielders and baseman.
Shortstop, back catcher, pitcher, and ump.
Field, centerfield, left field, right field, stadium
bleachers, seats. Cleats, hats, helmets, face mask, and
body protection. Teams, coaches, staff, manager.

Cutting players, getting new players, and
trading players. Making teams and making
the best team of all. Foul balls, strikes, and
balls. Stealing bases, taking home, and many other
bases. Yelling, booing, shouting, and much more.
Me and my mom love baseball and the Cubs.
There are so many, oh, so very many great fans,
Yet there are tons and tons of stands.

Beneath the sodden ground where she waits (a sonnet)
Aubrey M.

Beneath the sodden ground where she waits
Screaming with no sound, her rescuer came late.
She smiles while knowing his death is coming.
She sees the legs appear bloody & black
Unto his mangled body her eyes bore.
She spots the blood. She tugs the skin. Blood floods.
She whispers, you unlucky fool, dragging
Him to a shed where she begins her work.
In the shed she dismembers him alone,
She laughs wildly, tearing off limb by limb.
Bathing in the crimson pool, she smiles.
She throws the parts 'round the room, disgusted.
She walked away when the deed was done,
Couldn't bear to stay, she killed her own son.

My World (a sonnet)
Sabrina N.

When I walked in the kitchen door,
He ran up to me and gave me a hug.
For a second, I was holding my world.
He smelled like Tide with a touch of Downey.
We ran out the door and ran to the tramp.
Up. Down. We jump with glee. Up and down. Yay.
Flipping around. Having a ball. Up and down,
This long, brown, shaggy hair just whirling around.
Up the stairs and down to the basement.
Turn on the TV. What's going to happen?
We sit on the couch, so close together.
Is it true love or just a phase?
I hold him close as he cracks some jokes.
Someone is coming, we instantly spread.

Fine (a sonnet)
Jasmine K.

I'm glad you're happy, you say that you're fine,
I hope you prosper, come around in time.
I know I did it, I'm really sorry,
but something was never there. Feel it
too many things to think about. I can't
think about different emotions to you.
We were distant. Our interests clash much. I
feel our center of realization
wasn't in the center. I need to tell
you what happened, so you won't be mad. I
don't like wasting paper, so take the time
to listen. I'm sorry and we're still friends.
But phone calls and vocab words just must end
I'm good and over you, just hope you're fine.

My Dog Lela (a sonnet)
Christopher P.

My dog Lela is very stupid and
On Valentine's Day she will be Cupid.
My dog Lela is stupid, for she eats garbage.
We still like her even though she's childish.
Though she's outlandish, it's really okay,
For she's bigger and bigger every day.
She's the dog and we love her, hooray.

You darn dirty dog, you're badder than bad!
Now get to your cage, no food, so take that!
You think you've won, you think it's alright but
By my words, you're sleeping outside tonight.
Now get away, you have shamed me today,
But I can't stay made at you forever,
My love reigns over my rage forever.

Easy but Hard (a sonnet)
Elizabeth M.

I feel it, today will be a good class.
After our plié combination,
I balance in passé for ten seconds.
Relevé, élevé, for sixteen counts, repeat.
I have good pain in my lower body.
Arabesque, balance, relevé, hold, split.
Across the floor, tombé, pas de bourrée

I suck so much, I can't love it any more.
Penché, balance, I clatter to the floor.
I am doing everything wrong, crap.
Music does not work, I feel just like it.
I don't understand the words she's saying.
Turns, turns, pirouettes, I keep falling.
The girls in my class all smirk and laugh.

Finding the Light
Patrick T.

Dear Jesus, my Savior,
Please pray for me.
Don't know who I am
Or who I should be.
Dear Jesus, my Savior,
Please pray for me.

Don't know who I am
Or who I should be.

I walked to the valley
And to the church too.
Jesus, O Jesus,
Where are you?
I walked to the valley
And the church too.

Jesus, O Jesus,
Where are you?

I went to the river
And I stayed to pray.
My dear Jesus,
Hope I can find you someday.
I went to the river
And I stayed to pray.

My dear Jesus,
Hope I can find you someday.

I've been tryin' to be good,
Don't know if I can.
Lord, O Lord,
Give me a plan.
I've been tryin' to be good,
Don't know if I can.

Lord, O Lord,
Give me a plan.

So I'll keep on praying
In hope of finding the Light.
I'll say my Hail Mary's
And my Our Father's tonight.
So I'll keep on praying
In hope of finding the Light.

I'll say my Hail Mary's
And my Our Father's tonight.

Rock 'n' Roll
John M.

The screech of the guitar chords,
All the great bards coming back for more,
Touring throughout the night, travel across the country,
Have to catch next flight.
Album goes platinum, win an award.
Party all day, trash your best friend's Ford.
Such great music cemented into your soul.
Long live Rock 'n' Roll!

Untitled
Dan M.

The sight of death is all around.
My psychiatrist left me, he said he met someone new.
My lovely cat is planning its own quiet suicide.
I search my empty socks for hope.
Where did I hide the frozen peas?
I wish I may, I wish I might, but I feel nothing tonight.
You died upon the dock
But who cares.

Untitled
Elaine K.

A mother's moan rings out as a dog does at the moon.
A pool as deep as a fresh rain puddle lay
around her precious boy.
As the night pressed, that Hell was upon her.
As she sat by her boy,
lying on the ground,

her cooking apron quickly went from white to red,
her sorrow impaled her on spears,
her pain ripped out her heart,
her anguish wasted her life away
for she had no more without her son,
her only treasure in the world.
As she shut her eyes,
her life did the same.

Cat
Kenneth M.

The fur was orange
and beautiful as he strutted on
the blue banister
he leaped gracefully
down and landed on his feet
he galloped down the street swaying his tail
he went to his green bowl and lapped up his milk
with his eyes closed savoring every bit
he left his bowl and trotted through town
he passed the market which smelled of fresh fruit
he pranced around happily
but then he got tired
and he raced home to go to sleep.

Fire
Kevin C.

Fire is a wondrous element.
Still contains the wonder as
stonemen had on it as we do
today. Fire is neither gas, liquid,
or solid because it can't be contained.
We have enslaved the land,
sea, and even the skies but
fire will always be wild as a
mountain lion. Fire is as if
it came from a dimension where
fire is an element. Not even
the Greek gods were able to
contain the secret of fire. One
day Prometheus gave man fire
and the next day Zeus was
shocked as a father, with his son's
defeat. What he saw was
a civilized man, not the sane

primitive race. Man had constructed
ships, masts, cities, education, and
metal tools. In other words, fire
controls us.

Pointe
Lauren S.

　　　　As if the five girls were tall,
slender pillars, with pointed grace
and agility.

　　　　The music begins and they are
off, melting into the slow beat
and becoming one.

　　　　The glide gracefully across
the stage, like swans on water.
Strong and beautiful, they calmly
come together, moving in perfect
unison, like musicians playing one
grand march all together.

　　　　They pull into the final arabesque,
gracefully arching their backs into perfect
U's, like smooth bridges.

　　　　Then the music stops and they
fall back into the ordinary, short and
bland, just like all the normal people
in the ordinary universe.

Home
Enass Z.

The children play
in the sunshine,
the red sphere glides along
the brown & green Earth into
their hands.
Their feet hit the pavement
with a soft pound.
Another child comes
running along.
The pressure of two hands is
felt on my back.
The scene flew past my eyes as

I tasted the bitter taste
of dirt in my mouth.
My face is covered with the wet mud.
I get up with pain in my back
to hear the mocking laughter of children.
Soon my face is wetter. It's wetter
with tears.
My heart is pounding in my
throat from the embarrassment.
I turn around & pick up my legs.
I run to the soft heaven I call
Home.

Ballet Blues
Britt

I walk into the dance studio.
I am 5 minutes late & the teacher
Is about 2 tell me
That I can't stay, I have 2 go.
I have the ballet blues.

Then we start on pirouettes
And I try to turn & fall over.
I have absolutely no balance,
I need a 4leaf clover.
I have the ballet blues.

Oh, great, now we're doing splits
In 4th & almost half way down.

Favor for a Friend
Emanuel V.

Don't talk to me like you're better than me.
When you don't know anything about me, or what I stand for?
Making your generalizations based on the hypocrites that you know
really don't embody
what it means to be a Christian.
But acting like they are the norm, just to make yourself feel better.
I won't question you, if you don't question me.
My faith is mine, and mine only.
And yours…or lack thereof, is your business.
But if you do try to knock down these walls, you're going to find it mighty
hard.
You're not attacking the man, you're attacking the God inside.
You're a good person, and I hope you'll find the way.

But there's only so much I can do, before we go our separate ways.
I wanna see you there, but at this rate, I won't.
This cynicism is unnecessary, don't hold it against me, because I have
nothing against
you.
There's no reason for me to.
We are all equal under His eyes.
I'm sorry for the anger, it just hurts me so much
To see you writhing inside, and falling further away from the Path.
Anger and Negativity only beget more.
I just want you to learn a little more before you jump into the pit.
This isn't a situation where you take your information second hand.
This is way bigger than whether you like me, or whether you can be
bothered to dedicate
yourself to something.

I'm not trying to force anything on you.
In the end, of course, what happens with us is between each individual
and the Creator.
I'm just asking you to research before you take a stand.
Because I love you, and I want you to live.

School Books
Alex S.

The old words jump out from the page
yearning to be read, comprehended, and thought of.
The letters typed years ago
on a frail, yellowed page,
the small rips & tears from
countless students fingering through
them, frantically searching
for the right answer.
The old smell of dampness,
the dust blown off the cover.
Treasures within the old binding.
Words that shaped an innocent
child's mind forever
developing something fragile,
like a thin piece of glass,
the right words strengthening it
while the evil things of the world
scratch & crack it.
An innocent page of paper
filled with power:
to bore, to entrance, to teach.
A school book.

242

The Epiphone
Eric P.

Every day
It lies there so out of
place, a body in a coffin
with life still in it,
so out of place
in that case
tempting me,
taunting me,
looming over me
like the thought
of sleep on a late night.
Temptation overwhelms
me as I loosen my
grip,
my book hitting the
floor as I stop my
unwanted daydream,
I reach over and
pick it up by the strap,
I plug it in and
get my fingers ready.
After I stroke it, a sound
comes out equal to a
scream of a banshee.
As I sit back down,
I am filled with agony.

Little Peter
Vanessa H.

His smile, sweet
drool flows like a waterfall
it drips onto his chest
baby fat flows
over his little pants
and bounces as he hops into the baby pool.
His innocent eyes look at me
as he fills a cup with water
and runs it to the sandbox
he dumps it into the sand
like a tsunami crashing on
microscopic people
he throws the moist sand into
a bucket and crushes
it like a garbage crusher

he tips it over and slowly
pulls the bucket up.
A castle appears...
edges smooth as a still lake
he points at it and smiles
and then like a giant
wrecking ball he destroys his creation.

Blues
Gabe H.

When I woke up in the morning
I got up out of bed
I brushed my teeth and went downstairs
and then my mama said hurry up.

Cuz I got the blues,
the early morning blues.

Mama made me waffles
and chocolate milk and juice
I don't wanna go to school and I made a big old fuss.
Mama said to get outside, you gotta catch the school bus!

I got the blues,
the early morning blues.

When I get to school,
I'm still half asleep.
I have to write a poem in class and can't think what to write.
I throw the balls of paper into a rumpled heap.

Because I got the blues,
the early morning blues
I wake up every single day
with the early morning blues.

Broken Collarbone Blues
Jesse B.

The X-rays come back
And they made me pretty blue.
My clavicle was broken,
How could this be true?

I've got the broken collarbone blues.
Yeah, I'm gonna be out for a while,

I'm incapacitated with the
Broken collarbone blues.

There's no more football
And B-ball's got to wait,
Guitar's a little painful,
I've got this horrible, horrible fate.

After a month
I thought it was alright.
The doctor said, "No, sir,"
I cried all through the night.

Elimis
Liana M.

Every day, on my desk
Lays the mighty pencil,
Bright stark yellow
Like a daffodil rolled into a rope,
Pink eraser like the center of a flower,
Black tip like a clinging piece of dirt
Falling off the way we want on paper.
Pencil with a design is as a fake
Flower designed the way we want.
I take them all and sharpen them
And set them back, standing
Straight up
Like a vase of flowers
On a table in summer,
But as a time of forever to
Record our lives.

The Song
John S.

The piano with its ivory keys
like a train track
your fingers slowly move over
them as a train on its tracks
you play faster and faster
the raw notes become a song
you hear the slow humming of
the train's motor.
The train starts nearing
the intersection,
the roar of the cars gets louder

as you play faster.
Your hands are moving fast as is the train.
A car pulls onto the tracks,
it is not running. You play on,
in that instance you hit the wrong key
as all of your music goes sour
the car is in pieces,
things scattered all over the tracks
just like your music papers all over the floor.

Untitled
Rubye C.

Step into a new world,
where you get to discover more
it's an amazing Autumn galore.
Rays of green, yellow, golden & red,
then slowly a fallen leaf rests on your head,
gusts of wind enclose you,
warmth is what you're used to.
Now the chilling wind dances
and leaves join in like an enchantment.
One crashes against a defenseless cheek,
small, lively, and sleek.
The crunching as you walk on
directs the orchestra of a rhythmic song,
causing its victims to hum along
and you've almost reached home.
Now there's another world
once you've walked through the door,
you hear your stomach rumble
and your senses begin to fumble,
there's a warm mood,
look at all the food,
all the family members praising today,
thank God it's Thanksgiving Day.

The Pool
Jessica

The glistening water,
blue crisp water
like diving into a lake filled with sharks.
That is until we dive.
That once calm, collected water
is now like a jungle.
Water splashing everywhere,

People yelling and screaming,
But you seem to block that all out,
all you think about is surviving,
all you think about is leaving that jungle alive.
Then it's over, it's done,
just that quickly everything comes to a closing.
You get out, your body aches,
your muscles feel swollen
but you survived, you're alive.

Poetry
Matt S.

Been staring at a clean
Sheet of paper today.
Trying to figure
Out what to say.

Games
Brian G.

My games are fun,
like a sleep over at my friends.
When I play games my fingers are like cheetahs,
fast and reactive.

My eyes cannot move,
trained on a single spot.
My ears closed to the sound,
I am shut out from the world.

When I lose, my fury,
rises like an inflation balloon
then it pops and I fall back down to earth.

The Video Game Blues
Jaron A.

Woke up this morning,
took a bath,
went to play some games
but then there was something bad.
I got the video game blues
and it makes me feel so mad.
I got the video games blues
and I don't feel glad.

I got the worst kind of blues
'cause this game stinks so bad.
I tried to buy another
but I was broke.
I tried to earn some money
but all I got was smoke (nothing).
I got the video game blues
and it makes me feel so mad.
I got the video game blues
and I don't feel glad.
This game stinks the worst,
I really want to curse.

What If
Liz D.

What if rap didn't exist?

What if the only rapper
was from a candy bar?

What if when someone said
Eminem everyone knew that they
were talking about the candy?

What if R&B stood for Ray and
Bob, a new lame Fox sitcom?

What if Beyonce and Halle Berry
both had acting as their main career?

What if the only meaning for Hip-Hop
was a famous bunny dance?

What if rap didn't exist?
Our world would be a better place.

What If
Airica T.

What if Tupac was
still alive?

What if X-Zibit
changed his name to
Ponyman?

What if Ashlee Simpson
could actually sing?

What if Maya stopped
eating?

What if Terri Schiavo
lived and her husband died?

What if Liz
listened to Rap?

What if we all got
along?

What if?

What if?

What if?

Untitled
William M.

watch
a ball going back and forth
from hand to hand
slowly the pace quickens
left to right the ball suddenly gains height.

swish
is this not complete bliss
the descent of the ball to the floor
from the basket
is this not perfection?

squeak
shoes on the feet of those who play
driving to the hole
slowly elevating closer still to the rim
hands hanging on the rim
as the ball goes through the rim
ever closer to the hardwood floor.

Stick People
Dan E.

stick people are cool.
stick people rule.
stick people move.
stick people have a groove.
stick people spy.
stick people die.

Homework (My Blues)
June D.

Homework,
takes forever.
Homework,
boring.
Homework,
long.
Homework,
time consuming.
Homework,
when will it end.
Homework,
I'm done.

School Lunch
Lindsay M.

The school bell rings
it's time to dine.
When I eat and school lunch
and I get in the line
everyone's talking
The lunch smell fills the air,
it makes little kids choke
and the 8th graders swear.

I can't make up my mind,
what should I chose?
No matter what I pick,
I will lose.

The pizza,
no one can bear,
do you know why?
It's covered in lunch lady's hair.

Apples, bananas, and peas are rotten.
The meatloaf is bloody
and the pan they cook it in
is dirty.

The salad has bugs in it
and the leaves are brown.
The carrots are yellow and dry,
it's the worst in town.

The little kids chose the Sloppy Joe.
Big mistake,
they go to throw up,
I wanna have cake.

I throw away my lunch
and I sit down at a seat,
my friend has a Twinkie,
now that's an awesome treat.

Rumors
Allison L.

Passing lies
Being talked about
Talking about others
Suspicious looking eyes
Watching from the corners
Gleaming the squint of death
Hoping to get a glimpse
Of what is the truth
Knowing people know your deepest thoughts
Once it starts
You can only wait for it to die away
You can't put an end to the madness
You can't stop it
Rumors suck.

I Was Wrong
Amber J.

I walked in hoping for a carefree afternoon.
        I was wrong.
As if I could stop time and everything,
        I was wrong.
Everybody were angels.
        I was wrong.

The devils would be my undying slaves.
    I was wrong.
No stones turned, no item out of place.
    I was wrong.
Everything and everyone would be in
order, like a military line.
    I was wrong.
Every afternoon I take my reluctant
    steps into it all.

Blue Moon
April W.

Wednesday was a bad day,
My little sister wanted not to play,
My mother worked late,
My brother had a date,
My dad was out of town,
My whole world was coming down,
Wednesday, I could not smile,
Wednesday was a bad day,
We had a whole blue moon that day.

Baseball
Jarrett J.

As if a shaved apple,
bouncing of the bat.
A pack of red hots
and lots of hats.
This game is played
with 4 homes,
played outside,
or in a dome.
This game is like
a game of cricket,
but in this game
you do not kick it.
The ones on steroids
are Bonds and McGuire.
They say they don't take 'em
but they all are liars.
If you're wondering
what this game is called,
the name of the game
is baseball.

Untitled
Mariah R.

If I were a broom I'd be dirty all the time. I'd hate it because I detest un-cleanliness. It really annoys me how people leave me on the floor, and kick me, and then pick me up and make me dirty again by sweeping. Sometimes I even feel neglected because they use Mr. Vaccum more than me. They say he's better.

The Flight of the Flag
Killian M.

As I step outside
and the cold wind wraps around my face,
the smell of the fresh rain relaxes me.
I slosh through the mud.
I take a look around.
My head flaps up and down.
I salute above to the flag snapping all around.
I wait until my fingers freeze
to let my guard down.
A slight breeze carries the
perfect flight of the flag.
I go back inside and the leaves whistle goodbye.

JOSEPH KELLMAN CORPORATE COMMUNITY SCHOOL
Principal: Brenda Browder
Teachers: Ms. Gordon, 3rd, Ms. Taylor, 4th, Ms. Samuel, 5th, Mrs. McKinley, 8th

Jennifer Karmin, Poet in Residence

Jennifer Karmin is a poet, artist and educator who has published, performed, exhibited, taught and experimented with language throughout the U.S. and Japan. A Poet in Residence since 2000, she also teaches creative writing to immigrants at Truman College and was the recipient of The Poetry Center's Gwendolyn Brooks *Hands on Stanzas* Award for her work in the Chicago Public Schools. Intersecting writing with sound and image, Jennifer is co-founder of the public art group Anti Gravity Surprise and curator for the SpareRoom Time-Arts Cooperative. She earned her B.A. in the Poetics Program at the University of Buffalo and her M.F.A in the Writing Program at The School of the Art Institute of Chicago.

Jennifer says, "I want my students to be empowered readers, writers, creators, and critical thinkers. This spectacular year (my fifth as Kellman's Poet in Residence) the students and I discussed poems by Claude McKay, Langston Hughes, Gwendolyn Brooks, Adrienne Rich, Maya Angelou, Gary Snyder, Amiri Baraka, Lucille Clifton, Jayne Cortez, Quincy Troupe, Nikki Giovanni, Anne Waldman, Janet Campbell Hale, Víctor Hernández Cruz, Ntozake Shange, and Gary Soto. I am a poet and teacher because I have had excellent poets and teachers in my life. I dedicate my 2004-05 students' poems to my teacher Robert Creeley who always pushed young poets onwards."

When History Changes, People Change Too
Third Grade Group Poem: Deon A., Brandon B., Kayla B., Oddis B., Rico B., Kenya B., Kiara B., Colin C., Adrian D., Jasmine G., Amber H., Bakia J., Keiana J., Ryann J., Travoy J., Nkoya K., Andrea M., Paris M., Citron M., Tamia M., Jamal M., Caprice O., Damenicion S., Shaun S., Andy S., Joan S., Shimarr S., Justus S., Ashly S., Vincente T., Eboni W.

Do you know who made history?
Who made slavery?
History has changed these days.
Slavery is no longer alive.
Before blacks were slaves in the South.
They hit them for no reason and they wouldn't let them go.
They would whip them.
They treated them cruel.
My culture is good and bad.

History changed by blacks and whites getting along.
History changes by learning new things.
History changes by people inventing new things.
History changes from African American heroes.
History changes because I can become a hero.
I made changes.

Welcome to the history of black people.
Harriet Tubman was a woman who broke out of slavery.
Abraham Lincoln made history by making this a free country.
Rosa Parks was a woman who started the bus boycott.
There was a white man who took Rosa Parks' seat.
She didn't let him, she was sitting there first.
That's not fair.
I don't like what the bus driver did to Rosa.
He made her go to the back of the bus.
But Rosa helped us so we can sit where we want on the bus.
Martin Luther King helped us so that nobody will be judged
By the color of their skin.
He was a brave man who spoke out to blacks and whites.
They all stopped the bad treatment of blacks.
They all did something special.

History history you leave lots of memories.
Culture is history.
We speak many different languages.
History changes by different people doing things to help each other.
It is great to know about people who did things for you.
History is in my mom, my sisters and me.
History can be in your heart, history can be in your mind.
How did everybody change history?

We don't know who started history or will end it.
History is real – it can be in a book, on a computer, even from God.
History is not just in the past but we make history now.
History changes so that people can celebrate.
Everybody can change history, even me.
People make history change so I can become a leader.
History changed when black people fought for it.
Why did whites do bad things to blacks?
History is different from back then.

History changes in my imagination.
My life might be different everyday.
History changes because of your life.
It gets better or worse, it depends on how it was before.
History changes me and the world.
History means to move on.

Change
Rico B.

when I change I feel good not bad
bad is not safe
who helps me change
my mom and my dad and sometimes
I help myself change
we see change and I will change
I will act to change
everyone will change
my body will change my food will change
my face will change my hands will change
my hair will change my soul will change
that means everyone will change
their soul face hands and feet
together we will change

Are You Safe?
Kenya B.

We are together forever
We are safe
Safe is when you're far from danger
Do you have another person to help you?
I feel safe at home
I see if there's danger around me
If I can smell cigarettes around me
I'm sure that's not safe

I'm safe because I want to live healthy
I'm happy that I'm safe
I have protection
When I'm asleep angels keep me safe

Did I Change Yet?
Jasmine G.

I wonder what it would be like if I change.
Would I look pretty?
Did you change?
If I change, I would look like a butterfly.
Change can be good or bad.
Everyday I ask my mom, "Did I change?"
My dad says that if your voice changes
That means you are growing up.
I can't wait to grow up.
I can change myself if I want to
But it takes so long to change.

I Relax At Home
Nkoya K.

It feels so good and my cat comes to join me.
I always hear my cat running across the floor.
My mom says that I'm supposed to be cleaning things.
So I take the brush and clean my cat, so soft.
In my house, I listen to hip-hop and R & B music.
I talk on the phone a lot and hear my friends talking.
Home is a safe, cozy place.

Mystery Problem
Tamia M.

Sit back and enjoy my mystery case
I have to find out where the ghost is and try to save the day
There once lived far far away a ghost in a haunted house
My gang and I went into this haunted house
It was so spooky that half of my gang went back to the car
The rest of us went upstairs and heard a noise
We went to see who it was
It was a ghost
We ran back to the car
We were so scared

When You Change
Shaun S.

I am different
I am different
the people who helped me change are
my grandmother, aunt and mother
I see change
when people are helping others
change is sometimes bad
when you change sometimes you learn new things
paper changes when you draw on it
you can change good to bad
you can change ugly to pretty

My Help
Shimarr S.

When I get in danger, I call 911.
When I get home, I help.
When I get homework, I ask for help.
When you have a job, you get money to help.
When you are kidnapped, you need help.
When you are on the street, you might need help.
When I'm crying, I cry.
When I'm sick, I feel mad.
When there is a stranger, I run away.

Lies
Justus S.

I jumped off the Sears Tower but didn't hurt myself
The teacher made me get glasses
I was in a tornado
I jumped on an alligator
A lion tried to eat my head
I am a monkey
I have a tail
I am a hotdog
I am a fan
I am tape
I am a tape recorder
My chair is my girlfriend
I am spoiled
I am a mop

258

Looking Into A Young Soul
Ashly S.

When my mom looks into my sister's eyes
She's looking into her soul.
I know that my mom is looking into her eyes
Because she loves her.
I know that when she looks at me
She's looking into my soul.
I know that because I'm looking into her heart.
Sometimes I look into my sister's soul
And she knows what I'm doing.
My grandma tells me she sees my grandpa's soul
Even though he is dead.

I Am Safe In Wonderland
Vincente T.

I like to be safe
I feel safe
I'm the safest person
I am safe in my bed
Mom keeps me safe
My dog is safe
Help me be safe
I follow safe
Safe talks to me
I talk to safe
I keep safe
I keep safe safe
I keep people safe
Safe is my friend

History Has My Back When Times Change
Fourth Grade Group Poem: Rajae A., Rhainesha B., Kiame B.,
Jasmine B., Antoinne B., DeMacio F., Christopher G., Jerome H.,
Tyrek H., Devante H., Anton H., Demonta H., Erin H., Eric J., Devin
J., Kendra J., Keith L., Diamond L., Daija M., Parish M., Nicco M.,
Mykia M., Kaylah M., Erica P., Forgae S., Martrese S., Damari T.,
Jeremy T., William T., Tania T., Kevin W.

History history history isn't just about black people
Can you hear the wind?
It's sending history to me
Can you blow history out?
My history, your history, our history

I remember history
There was a time when the slaves were captured
History looks like the great migration
I was brought to this world

When was history made?
I want to make history
History is like a kid who makes something up from the top of
her brain
I think about flying with all the people who helped change
history
History is Matthew Henson, one of the first men to discover the
North Pole

Why were African Americans slaves?
Why was it so hard?
Why did people get taken away from their families?
History smells like cotton
Because the slaves picked it
History tastes like soul food
Because the slaves would gather every Sunday and
eat together

Is history a person or our imagination?
Jean-Baptise DuSable a pioneer who discovered Chicago
Harriet Tubman and Frederick Douglass freed our ancestors
Dr. King went from a no one to a some one
He got thrown in jail, hit with a brick, his house burnt down
And he stood strong
Jesse Jackson helped people to go out and vote

Our ancestors worked hard to acquire freedom
We are free to play baseball and sit in the front of the bus
Thank you all of you for our rights
We love you
I come from a black family
My whole family is black
I love being black

History is here, history is there, history is everywhere
Blacks and whites, we're all the same
We can be friends
That's why people came to fight for us
Power to the people and nothing more
From George Washington to hip hop artists
History is the bill of rights, civil rights
Suffering, abolitionists, freedom, marching
We never gave up
We told people who tried to stop us

260

To shut up

Do we make history or does history make us?
Changing history was powerful
Changing history was confusing
Changing history made freedom
History is the past but we still make history in the future

My life is history
I can feel it, I can see it suffering
I go home and think about history in my head
My grandma told me a story about when she changed history
My ears were open and I was listening

Who can understand history?
Just like that history changes
In a blink of an eye
One day you are going to change history
It is up to us to carry the torch with pride
You can stomp and romp with us
We make history go bump

In The Beginning
Rhainesha B.

the beginning smells like hair
it looks like a clip
it sounds like an air conditioner
it feels like smooth skin
it's so colorful like a butterfly
in the beginning I was chillin
outside with my dad
it looked like a melting ice cream
yummy yummy yummy

Think About Decisions
Kiame B.

When you make a decision, you have to focus.
Think and don't get frustrated.
Make a good choice.
Why do people make decisions?
They want to do the right thing and not the wrong thing.
Decisions are good to make.
When you make a decision, you may fly anywhere.
You may go.
Remember don't hit your toes.

Makes Me Feel Relaxed
Antoinne B.

the sounds of the birds chirping
when I dream, I feel relaxed
when I look at the sky, I feel relaxed
when I feel stressed, I say wooozaaa
relaxing smells like milk chocolate
feels like I'm at six flags
sounds like the jungle
looks like fresh oranges
makes me think of when I was three

A New Place
Devin J.

A new place is scary.
A new place is haunted.
A new place has ghosts.
A new place has a floating head.
A new place has monsters.
A new place has a mummy.
A new place has a graveyard.
A new place has a big, fat spider.
A new place hates people.
A new place is horror.
A new place is evil.
A new place doesn't love.

Magnificent Work
Parish M.

Work is school
School is work
Work is easy
Sometimes work is confusing
I always put lots of effort into my work
Work makes me go up, down, side to side
Work is me
Work is my thing
Work work work
Poetry is work
Scientific, intelligent, stupid, boring, crazy
Wet, dry, black, white, tick, tock, strategies
Work looks like fire

Why Do People Sing and Make Noise?
Mykia M.

voice is a beautiful sound to my ears
sometimes noises get on my nerves
voices make me want to sing
some people sing because they're happy
most people sing because they're free
why don't people speak louder?
some people are shy
some people talk a lot because they love their voices

I'm About To Fly
Martrese S.

A poem that makes me feel
Like I'm flying in the sky.
An excellent poem reminds me of
The 5 senses, stanzas and imagination.
When you write a poem
You need a title
Not anything
An interesting one.
You can rhyme
When you write your poem.
You have to use lines
Not a paragraph
Use stanzas.
Have a strong ending and free verse.
Describe and ask questions.

Work Is Boring And Fun
Jeremy T.

Work smells like fried chicken
Work sounds like hip-hop
Work feels smooth
Work looks like Missy Elliot
I work because when it's all over
I can be proud of myself
And have the feeling of accomplishment
When I work, I put 100% into what I do
Work is something to learn lessons from
And something to keep you busy
You could get a message out of it sometimes

A Brand New Decision
Tania T.

A brand new decision is hard.
A brand new decision tastes like ice cream.
A brand new decision looks blue.
A brand new decision smells like chocolate.
Everyone makes decisions.
I hate new decisions.
A brand new decision is a picture.
A brand new decision is a choice.
A brand new decision shows respect.
A brand new decision gives you money.
A brand new decision is focus.
A brand new decision is everywhere.
A brand new decision comes out.

Energy The Mighty Energy
Kevin W.

energy is the main thing
it makes you jump and sing
energy is everything
it's like you are a machine
when you are out of energy
you go to sleep
but when you wake up
you are filled with it
energy is fun in the sun
feels like a machine gun
energy is to run
while you are a kid
just have fun
energy doesn't just come
from a hamburger bun
don't forget to tell your son

History Is In The Making

Fifth Grade Group Poem: Shelby B., Richard B., Brianna B., Crystal C., Anglena C., Amber F., Al H., Xavier H., Jibreel J., Malik J., Leon J., Diamond J., Michael L., Jaques L., Janaé M., Lauren M., Brianna M., Sabreen M., Abria M., Ireal M., Jasmine M., Brianna P., Naquesha R., Antoine R., Derrick R., Rochelle S., Elliot S., Mariah T., Cahara T., Anthony W., Piniece W., Deandre Y.

If you don't have history, you don't have a past
History is my past and future
History can change in a week
History changes when we go to school
I'm history in the making
I'm the history of the year
My history never ends

        Take a look back into time you will see
        Easily it changes your mind
        Ancestors are from ancient history
        It might be a mystery
        They shed their blood to help us breathe

Cause and effect for us and our ancestors
Old history, old people, soul mates and lovers
Old history is blood
People were wrong but we were strong
Dr. Martin Luther King had a dream
Bus boycotts and marches to help us get our equal rights
Have the same jobs and use the same bathrooms
We struggled
Jacqueline Cochran was the first African American woman pilot
I will make history
Now we have an American dream

        We need a hero
        Someone to comfort us
        Someone who cares
        Keeping us safe
        Such as Harriet Tubman
        She didn't come to this world to be a slave
        She wasn't going to stay one either

Freedom impacts everyone's soul
History did a lot
It got me to be free
Let freedom ring
Let it be a ring of justice
Freedom impacts my beautiful soul
I am black and beautiful

Come with me and be free

Get up
Stand up
On your feet
Quick
Look outside
Time travel

My Black Soul
Brianna B.

My soul is black with a dark hole
My soul is dark as night
My soul is dark
My soul is my heart
When I'm hurt
I'm sick to my knees
My soul eats my heart
Then I begin to cry
Tears all down my eyes
It's like clouds
All over me
The water is cold
All down my back
My soul is black

I Know Change
Amber F.

I know change
change is very funny
sometimes it can be sad
change looks like sweet pie
change tastes like nachos with cheese and meat
changes sounds like a beautiful blue jay singing
change feels like money in your pocket
change smells like a rose in a flowerpot
I am change
I love to change
if I could
I would change everything

The Great Migration
Al H.

The Great Migration makes me feel great.
It smells like roses.
It was the best thing ever.
I can see my ancestors.
It's like they are touching me.
I wasn't born yet but my ancestors told me all about it.
They were happy to get to the North.
The Great Migration makes my family feel elated.
When I heard it, I felt sorry for my ancestors.
I was glad it wasn't me.
I can hear my ancestors screaming and celebrating.
We are free at last.

I Love Freedom
Jibreel J.

How about you?
Do you like it?
It is the best of the rest.
It has feelings like you and me.
It smells like the fresh breeze of a hot summer day.
It feels like heaven.
My great great great granddad didn't have freedom.
But I am here to tell him it is wonderful to step outside.
A life without people harassing you.

Just Relax
Malik J.

I love to relax
I rest my back

                    It smells like cake
                    Cooked and baked

It tastes like pie
I'm not telling a lie

                    It sounds like a voice
                    Calling my name
                    I'll tell it all
                    I'm not ashamed

I remember when I was little
Resting on a beach
At that time
No learning
Nothing to teach

The Way To Be Free For Me
Janaé M.

Did you ever see freedom?
You tell me.
Freedom is fun.
Freedom for everyone.
Freedom makes me sing
Do, re, me, fa, so, la, ti, do
All over my soul.
It smells like oranges.
It feels like a bed of flowers.
It sounds like summer.
With laughing kids from around the world.
It looks like a place that is alive.
It reminds you of a love.
It makes the black holes in your soul
Go away.
You think that every ancestor of your past
Was just here for you.

My World, My Life
Abria M.

I would like to change the world
I would like to change my life
I would like to change the way people die
I'll stop the violence and live a happy harm-free life
if I could change the world
no one would ever die
if I could change people
no one would get fevers
if I could change our character
no one would ever walk barefoot
we would live in a free world
all the poor people would have free homes
no one would ever be alone

268

The Past Is Gone, But The Future Is Here
Naquesha R.

The past is a passion, but the future came here.
The past is right next to you or it might be near.
Past is like cherries on a cherry tree.
It makes me feel possible and set free.
Past sounds like bells in a box.
I'm not at the bottom, but at the top.
Past is from friend to friend.
It puts me first not at the end.
If you see the past, jump in it.
It will give you power so you can last.
Come on everyone, let's go to the past.
Come back in time and remember your mind.

Please Don't Tell
Anthony W.

I won't tell that you wet the bed
Will you tell if I hit you on your head?
If you got a beef
Don't mess with the chief
I'm the king of the town
When I make my verses
I make them with verbs and nouns
5 times just 1 more
When I get done

Hot Cocoa For The Winter
Deandre Y.

my favorite season is winter
I can play in the snow
throw snow
at cars and people
run
when I get to the house
I make hot cocoa
take a nice long nap
then I go back
outside
throw more snowballs
go back into the house
take a hot bath for two hours
and make more hot cocoa

Take Care Of What You Know
Eighth Grade Group Poem: Gabrielle Banks, Donshaya Beene,
Harold Carter, Demond Coffee, Chauntenee Cox, Jasmine Davis,
Ashley Fisher, Thoth Gunter, Jonathon Harrison, Antonio Johnson,
Vincent Johnson, Geraldine Junious, Jennifer McCullough, Darrius
McNutt, Novia Moore, Alexandria Ownes, Ricky Pace, Jacar
Robins, Keona Robinson, Stephen Scott, Jade Skinner, Chauncy
Starling, Tyjaun Stewart, Vernette Swanigan, Amy Travis, Anthony
Travis, Keionna Walton, Jeramey Winfield

History, the key to the past
    Does it mean the old days or the dark ages?
Eons and eons ago there was a discovery
    the evolution of culture
Each day history is made
    The things you won't forget
An antique like my grandmother's locket
    Inside a black and white picture of my great great aunt

I'm walking the path that our heroes have paved
    Blast to the past
The laugh, the cry
    The brave, the pride
Rumor has it that we're part of history
    Some days full of joy
Thoughts full of misery

    You need to know
        About when slaves used to plow the fields with a hoe
    Back in the day
        Our fellow brothers and sisters were strong
    Didn't moan
        Disowned their captivity
    Like reliving the days of Nat Turner
        He went to the Supreme Court for his freedom
    Don't think it's a joke
        Wars and fights
    Struggling hard for our rights

Over the years people slaved
    Working hard nights and days
Over the years many mothers cried
    Their children stealing and killing just to survive
Over the years people shunned each other
    Never knowing when to love another
From Martin Luther King having a dream
    to the beating of Rodney King
To Emmet Till becoming an unsolved mystery

The old days
They used to call it
Beginning, walking, slavery
War, fights, hate
Civil rights, punishment, deceit
Life, death, end
Past, future, hope
Segregated, incarcerated, community
Dream, justice, forgiven
The history of me

History is us
History is what creates us
People who are important to me are people who teach me how lead
Who open my eyes so I can see bigger and better things
If it weren't for them, African Americans would not have succeeded
Never forget your history
it will always grow
What happened back then is still important today
How black people paved the way

Many people think we are coming to a better day
Is it the same everyday?
The same dark clouds?
The same wars?
The same score?
Years go by silently
Waiting for a new struggle
Past tense never coming to the present
History isn't the same
Have things remained?
The next thing you know you're gone

Deep, deep is history
Years and years have passed
Days and days have gone
Hours and hours and minutes and minutes have flown
We're making discoveries everyday
About how evolution occurred over the years
We've conquered our fears
We're giving cheers
Lift every voice and sing
We're history
New electricity
Old electricity
Black and full of beauty
Patience

The meaning of history

Tells us how we're set free
It opens our eyes
History, what keeps us together
To be known for doing some remarkable thing
Light a match and watch it go
Across the world with a glow
Bright as the sun
Hot as fire

Types Of Voices
Donshaya B.

Tone
The note of your voice
Vocals
The way you sing
Loud
A volume of your voice
Opinionated
Sing what you want to sing
Sounds
Things you hear
Silly
A way of acting goofy
A cappella
Singing without instruments

Life Of A Working Person
Harold C.

what time do you get off work
you look exhausted each and everyday
working 8 hours a day
always contemplating
about quitting or leaving each and everyday
always complaining to your boss
to raise your pay
at the end of each day you say
work is less exciting each and everyday
but all in all you still go to work
and have the same conversation over and over
each and everyday

Personal
Jasmine D.

For me to know and you to find out
Who I am, what I'm about
My dos, my don'ts
My wills, my won'ts
Oh well!
That's personal

Let's play a game
Called think and tell
If you tell what I say,
You're going to jail

Here are the directions
My rules, my game
What I say goes
And that stays the same

Tell me your secrets
I'll tell you mine
If you feel embarrassed,
Don't worry, it's fine

I can tell you anything
Well that's what I think
After one secret, there's another
They're together like links

For us to know and them to find out
Who we are, what we're about
My dos, my don'ts
My wills, my won'ts
Now you know -----
My personals

Locked Secrets
Thoth G.

The hot, wet, sticky feeling of secrets
The burning pain and cries from the unknown
The quiet whisper of secrets that are locked away
　　　　What does it mean to know
　　　　　　　A secret
Secrets of dread and the dead
Secrets that kill
Secrets that steal
　　　　What does it mean to know

A secret
What to live with
A secret
Can you feel a secret
Creeping down your arm shaking your soul
Comes to your bed making you cold
Some cower away
Some grow bold
What does it mean to know
A secret
Secrets that make you scream
Secrets that can cut your spleen
What does it mean to have
A secret
To lay and wonder
To the dark thunder
To feel as if you've killed
To jump by a cold touch
What does it mean to be
A secret
I the unknown
I treated like stone
I the secret
I the unknown

Young Things
Antonio J.

Young fool
Young cat
Young dude
Young bat
Young dirt
Young flirt
Young rapper
Young shirt
Young girl
Young boy
Young world
Young toy
Young rules
Young shoes
Young lives
Young goals
Young souls

My Eyes Can See The Scent
Novia M.

Mission impossible for some
Youth to be strong, humble but numb
Eager to see the sweet humming bee
Young but wise so open your eyes
Electric flame surpasses the stream
Social bug flies through pain
Candy so sweet, floats above me
Artistic mind searching for a soul
Noisy, but low
Suspense heard in ears
Elegant glow to the face of bold
Essential, as water
Thievery not needed but is succeeded
Hot shivering cold can be noticed by a touch
Evening lights as bright as a smile
Scenery poor, but is smells of rich passion
Critical thinking, thinking critical
Each day goes by
Nice decision to make at a bad time
Tragic, imagination so long so gone
A simple touch so soft but mild
Goes a long way with eyes of scent

Better Days
Ricky P.

Today is the beginning of a new day
All my troubles have flown away
Things have gotten better
So better that the air has gotten fresher
No more worries
No more sad stories
Children outside laughing and having a good time
Adults standing on the corner listening to the poets rhyme
We don't have to worry about violence
We don't have to bow our heads in silence
Things are starting to get better in a new way
Because today is the beginning of a new day

Listen And You'll See
Jade S.

My voice may be loud
That's if I please

My voice can be low
Or even silly
I can make my voice quiet
It can even be squeaky
Or if I like country
Whatever I choose
Is up to me
Crazy
Lazy
Even mean
Every voice is different
All are unique
All you need to do is talk and you'll see

Confessions Of A Young Mind
Tyjaun S.

A young mind always turning down responsibility.
But the young mind is always learning new capabilities.
That's what makes a young mind so unique.
The creators of the creative game hide and seek.
A young mind is always willing.
Giving a young mind joy can be healing.
A young mind as sharp as a tack.
But the feelings of a young mind as short as a mat.
Young words can be silly or deep.
The words may make you laugh or
They can make you weep.
These are the confessions of a young mind.
Thank you again for giving me your time.

Young Child
Keionna W.

Free as a bird
        Growing tall as a tree
A very little soul
        As frantic as can be
Energy of a child
        Mind of a grown up
Reaching for the stars
        Hands folded in like a cup
Victorious mentality
        Never like reality
Children across the world
        Millions of boys and little girls
Little squeaky voice

Because it's their choice
Love life to the sky
Imagination very high
Little but strong
Always hate to admit when wrong
Yes, I know the mind of a child
Because I once was one
I like to run wild

OFF THE STREET CLUB
Club Director: Ralph Campagna
Assistant Director: Arnette Morris

Toni Asante Lightfoot, Poet in Residence

Educated at Howard University, George Washington University and
Cave Canem Poetry Workshop, Lightfoot is a seasoned creative writing
instructor. Having taught through ETA Creative Arts Foundation, Young
Chicago Authors, Writerscorp, and the Guild Complex, where she was
also Outreach Manager, Toni has developed curriculum that highlights
the interdisciplinary uses of poetry in the classroom. Lightfoot
contributes regularly to *Black Issues Book Review*, has been featured
on Def Poetry Jam, and performed her poetry at The National Theater,
The Lincoln Theater, and The Democratic National Committee
Headquarters.

I am...
Candice B.

I am a black smart intelligent girl;
I am a girl that speaks her mind
and tells it like it is all the time.
I am a girl on top of the world shouting hi!
I am a dancing diva.
I am Candice, which means Queen!
I am a bird that fly's so high.
I am a doll with stilettos pumps on.
I am star that's in the sky
that every one wants to wish
a wish on.
I am, I am ,I

Epistle For My Father
Breanna J.

There is something between us that is keeping us from each other. I
wonder do you want to see me, do you want to talk to me, or is it that
you just don't love me? I feel like you have turned you're back on me
since day one. I loved you and still do but my heart is telling me to be
strong for my family and myself. I always wanted someone like you but
you didn't come around me or call me Do you think you don't have any
children? Well yes you do? Are you having that much fun you can't call?
I wish you were here to see me grow up because I want you to be there
for my graduation but I know you won't come. When I get older I will
become a pediatrician and help babies because you left me when I was
a baby. Even though you left me I still love you.

Sophisticated
Breanna J.

I am 14 years old
I love to read.

I am a person who loves to make new friends.
                that loves to write.
                who likes to talk on the phone.
                who loves everyone.

I am a person who likes to listen to music.
                likes the color purple.
                likes an artist named Razz-B.
                loves poetry.

I am a person who likes Winnie The Pooh.
        loves the smell of red roses.
        will achieve my goals.
        will become a pediatrician.
I am a person.

What Brought Me Here
Taynyia H.

Well, if it weren't for my Grandma, I wouldn't be here. If it weren't for my Grandma I don't know where I would be right now. That's why I love her.

It all started when my aunts, uncles, and cousins used to come here. They encouraged us to come here and they have encouraged us to stay. I've been here at the club for some years and I love it. It is keeping me off the streets and out of gangs. I am going to keep coming back.

I am
Tangela H.

I am a pair of soft, cute looking socks that slip on my beautiful, comfortable feet.

I am sausages that fall right down on the pizza having a great time.

I am a sweet, friendly kitty that loves to curl up on someone warm and cuddly.

I am a pink flower that shines bright when it sees cute adorable girls just like me.

I am strawberries that are ready to fall from the sky on its way to fall in delicious chocolate.

I am a comb that is ready to go into a wonderful ladies hair.

I am as fast as a Leopard chasing after its prey.

        I am Tangie

I Stop Running
Tangie H.

I stopped running when I went to see the most wonderful girl in the mirror, me
I stop running when I go shopping with my friends
I stop running when it starts to blizzard

I stopped running when I got a B in social studies
I stopped running when I heard the soul of my grandma YaYa speaking to me in my dreams.
I stop running when I got to be in the Spelling Bee
I stopped running when I my reading skills got higher
I stopped running when Jesus came down and helped me bring knowledge to a new level
I stopped running when I felt myself coming to a new world.

Today
Tangie H.

Today, I had a wonderful day.
I did well in the spelling bee.
My mom and dad were really proud of me.
I felt so happy that everyone was cheering for me.

I did well in the spelling bee,
I was so happy to make my mom and dad so proud.
I felt so happy everyone was cheering for me.
I can't wait to see how tomorrow is going to be.

My mom and dad were really proud of me.
My parents were so happy they gave me money.
I can't wait to see how tomorrow is going to be.
I hope that I can to do something fun tomorrow.

My parents were so happy they gave me money.
I felt so happy that everyone was cheering for me.
I hope that I can do something fun tomorrow.
Today, I had a wonderful day.

What I did today
Tiffany J.

Today, I had fun day.
I was in the Spelling Bee
for the 4-8 graders.
I was really nervous.

My heart was really pounding
like it was on its way
going down the deep ditch.

My mom and dad,
teacher, and classmates
were cheering for me
when I was on stage.

I felt happy for myself
because everyone
was cheering for me.

Spring Is
Taynyia H.

Spring is like a rain storm that doesn't stop
The next thing you know the flowers begin to grow
Spring is like a big pop sometimes its cold sometimes its not
In the spring it's a mixture of weather
Just the other day I found a wet feather

I love spring
Spring is very cool
Sometimes all you see are bird's wings
It's too cold to get in the pool

Spring is sometimes very fun
Rain, Rain, Rain
To be for real through rain
sometimes brings you pain.
You know when it's raining
you have to get work done

Portrait of Tiffany Nicole Jackson
Tiffany N. J.

I am a blue silk shirt that shines so right
I am a slice of pizza in my mom's kitchen that's bring me warmth
I am a cat pearling on my mom 's shoulder in the morning
I am a baby blue button on my coat
I smell like a watermelon with strawberries on top
I am fast as a dog
I am Te-Te

Spring To Me ...
Tiffany J.

Spring is very fun
sometimes
we don't have to
wear big coats
we can came out
with just our clothes

spring is when flowers
start to bloom
it's very warm outside

spring is the type of weather
that everyone can enjoy .

This is what spring is ...

Why I'm Here
Antoinetta B.

Off The Street Club was founded in 1900. When my daddy
was a little boy and my mommy was a little girl they used to come to the
Off The Street Club.
So now it is me and my big brother's turn to go to the Off The Street
Club, and soon it will be my baby brother's turn. So basically it is a
tradition starting with My parents. So I guess I am here because of
tradition.

I am...
Breana M.

I am brand new pants that look very well.

I am a huge dinner, a masterpiece that tastes really good.

I am the lioness that all obey.

I am the color of a slanted pink hat.

I am the scent of a fresh lemon tree

I am the texture of a quilt that has love in every stitch.

I am the speed of a furious cheetah.

I Stopped Running
Jasmine S.

I stopped running when I had my first Asthma attack.
It became hard for me to breathe and my body function began to slack.

I passed out a was going through a trance.
When I woke up I was in an ambulance.

I was in the hospital mother said that everything is alright.
I felt even worst at the end of the night.

When I woke up I felt a thousand times better.
I had to write my new experience down in a very dramatic letter.

And when I finished writing I thought about something
That never again will you ever catch me running.

I Am
Annonymous

I am

I am a kitten and I do a lot of playing.

I am a happy red devil because I love to write.

I am a fast angel in the sky.

I am the quick wind.

I am the sweetest strawberry.

I am you and

You are me

Now tell me

Who am i.

**I Am
Marquita S.**

> I'm a dog living in a house.
> I'm a pink heart.
> I'm the scent of strawberry.
> I'm soft as a book.
> My name is marquita shontrell sims
> But I am quita.

**I Am
Shavonne W.**

I am pair of leather pants dancing at the club.
I am a bowl of ice cream at baskins robins.
I am a Cheeta standing in a jungle.
I am the color pink the texture of a bowl.
I am the scent of strawberry inside of a cheesecake.
I am a soft texture of a pillow.
I am as fast as a racing car.
I am Shavonne Marquis Walker
Bonnie.

**I Am
Patricia G.**

I am a silk dress
On prom night all pink and white
I am the scent of strawberry with
Whip cream on top at night
I am a pink Tricia shirt
I am Tricia!

**I Stopped Running
Taynyia H.**

I stopped running when I heard that my sister had pneumonia. I was
shocked. I was scared because they said she could die. I love her and
she is the only sister I have. I went all the way to the Southside over to
my mother's house. She was so happy to see me and I was so happy
to see her. I was even crying while I was holding her. I didn't want to
come back home. When she was back to her normal self I told her "I
love YOU!"

Pantoum
Shavonne W.

I was so happy today!
We didn't take our Social Studies quiz.
Today was a great day!
We didn't go to Science or Reading!

We didn't take our Social Studies quiz.
I went to the Spelling Bee.
We didn't go to Science or Reading!
A lady from Robert Crown came to our class.

I went to the Spelling Bee.
I came to Poetry class.
I thought about the lady from Robert Crown
I was excited.

I came to Poetry class.
I wrote that today was a great day!
I was so excited!
I was so happy today!

Past Me, Present Me, Future Me
Candice B.

I was a little girl with a mind filled with imagination.
I was a goofy girl who had lots of dreams
    and thought all kinds of crazy things.

I am a pretty flower that smells like baby powder.
I am a shiny star that never stops shinning.
I am a beautiful, black, intelligent, little girld
    \who has lots of dreams still to follow.

I will be a successful independent woman.
I will be a fancy young lady too!

Now it's your turn, who were you?
Who are you?
Who do you want to be?

Future Me
Chamika A.

I want to be a veterinarian when I grow up.
I love animals.

I don't want to be a veterinarian because
I don't want to have to do any euthanasia on animals.
I don't want to put pets to sleep.

If I am not a veterinarian then I'll be a regular doctor.
I think doctors do interesting work.

Another reason I want to be a doctor is because I like to make people feel better.
Also, if my mom got sick then I could help her too,

JOSE CLEMENTE OROZCO COMMUNITY ACADEMY
Principal: Coralia Barraza
Teachers: Mr. LeMoine, Academy Day, Ms. Briseño, 6th, Ms. Creed, 8th, Ms. Hernandez, 3rd, Ms. Rihani, 7th, Ms. Visinaiz, 8th

Jennifer Karmin, Poet in Residence

Jennifer Karmin is a poet, artist and educator who has published, performed, exhibited, taught and experimented with language throughout the U.S. and Japan. A Poet in Residence since 2000, she also teaches creative writing to immigrants at Truman College and was the recipient of The Poetry Center's Gwendolyn Brooks *Hands on Stanzas* Award for her work in the Chicago Public Schools. Intersecting writing with sound and image, Jennifer is co-founder of the public art group Anti Gravity Surprise and curator for the SpareRoom Time-Arts Cooperative. She earned her B.A. in the Poetics Program at the University of Buffalo and her M.F.A in the Writing Program at The School of the Art Institute of Chicago.

Jennifer says, "I want my students to be empowered readers, writers, creators, and critical thinkers. This spectacular year (my fifth as Kellman's Poet in Residence) the students and I discussed poems by Claude McKay, Langston Hughes, Gwendolyn Brooks, Adrienne Rich, Maya Angelou, Gary Snyder, Amiri Baraka, Lucille Clifton, Jayne Cortez, Quincy Troupe, Nikki Giovanni, Anne Waldman, Janet Campbell Hale, Víctor Hernández Cruz, Ntozake Shange, and Gary Soto. I am a poet and teacher because I have had excellent poets and teachers in my life. I dedicate my 2004-05 students' poems to my teacher Robert Creeley who always pushed young poets onwards."

288

From Love To Death
Academy Day Group Poem: Mr. Andre LeMoine, Sara A., Daniel C., Angel H., Teresa L., Jamie M., Lucia M., Mercedes O., Edith P., TraVera S.

History changes when love meets up with time
History is made every single day
From the Chicago fire to transformation
Now if only we could change it
The parts we don't like

War and soldiers
Fighting and getting killed
War is full of blood
A fight for evolution
Lots of people have sacrificed
Their blood, sweat and tears
Even knowing all the dangers
There's so much revolution
To fight for evolution

We stand, sit, watch
While it keeps going on
We wrap ourselves in flags
To insulate ourselves
No longer seeing or hearing the war
That is right outside
Protest transporting us through time

Revolution is what George Washington fought for
He won our freedom with so many casualties
The founding fathers declaring
All men are created equal
But the beauty was hidden by discrimination

I can feel Rosa Park's chill
When the bus driver told her to get to the back of the bus
The chill from her head to her toes
Freedom shouldn't come and go
Martin Luther King didn't really get free from discrimination
He freed his people from it

The world revolves
The sun changes
Making day and night
History is never the same
Something new is always happening
Time flies
When you're living life

289

Without History Nothing Would Exist

Third Grade Group Poem: Donovan A., Rosalía A., Jazmine B., Jorge B., Jorge B., Martín B., Brian C., Mayra C., Cynthia C., Uriel D., Carlos E., Cristal G., Damaris H., Víctor M., Heidy M., Jesús M., Cecilia M., Hugo N., Brenda N., Ashley N., Maya O., Cristal R., Alejandra R., Juan Carlos R., Mónica R., Melissa R., Francely V.

History was changed by people
We use imagination to think about history
Questions of history
How did the Aztecs change history?
The Aztecs made pyramids
If it wasn't for history you wouldn't have as much fun as you have
Special things that people did that almost everyone knows
Happy people thank them all around the world
Telegraph, cell phone, telephone, morse code
A good inventor makes handy inventions for people
History changes something or someone
What people are in history?
Jackie Robinson was the first African American
To play baseball with white people
He made a lot of home runs
Louis Armstrong liked to play jazz music
He liked the sound of his trumpet
If it weren't for those people
History would have never changed
People even change the way they look
Destruction changed history
Some laws in the past were not fair for the world
People who break the law are sent to jail
Do wars really change history?
Why do people fight?
No one knows
War changed the life of people
It made civilizations
The North and South fought the Civil War
War changes life
A lot of people die
People are at war now
When I hear the sound of a bullet
I get scared
I wonder why guns were invented
They just cause danger for people
Why did Martin Luther King die?
Somebody shot him
The memories of history
You don't feel it when you change
We can see history
One day you can change history

Do something incredible
History will always be changing around the whole world

The Strongest Person
Rosalía A.

He is big.
           He is strong.
                      He is the most powerful in the world.
He is nice but scary!
           Who is he?
                    What is he?
Is it even a he?
           Maybe he isn't even human.
                    I don't know, go ask your mother.
O, but I know!
           The strongest one, I weigh 4 tons.
                  Do you know who I am?
An elephant!

Baby Blue
Jazmine B.

the color of some books
the color of a book bag
the color of construction paper
the color of water
the color of chalk
the color of the sky
the color of school pants
the color of the chair
the color of a flower
the color of my folder

My Strong And Interesting Energy Poem
Martín B.

Is my friend strong?
Yes, I saw him on the bus.
He spends four hours a day exercising and playing.
He gets hungry if he doesn't eat breakfast.
He does not eat candy, only fruit.
My friend's dog is strong, he can lift the whole planet
And even the sun with one hand.
My friend saw a frog that was so strong that he got scared.
He went home screaming.

Is Working Hard?
Brian C.

Hard work is good for all people
   Working is fun
If you want to work, you need a lot of energy
   Working for some people is so boring
Working tastes almost like nothing
   Working smells like inside
Working sounds noisy
   One time I was working in my house
I got some money from my mom
   Work for adults is hard
They have to work eight to ten hours a day
   When I was born, it was work

New Things For Me
Uriel D.

When I change schools
I like it
I meet new friends
I like new food
If I could invent something new,
It would be a big dinosaur
That could talk with batteries
I have tried spinach
I don't like it
I have tried new kinds of pizza
It tasted good
It looked like a big, round circle

How The World Has Energy
Damaris H.

People have energy.
We all have energy when we wake up.
We are all like energy.
Energy for me feels like I'm strong.
When you have energy, you are powerful.
When I'm powerful, I feel proud.
When we are working, we have energy.
I imagine how the earth has energy.

Secrets Make Me Think
Víctor M.

I get a treasure, new house, new world
        I feel cool, big, like a giant and great
        I wouldn't know how to write my secrets
I look and feel proud
I wouldn't tell someone my secrets
        That I am Santa Claus and the Grinch
        That I hate Christmas
I feel like I am a robot
My secret in a poem
        I have eaten the food in the icebox

Everybody Needs Help
Jesús M.

I need help
even the teachers do
you can hear help anywhere
with anybody
when you need help
ask for help
help reminds me
of being young
when you were young
you asked for help

Best Friends
Hugo N. and Juan Carlos R.

Friends are the best to all the people in the world.
It's fun having friends.
Friends care for each other and help one another.
Friends are important.
When we don't have friends, we won't have fun.
We will be lonely all the time.
Friends are helpful.
They can help you with anything.
One time I had a friend who moved to another house.
When friends are nice, you can see them smile.

Black History Month
Maya O.

A special celebration
African Americans were slaves
Some slaves got free and some did not
Martin Luther King helped people to get together
Luis Armstrong played jazz music
Ella Fitzgerald was a singer
Ray Charles had great hits in music
2Pac was a great rapper

Poem About Me
Alejandra R.

I like dolphins.
They are my favorite animals.
It makes me write poetry about them.
I express my feelings about my favorite animal.
My secrets are my favorite things that I like.
I like watching the stars in my room from the window.
The ocean is my favorite thing to see.
I have one brother and one little sister.
I want to know what is your favorite animal.

Super Hero Energy
Francely V.

Do you have energy?
Sometimes everybody needs energy.
I love super duper energy power!
Going to rescue when someone is weak.
Super Energy to the rescue.
By running, jumping rope, walking.
If you try, you might have
When you are weak or sad
Energy is strong, powerful

I do!
I don't like weak, slow energy.
I wish for a super energy hero.
Ta ta ta dahhhh!
How do I get energy?
It can be hard to have energy.
Super Duper Energy Power!
You need energy to cheer you.
Strength and bravery.

The Future Is The Past
Sixth Grade Group Poem: Araceli A., Lillian A., Dayant A., Evelyn B., Jaime C., Joshua C., Noé D., Sandra G., Rafael G., Deshonda H., Christopher J., Christian L., Jorge L., Diego L., Crystal L., Mayra M., Dehjua M., Martín M., Irving N., Abram O., Mercedes O., Mercedes O., Alvaro P., Jeanette R., Jocelyn R., Zulema R., Miguel S., Michael S., Javier S., Azaed T., Ariana V., Daniel Z.

History happens in all countries
It happens on the news, at the playground, in your home
It can make you proud
Why do we need to remember?
Our history might change
It is a way of life
History is learning about ancestors
We can learn what is going to happen during our time

Why is history war?
History is bloody
War kills innocent people
I respect the soldiers who help fight back
Atomic bombs all over the place
Bodies in the air
Like the underworld
There's people dying
There's people crying
War is an ugly thing
You can't forget it
Bloody soldiers running
Tanks, weapons, chemical explosions

It's better when people have energy
People have passion for their rights
They don't let anything get in their way
Harriet Tubman helped slaves escape
She wasn't scared
Abraham Lincoln tried to free all the slaves
People wouldn't let them go
Rosa Parks did not want to give her bus seat away
She got arrested
Martin Luther King proclaimed "I have a dream"
I wish I had met him and helped
There is no difference in people
But there were fountains with signs saying "white only"
African Americans couldn't drink from the same water fountains as whites
Some people change history more than the presidents do
Passion takes energy
Not to hate but to be become better

What is your discovery?
History is creativity
History is energy
Life is like a kite
What is the meaning?
Can life be changed?
Now is different
Things change whether you like it or not
It's hard to save history
You can only control yourself
Remember what I'm saying

Teasing Your Friends With Secrets
Lillian A.

I have to tell
you a secret. But
I don't know if you can
keep it. You might want to
tell somebody but guess what?
You're going to have to sneak it.
Should I tell you if it is good
or bad or very sad or maybe it
will make you mad? Well, let
me tell you this much —
it ain't about your grumpy old dad.
If I tell you it might make
your day very sad. I don't know
if I can trust you, you might be
telling somebody and I might
bust you. Well, by the way
a secret is something you
should keep not something you
should tell you buddy on
the sneak peak.

Myself / My Life
Evelyn B.

I like to play basketball
I hate when girls give their attitudes
And they are talking bad about my friends or me
My best friends are Lillian and Araceli
When I do something good, I feel proud
I like helping my friends
I'm proud of myself and who I am

Help Me And The Other People Around You
Joshua C.

Help means that you have a problem and you need help
I picture help as someone helping me
Then, I see them and I help them
You can ask questions like
Can you help me?
Or
Can I help you?
You might need to ask these questions
Once or twice
Everyday people need help all around us
You might say
I never help
But one day you will need help yourself
Maybe people will need your help
Always help people around you
Help them be safe
Be safe yourself

Big Energy Little Energy
Jaime C.

I have energy.
Everybody has energy.
Energy makes you happy
And happy again.
Sometimes energy makes you hyper.
It is part of vitamins and minerals.
When you do not have energy
You feel weak and sad
Or you just don't want to move.
When you have a lot of energy
You have to do something active
So you won't be nervous.
It's really hard to control energy.
You have to run around or play with something.
I just used up my energy
Writing this poem.

Hopping In Rides
Noé D.

some rides are fast
        some are slow
there's some that make you go wow

```
                low riders are the best
they hop down the street
                and say this is me
cars are like art
                they express your feelings
you can do anything
                if you have imagination
just style up cars
                if you can
some are so good
                some are just wrong
some make you look cool in the hood
```

A Perfect Place
Sandra G.

A relaxing place
Where nobody tells you what to do
Where you can read
A room with books of imagination
A chair with a desk
A tv of your own
Just relaxing there
Not doing anything that bothers you
Enjoying the lovely peace

Green
Rafael G.

```
                    Reminds me of grass     Of trees
Feels bright                Happy
                    See it in the Mexican flag          In a rainbow

Aliens                          Money
          Feels bright inside          Really really surprised inside
```

Things That Will Contest Your Mind
Dehjua M.

mind what is that?
a
nut in your head
a
clock ticking
wanting
to get out of your head

decisions do they come
out of your head
do you feel
your mind
when you're knocking
back and forth

how is my mind?

big or
little or
even small

I know they are
the same
but in my
mind
small is
smaller than
little

I just
can't wonder
what's
in my mind
anymore

Young Meanings
Martín M.

Young is playful.
Young is being kind.
Young is to be exciting.
Young is loud and loud.
Young is courage.
Young is to be joyful.
Some parents say they wish to be young again.
Young is to enjoy, to feel, to play, to have energy
And to still be young.
If you wish to be an adult, so be it.
But you will always remember me as young.

My Super Dream Relaxation Spot
Mercedes O.

A relaxing spot for me would be
In Spain, Miami or downtown Chicagotown!

It would be over there, high up in the air
Where there are beautiful sceneries, on the beach.

When in the morning you see the sunrise shine in your eyes,
Pastel colors of bloody red, soft violet, and aqua in the sea.
At night you see the sunset while everyone gets slow,
See the bright watercolors of baby shocking pink,
Slow and mellow baby blue,
Green as leaves with ivory,
And shiny pond water with emerald green.

My relaxing place would have a soft baby feel like a hammock.
There's my own refrigerator with tons and tons of food
To feed 10 people for a lifetime,
A radio to listen and dance to soft classic R&B,
Rap and hip-hop to bring me to life
And alternative rock to relieve my anger and miserable life.

My relaxing spot will have 4 guys all doing what I say,
One for feeding me the most delicious mouth watering grapes,
One for keeping me cool while the scorching hot sun blazes down,
One for massaging my aching back and legs,
And one to be my bodyguard against all those who are jealous.

Though I know this is my super dream relaxation spot
I must wake up now for my own good sake.
Or do you know that this might be real?

To Envision Or Not To Envision
Alvaro P.

you might think I'm different
just trying to envision
this being the last time
maybe the last rhyme
I don't do crimes

you might think my rhymes are lame
I don't mess with games
peeps trying to step to the plate
I might not be straight
I'm not a fish who took the bait
I might be late
I'm not a hero
neither a zero

I went packing
I began grabbing

300

my feelings are tapping
I might stop rapping
as soon as I stop lacking

I got some stitches
I don't eat fishes
I don't believe in superstition
I gave the food in some kitchens
there are no real riches
it's not delicious
don't put me on stitches
I need a prescription

I'm not going to fight this life
you mess with that
you mess with me
you mess with my brother
you mess with my family

Raphie's so bony
my rap ain't phony
I could move a boulder
I'm just a soldier
I eat beans
I like the marines
I'm not a copy cater
my life never shatters

I Have Energy
Jeanette R.

To play and laugh
I am enthusiastic
I get hyper and crazy
I begin to giggle and to scream
On vacations and Fridays
I get wild
Saturday is time to scream
Party time
Sundays I have little energy
Mondays I say goodbye to energy
Time to go to school

History Is The Beginning Of The World
Seventh Grade Group Poem: Miguel A., Jennifer A., Amanda A.,
Darlene B., Luís C., Alejandra C., César D., Peter G., Manuel G.,
Agustin G., Viridiana G., David H., Reginald M., Marco O., Jesús O.,
Virginia P., María D., Miguel R., Consuelo S., Michelle S., Orbel V.,
Lizette Z.

History goes in a pattern
Everyday something becomes history
Everybody makes history in the world
It catches people's attention
Even if you're not famous
You are history to your family
Without history we wouldn't know
What happened back then

People, past, culture, religion
Cavemen made caves
Egyptians made pyramids
3 nickels would make you rich in the 1600's
3 nickels now buys you a piece of candy
The kings and queens of Europe
The democracy of America
All that happened a long time ago
Everyday someone invents another thing
First things are new
Later things are old
Without technology we would not know
What is going on in the world

History is shown with violence
The worst things that happened to the history of the earth
It's just not right
Why enslavement?
Why not freedom?
Why were we so ignorant?
Hiding us from the truth
Covering things up
We sat there with heads in the sand
Until the people spoke and became free

We have different opinions
Violence, law, immigration, money
Have you ever thought of changing history?
Going into the past and making a difference
If we get smart enough
We can make a time machine

Being Helpful
Miguel A.

all around the world
people always need help
they ask for help
they call for help
sometimes even scream for help
I saw a lady fall
I asked her
do you want me to help you
if you help a person
you feel very good inside
helping friends and neighbors
everybody that needs help
a person might help you

It's Love
Amanda A.

It's something you feel.
It's something you fear.
Some people think it's beautiful.
Some people think it's horrible.
You think it's scary.
You think it's lovely.
It's like a beautiful dove.
At the end you know that it's love.

The Years Pass Us By
Darlene B.

The days pass
New faces we see
Being young is fun
Being spontaneous and being me
   No one wants to grow old
   Everyone wants to stay young
   The teenage years
   Being little
Growing up is only responsibilities
From going to work to paying your bills
No time to be a kid
Your youth will stay with you
   As the years pass us by
   The candy, the nicknames, the friends you had
   It all turns into a memory

But you're a kid in your heart
As the years pass us by

No More Secrets
Alejandra C.

I don't have secrets
I always let everything out
I never hide anything
I mean, for what

If everyone had secrets
Everyone would be curious
So let it all out
Before someone gets furious
Say your secrets and be truthful
Secrets can be really hurtful to express

Sometimes secrets become lies
They get discovered and spread like flies
People start to regret those secrets
At the end you are all alone
Without a friend or a soul

I don't have secrets
I always let everything out
I never hide anything
I mean, for what

Decisions Are Options
Agustin G.

you have something   to choose
          making a decision   leads to responsibility
some are easy   some are hard
          some give you time   to think
so make it choice   slow or fast
          either way   it's your decision

Life's Decision
Reginald M.

A decision to be made
To show how life should be made
Even with your family
You know how you would be

Just look deep inside
See what you find

Taking all your time
To make up your mind
When it's right in front of you
You can't tell the truth
No matter how far
Just be who you are
Just know you
Tell the truth

You may have to choose
It may give you the blues
You want to look for love
Just look above
If you're lost and need to be found
Know that your family is around

The Only Person I Trust
José M.

Tim was like a brother to me.
He looked out for me.
I looked out for him.
We were in the same class for 4th and 6th grades.
We would always hang out.
We would always chill out at his crib.
We would watch tv or go to the park.
Whenever Tim had a problem I would help him.
When I had a problem, he would help me out.
Sometimes we would argue.
But two or three days later, we would be friends again.

Hawaii Waves
Marco O.

smelling the ocean breeze
sleeping in a hammock
eating pineapples and coconuts
swimming and playing volleyball
waking up in the afternoon
building sand castles
messing them up
surfing for a long time
then wiping out
on hawaii waves

Feel What I Feel
Virginia P.

In a cage
I can't get out
Set me free
Set me free
Is what I say

No one can hear me
I can't hear them
I see the world
All the horrible things in it
People can't see what I see

People have shown me how hard the world is
I see what I need to live
I've shown myself that I don't have to be like you
I don't have to think what everyone wants me to think
To survive

I've shown you what I feel
So you can feel what I feel

How Birds Fly
María D.

The birds are up and alive
You wonder why
You've never thought of them before
Even though they're right outside your door

Now they chirp and they sing
Fly up with their magnificent wings
They soar through the sky
In a blink of the eye
You wonder how they fly
Like graceful creatures
Through the sky
Is it magic?
Is it faith?
To fly it must have strength
Power and courage within
A truly amazing creature that it is

Punk
Miguel R.

we aren't crazy
just a little
    we don't
want to be the same
    why
are we to blame
we're not deadly
    yet
we're not quite
    friendly
don't misunderstand us
    maybe we
    are freaks
but inside we're
    all the
    same

When You Are Young
Michelle S.

When you are young you have fun.
    First you learn to talk.
Then you learn to walk.
    Soon enough you'll learn to run.
You make up stories.
    You have adventures.
Let your imagination run wild.
    You're a princess,
A pirate,
    A king or queen,
Or maybe a monkey at the zoo.
    You play a lot.
Then you go to school.
    You learn new things.
You make new friends.
    You smell the flowers of a spring morning.
You want to play in the mud.
    Winter comes, you want to play in the snow.
Another year has passed but you are still young.
    You make more friends.
You go out.
    You meet new people.
They become your friends.
    You learn to like them more than just friends.
Your heart is broken.

You run to your mother's arms.
She cradles you and says everything will be all right.
You wish you were a baby all over again.

The Clock Is Ticking
**Eighth Grade Group Poem, room 204: Silma A., Jesse A., Mayra A.,
Marisol B., Julie D., Isaac H., Mayra M., Miguel M., Ivan N., Yesenia
O., Jose R., Tania U.**

History is a big, fat mystery
History is a word that sounds really old
The world is changing
What changed history is people
What passes right now becomes history

Who   What   When   Why
      Where   How

In the past girls always used to wear dresses
Now we wear jeans
When people took pictures they were black and white or people painted
portraits
Now we have color pictures and digital cameras

One thing remains the same – war
We go to war for stupid things
We attack with nuclear warheads
Then wonder why the ozone layer is breaking apart
Kill and kill and kill
Power in the world is war and money

Will wars ever end?
Will our soldiers come back?
Will racism continue?
Will women get the same rights?
Will robots take over the world?
Will we live on mars?

Time never stops
You can be in the present and never have the same old life
You never know who will make the future
It will be different from the past
We do not have to look for history
We make history

The Effect Of A Decision
Silma A.

The decisions I make
are the consequences I take
for acting so selfish
     I had no choices
     In my life my present
     is part of the choices I made
     the past good or bad
          My choices that always feel so rough
          effect my future by leaving a tough space
          inside my heart
               A teardrop away
               is a sense of sadness
               a teardrop to stand for
               a quick feeling of pain

This New Thing
Jesse A.

New, the sound I hate the most.
Where something is always taken from you.
Thrown away and replaced with something new.
The touch you can't bear.
The sight is spine tingling.
The taste you hate for it is so yucky and mushy.
The smell is stomach wrenching like fire burning trees.
You hear the dark voice of this new thing.
As it speaks everything goes pitch black.
For you hate this new thing.
You toss it, trash it, destroy it, burn it.
Throw things at it, break it, rip it.
But no matter what you do it always comes back.

The Beach
Mayra M.

the smell of the water
the shinning sun
the sound of animals all around
the smell of great food
a great place to relax
don't think about work
nobody is talking to you
no sounds of cars or trains
just bright colors
fall asleep

What I Hear Everyday
Miguel M.

       Help, a horrible word
Do you want to know why?
       A guy saying he needs help with his wife
A neighbor saying his life is like living with pain
       Do they think about how others feel?
No more, I won't help another soul
       As long as I live
No more, I will not
       No more giving
Man, I need help

Breaking Your Head
Ivan N.

Decisions, decisions
So many things to think of
So hard, so difficult to decide
What side to choose?
Good or evil, black or white
What choice could lead to trouble?
What choice could lead to anything?
So hard to decide and nothing to do
But to decide
Ying and yang, enemy and friends
Break your head just to say yes or no
You may end up dead or alive
You circle around the room
Pacing and pacing and pacing
You throw yourself on the bed
Roll yourself around on the floor
Think until you break your mind
A war in your head, voices in your head
Run around and hit the wall
Yes

Relaxing Mind
Yesenia O.

my relaxing place   my mind, head or whatever you call it
     my mind has all   my thoughts, feelings and memories
my mind is big enough   to imagine every little thing or big thing I want
     my mind is like a perfect dark cave   a small one
I can just sit and express myself   think to myself
     do whatever I want   I sit back and go inside my mind
imagine   a perfect relaxing cave

310

Our Roots Change

Eighth Grade Group Poem, room 213: Ms. Dawn Creed, José Bahena, Ariana Calderón, Erica Castillo, Danny Cervantes, David Crisantos, Lorena Delgado, David Díaz, Marcus Elston, Daisy García, Pedro Hernández, Michael Higgs, Omar López, Elizabeth Márquez, Eduardo Méndez, Isabel Montalvo, Jazmín Navarro, Erik Ojeda, Jacqueline Omana, José Peralta, Estefani Pérez, Daniel Rico, Gilberto Robles, Carina Rodríguez, Uriel Sánchez, Jazmín S., Sandie S., Andrea S., Jorge T., Mayra V., Raquel V.

Metamorphosis
When an animal evolves, it changes
History is everywhere
Look at the smallest thing
Look at any simple thing
Everything becomes old
You will see that it has history
Rap has a history
From the underground of New York to the mainstream
Plants change the environment
When I go to Mexico, I see changes
Even when little Timmy took his first steps
Wherever you go, there will be changes

Our history, their history, everyone's history
Everything around you is always changing
Things you will remember in your life
People change and realize how much they love their families
Our lives change in one way or another
When people die, a new life begins
New people come alive to be happy or suffer
Time goes by
People try to hurry before the sun rises
Time flies so fast
First you're born and the next thing you know you're gone
Are we on a hamster wheel going round and round?

History is America coming to be
When I first heard of the Underground Railroad
I thought it was a real railroad
But it was actually a route slaves took to escape slavery
History is 9/11, the planes hitting the World Trade Center
New York changed with a lot of panic
Revolutionizing people
Wars are started by people who don't how to think
Who kill and die
Without war we could have a better environment
Is history a mistake?
You can never go back and change it

Technology makes things fast or slow
The first stove was invented
The first car was invented
The first tv was invented
Technology is good and bad
Helps us to save or destroy nature

History is like a book
If you want to see the future, turn the page
A new chapter will be born
A new chapter for all our lives
It is a gift, it is a chance
To be known as a leader
A person who does something amazing
Unbelievable

Change history
Change lives
Change feelings
Change people you love
History changes because of our decisions
Our plans for global brotherhood always change
Could I change people?
What do you to change people?
Banish the bad, evil, dark things
Like an endangered species
The smell of a new evolution
Years go by, a new life
Ignorance is a thing of the past

Don't You Ever Get Tired
José B.

I will fly in the sky
jump over the moon
happy all over me
let's play
come on
no, yes, no, yes
let's go swimming
or even run as fast as a car
I touched the sun when I got to the other side
I like everything
I am a battery that gets recharged and keeps on going
yawn
call the ambulance
I'm getting tired
I will fall from the moon

312

turn to mud
I'm
falling
asleep

Tired Man
David D.

You are home on the couch watching tv
A bag of chips in front of you
A can of pop at your side
Just sitting
Not doing anything
Being lazy
Other people are outside
Full of energy
Running in the park, laughing, talking
Smelling fresh air
Tasting clean, cold water from the fountain
You are at home
Your house is dirty
Trash everywhere
Smelling the same old air
No energy, no strength
Going to sleep
Turning off the tv
The next day is a different day
Outside is raining
No one is outside
You feel better
You clean up and go downstairs
Full of energy
You open the door
Run outside in the rain
Run in the park
Smelling the refreshing air
Going home to sleep
Waiting to see how the next day will be

Soulife
Marcus E.

it comes in many forms
art that is truly from the heart
on paper, walls, murals
it can be expressed in a painting
on a graffiti wall

313

it can come in gifts or a celebration
known for culture
it reduces static
so much style
fresh breeze is what you
smell, taste, hear, feel, and see
a soul in me
maybe there's a soul in a tree
why not
it grows up like me

Swallowed By The Water
Daisy G.

Midnight
I'm walking down the beach
All of a sudden, I see someone
Calling out for help
Should I help them?
There's no time to think
Not even time to blink
I open my eyes
I'm already swimming towards the person
But wait, I can't swim
Help, help, help
There's no sound, only silence
There's no light, only darkness
Who will want to help us?
No one, I guess
We've been swallowed by the water
No help comes to us
I was trying to help but who helped me?
No one
Why didn't they help us?
I don't know
I'm not their conscious
Deep inside my heart
Tears are falling apart
Like a broken crystal
I'm still waiting for help

Army Of White Shirts
Michael H.

All throughout school there is an army.
An army of white shirts.
They report to their classroom base.

Where they sit in rows like sardines.
They report to their general teachers.
Go to the hot, stuffed cafeteria and eat grade F food.
They have little time for homework due the next day.
No fun or activities.
They get shipped off.
To the war of everyday life.

True or Lie
Elizabeth M.

I am 13 years old.
I am the tallest in the world.
I am from Durango, Mexico.
I am the best writer.
I went to see the president.
I have 10 friends.
I am strong.
There are 5 members in my family.
I have the best imagination.
My favorite class is math.
In all my classes, I have an A.
Today is my birthday.
I am in the eighth grade.

Bigger Thing
Eduardo M.

you're high but you're never low
peer pressure is always near you
forcing you to what you never wanted to do
in the end, you always end up doing it
you get used to the smell
you like it when it touches your lips
you always want to do it
but there are people near you
after a while, you need it stronger
you never realized you're a junky
it's the life you chose

I Want To Runaway
José P.

Time is just wasting
I'm here wasting it
With nothing to do

Just sit here and listen to music
To cry for what I've done
Fighting with friends and breaking our friendship
I imagine myself walking alone in a dark hall
With no walls
Could running away get my problems out of my head
Instead of remembering the past
What I did
I can see myself in a better place with no problems
I will remorse about what I did
I never thought it would happen
Those who cared for me will not care any more
Time will pass by like time through a window

Shhhh!!!
Sandie S.

I have a dark secret
I must confess
but promise me you won't tell

That icky, stinky soup
my aunt made me
I never ate
I simply got up and took the smelly green soup
and flushed it down the toilet
all that was left of that soup was its icky, smelly smell

Please shhh! shhh! shhh!

Wait, don't go!
I have another secret
I must confess

I have a crush on shhhh!
because shhh!

OK, OK
promise me not to tell
on my science test I cheated
I copied off my friend and we both got an F!

That's all for today my friend
please shhh! shhh! shhh!

Wrong, Right Decisions
Andrea S.

Decisions are right, wrong, good or bad
        They involve consequences
After your decision, the consequences come
        The decisions you make hope they are correct
If not, you're going to end up with negative consequences
        You could be in a lot of trouble
Jail, dead, or end up on the streets asking for money
        Positive decisions bring positive consequences
They might help you in your future or now
        Make good decisions that come from your heart

What Is Energy?
Mayra V.

Energy is the sun rising up
It can be dark and tiring
It can make you feel good or bad
Energy is a herd of horses on the horizon
Energy can smell like your boyfriend's cologne
Or it can smell like the person you don't like
You can get energy everywhere
Why are you tired?
Is it because you ate too much?
Is it because you are depressed?
Energy is the wind
Strong and clear
Do you want energy?
Look around you and catch it with your hands
Energy is anywhere you can think of
Just look deep inside

I Am
Raquel V.

I am young, energetic and confused.
I am a rose bud with bees buzzing around me.
I am starting a long, new, hard journey.

I am energetic.
I love to party, I love to laugh.
My soul wants to jump out and run around.
My heart pounds faster and faster, impatient.
Makes me smile.

I am confused, I am confused.
Love or lust.
What is love?
How do you love?
Must be lust.

Sad and mad.
I want to cry a river.
I want to scream until my lungs blow out.
Bees sting my burning heart.
I want to punch a hole through their hive.
Grab a handful of bees – including the Queen.
Let their life pass through my veins.

Tough but strong.
Should I do this?
Is it right or wrong?
What will tomorrow bring?
And the day after?
This is so hard.
Please help.
Wait – I can do this all.
Don't cry, can't cry.
Everything comes with a price.
I'll pay for it all.

My petals have barely bloomed.
The wind blows my body about.
Feeling runs down my stem.

I am young, energetic, and confused.
Who are you?

ORRINGTON ELELMENTARY SCHOOL
Principal: Holly Murer
Teachers: Mr. Sigan, 5th, Ms. Hudson, 4th, Mr. Likhite, 5th, Ms. Rich, 5th, Mr. Wilda, 4th

Cindy Sigal, Poet in Residence

Cindy Sigal earned her M.F.A. in Poetry and B.A. in Creative Writing & Child Development from Sarah Lawrence College. Her poems have appeared in *Mudfish* and the *Sarah Lawrence Review*.

This was my first year with the Hands-on-Stanzas program and it was fantastic! The kids at Orrington were wonderful. My goal with each class was to create a community of writers and readers. I worked with each child, wherever they were in their learning process, to help them connect to the poems and ideas presented. Poetry is a natural learning medium because it mirrors the way language, thinking, and feeling exist within us as an interactive, dynamic whole. Teaching poetry is great fun and full of surprises-- often the kids themselves are the most surprised by how good their poems are or by something that they have never thought of before.

Poetry
Cara H.

The rain soaks everything,
filling all it touches
with life.

When it stops
a spirit
dips down to drink
from the pond.

A beaver swims by
and is filled with
a happiness that will never leave him.

Untitled
Aaron H.

I'm in Pearl Harbor, December 7, 1941,
playing the coconut game.
You throw coconuts at each other
like dodge ball. A plane
flies over head, it has the Japanese symbol on it.
Next thing I know, everything explodes…

I wake up in a hospital
with my friends. I was so happy
but my dog, smige
didn't make it.
64 years later, sometimes I think
I feel smidge resting his chin on my lap
as I eat my dinner.

The Message from the Old Man
Sophie Z.

I'm a small old man. Grinning
or frowning they write about me.

I wish I could have a young lady with the whitest smile in the sky.
They'd write about what she could have been.

Come here my child and tell what is inside.
Come here, no one can hurt you, come here and say what's inside.

Inside Me
Ben G.

Inside me is a bad image of a soccer game.
A picture of Hitler torching flowers,
a dark cloud of math, and a pit bull tearing
at my shoes profusely. Also, a Dorito of terror.

Or maybe a Dorito of happiness. My cat is evil
and has a lot of fur so I call her a dark furball of evil.
I feel like a girl when I skip
through the meadow of flowers! And when I'm happy
well, lets just say that I feel like a title wave of happiness!
And when I'm mad I'm like…
my cat unfortunately.

Inside Me
Tunde O.

Inside me there's a monkey.
Inside me there's a puddle.
Inside me there's a dragon.
Inside me there's a shoe.
Inside me there's a BMW.
Inside me there's a dark ball of fear.

Diving Board
Ella L.-U.

I try again and again
the saddle ready to put on,
It's on… the bull rears and
throws…Splash!

I get on the bull's back
ready for a ride.
He rears and throws…splash!

I get on the diving board
ready to dive.
Get ready… Go!
I hear a whistle: I dive—

Ode to my Rap
Vashon B.

Zoe-Zoe you mommies out there, you mommies
out there and yo dopman you think you're slick.
You sold crack to my sister and now she's sick.

If she happens to die because of your drug,
I'm putting in the pulos for 38 slugs.
Bang bang, choo choo train let me see you
do that woo oh woo, woo oh woo

peanut butter and jelly time peanut butter
and jelly. Let's go chups, chups chups
chups. If you want it, you can get it
let me know. I 'bout to break this thing up.
Let's go get it.

Stars
Shannon E.

I know what stars dream of--
they dream of people singing,
even people eating.
they dream about other stars
and people on the monkey bars.

Untitled
Clay C.

The sunlight beams down on a puddle
making the puddle orange, it shimmers
as the wind blows.

A coyote walks by looking for food.
It starts to get dark. The coyote howls
at the moon, walks across

the puddle, then stops
and pounces.

13 Ways of Looking at a Photo of Termite Mounds on the CapeYork Peninsula
Ina C.

1.
The termite mounds rise like pointy needles.
2.
The air seems cold.
3.
The termite mounds look like chopped down trees.
4.
There is no sun.
5.
The mounds look like they are in quick sand.
6.
The sky is dark.
7.
Some of the mounds are big, some small.
8.
Some of the trees look like they are going to fall.
9.
There are termite mounds that look like rocks.
10.
The ground is very dark.
11.
The wind is very strong.
12.
Some of the trees have fallen.
13.
No one is around.

From the Bottom of My Heart
Joey G.

Sometimes I think my aunt is going to come back
out of her grave. If she did—
flowers would sprout and the trees
would bloom and my family would be happy.

Happy
Jackie G.

There's a flower of friends growing inside me,
they fill up the darkness.

There's a tree of happiness. I feel like a part
of heaven has gotten inside me, pushing out

all of the hatred and sadness like a volcano
pushing out all the lava.
The American Flag has unrolled inside me,
releasing its freedom, power and happiness.

It Happens Again
Michael D.

Keeping your puddle of sadness in too long
about to erupt with anger,

diving into the hole of the volcano-
it finally erupts with anger opening the door to heaven,

then being swallowed by the eye of a hurricane, buried
under earth's core.

Inside Me
Isabel S.

Happiness runs through my blood.
Madness through my germs.
And things in between like…

A film of my past, going
through my memories,
a blizzard of hate.

A cloud that makes
endless rain of emotions,
a mirror of the future.

A peek of sunlight,
stopping hatred,
a waterfall of tears.

A dark corner of war.
A centered area of peace.

A cabinet of fun things.
A volcano of frustration.

All these bad
and good things
run through my blood
to my heart.

324

Inside Me
Sammi W.

Inside me there is soccer and someone tired of running
or someone who is happy that they made a goal.
A picture of the goalie missing a shot. Bang!
it hits the back of the net, the score board goes up one point.

Inside me there is a violin. Pretty music. Someone playing
at a recital. Someone not making any mistakes and hearing
the audience clapping for you.

Inside me there are feelings. Jealousy of someone's room—
how it's so cool. Sadness that my dog honey died.
Mad that my sister is in college and not home. Happiness
that I'm loved.

Inside me there's a heart
A heart filled with love.
Love from my family, friends
and my pet, Rocky.

Being Tortured
Jabari G.

I don't know how Nazim Hikmet felt when his tortures
made him stand in human excrement, but I imagine
it would smell bad and you might fall in it because it's kind of like mud.

I don't know how it is to be a piece of paper,
but I imagine it would hurt
because some people write hard.

I don't know what it would feel like to be cut in half
but I imagine that it would hurt
and I wouldn't be able to do things.

Inside Me
Khalil P.

Inside me is a dark cloud of hatred.
Dogs that lick until it's time to leave.

Inside me is a big black hole that came with my soul
and a puddle that gives me love.
Inside, cold air haunts me

There's jealousy of my cousin Akil
and a pit bull chasing me forever.

The Birds
Kaigh W.

I feel like there's a bird trying to escape
the cruelness of the world,

the hatred of people, the death
of war, the pure hell of violence.

The bird is trapped in a cage
of the world; I want to fly away with it.

Wonderful Poetry
Roman K.

Poetry can be as strong as a wall
and as weak as a piece of paper.

Poetry is the door to the impossible,
unpredictable and the wonderful.

It makes you relax and float off
into another world of sad and happy feelings.

Ode to Chocolate Croissants
William B.

Chocolate tastes so good. In bread
it's only better. A Croissant au Chocolat
and all that tasty butter—

Just thinking about it, the hunger
destroys me, my stomach's gurgling hurts!
I feel like I haven't eaten in years!

Ode to Video Games
Sam M.

Oh Video games, plentish me of your endless games.
Your colorful screens remind me of time-warping (Wait.
That's impossible.) Your never-ending fun is too delightful.
Your unforgettable stuff is so unforgettable (Wait, I already said

unforgettable). You are just too good of an invention!
You stop my boredness!

Untitled
Navy T.

Hey, I'm an alien
an alien that can't see
but I have a feeling that I'm not on Saturn.
What are you doing? No, no, no, noooo---
Where am I?
"You're in Heaven."
Why did I end up here, I wanted to be on Saturn.

Poems
Peixian W.

Poems are like me flying in the sky,
going in a black hole, experiencing a new place,
like being mad at nothing,
or feeling dumb when your smart.
A poem can take you to a place
where you have never been.

My Cat
Patrick W.

Soaring as an owl,
leaping like a leopard. Patient
as a fox. Ready to attack like a tiger,
to run like a rabbit.

The Eye is a Star
Adam C.

The eye is a star looking
down at us. The wind is like
a ballet moving through the air
too fast to see. History is time
that has or hasn't happened.
The moon is a mirror reflecting
the light of the night.
The sun is a hero
with its light everything is bright.
The sky is like a never ending adventure.

My Third Eye and Second Eye Sees
Oladapo O.

My third eye sees the past and future.
My two eyes see cake.
My third eye can see through anything.
My two eyes see happy people.
My third eye sees what's going to happen.
My two eyes see a handsome man.
My third eye sees if you are guilty or not.
My two eyes see if you are happy or sad.

Tye-Dye
Rachel J.

A swirl, a splash
a mixed up memory.
A boom, a crash,
the monkey's paw.
A volcano erupting,
a colorful page from a book.
The amazing bright colors of Kool-Aid
mixed together, spilling
and staining my shirt.
The colorful inside of a rock
split in two.
Leaves in autumn,
falling down to mix together.

A 10 Year-Old's Way
Hannah G.

Me and my friend Walter were going to run away.
We packed all the stuff we needed:
game boy, swim suits, junk food, laptop, ipod,
baseball-pitching machine and a portable TV.
I grabbed my floating skateboard with rocket boosters.
We found an island with nobody on it
and turned it into an arcade.

Listen To Me
Jeremy G.

I have a power, the power
to disguise myself without a disguise.
I will walk unknown.

I will cause trouble without paying the price.
I will act badly to people without them hating me.
The power will only be given to true mischief makers
who can manage their mischief.

Untitled
Ariel K.

I know that no one knows how it feels to swim away
from the Lockness Monster, but I think it's like you feel
like your not enjoying the dinner because you are it.

Also, I don't know how it feels to be in the underworld,
but it must be like you want to go back to the outside world.

How does it feel to be smashed by a giant? Terrible!

Poems
Yvettang G.

A magical palace
like little fairies in heaven
Or twinkling stars in the moonlight.

Untitled
Chyna M.

I'm in a world with no killing.
I'm in a world where people can never die,
or curse, or steal or go without poetry.

Untitled
Zhong C. O.

If you wake up early
can't you see the orange sun
rising up? I know you did.
It's God eating an orange pineapple, drip
by drip.

Cries of Misery
Jane S.

I feel sadness when something else is not surviving.
I get the cries of other people.
I can feel the pain and misery of others,
although people look right through me.

I see the tears right in front of me
like blood from a paper cut.

I see people in other countries surviving
on a crumb or two.

I have the power to hear the suffering
of others but I don't know why--

HELEN C. PEIRCE SCHOOL OF INTERNATIONAL STUDIES
Principal: Paula Rossino
Teachers: Mrs. Ramos, 3rd, Ms. Rivera, 4th, Ms. Rosenthal, 5th

James Shea, Poet in Residence

A graduate of the University of Iowa Writers' Workshop, Mr. Shea has published poems in numerous journals, including *Bridge*, *Crazyhorse*, *jubilat*, *LIT Magazine*, and the anthology *Isn't It Romantic: 100 Love Poems by Younger American Poets* (Verse , 2004). He currently teaches writing and literature courses at DePaul University and Columbia College Chicago.

Mr. Shea says, "I would like to thank the teachers and staff at Peirce for welcoming me into their community. It has been a pleasure to encourage the young poets at Peirce to write a new poem each week. From the direct honesty of Eva Guadarrama's haiku ("Winter is boring.") to the expansive imagination of Marc Coss's "Lie Poem," ("A black rhino threw / a hamburger-shaped bed at the tiger." to the subtle ending of Jessica Avila's "Poem" ("I can carry / 400 desks / in only one hand, / some in the / other hand."), all my students discovered a wide range of emotional registers. I hope that they may continue to train their ears, and write poems that delight and surprise.

Skeleton and Pineapple
Juan M.

Pineapple, are you in another
House? How come you didn't come?

Dear Moon
Araceli A.

How are you doing
tonight? I am glad
to be your friend.
Love, star, your friend.
I live where you
live in the sky.
I came out in the
night every day.

Untitled
Christopher C.

A dog comes to a cat
and the cat runs up
to the tree and the cat
stayed up and the dog barked
all the day and a
big dog came and
barked at them and he jumped
up the tree.

The Sun
Victor O.

The
up sun
the sun so
red and beaming
the sun is up the sun is red
I to a sun

The Loud Cowboy
Julio R.

The loud cowboy is so loud.
But he is happy, a birthday.

But the man goes slow.
And he is scared of October. (Of Halloween)

Untitled
Raul L.

I took a donut
of my brother
and then I

didn't say
sorry, then
my brother

said, who took
my donut, then
I said I did.

A Shadow
Raul E.

There once was a boy
That was not very good at making shadows.
His friends knew how to make shadows
But he cannot make a shadow.

The boy knew how to make toys and origami.
His friends did not know how to make toys or origami.
His friends were very, very jealous.
They were friends again.

There was a guy that stayed in bed.
He was lazy.
His brother told him to get up.
He did not get up.

Play Station Day
Diego R.

The world plays Play Station 2.
I play Need for Speed.
I play Need for Speed Underground.
I play Need for Speech Underground 2.

A Wolf Has Blue Fur
Eduardo C.

The wolf has blue teeth.
The wolf has a blue eye.
The wolf is unafraid of animals.

In the Night I See
Gaspar F.

Before my bed
I see lights.
When I
sleep, I think
about the haunted
houses. When
I sleep, I
hear talking.
I dream that
I'm home.

Untitled
Rogelio H.

It feels like
someone died.
and they are
dancing. From
a long time
ago. With a
flute. It is
fall. And
the leaves
are falling
down off
the tree.

The Dinosaur
Katherine F.

A dinosaur is red and black with spikes.
A dinosaur is a cool animal.

Moon and Star
Christina C.

How old are you, star?
Why are you big, moon?
How are you, star?
And you too, moon?
Why are you a girl, star?
And why are you, too?

Frog and a Fish
Nancy B.

A frog comes to
A little fish's feet.
And they were
Looking at each other.
And they were beautiful.

The Lying Animals
Ricardo A.

The blue tiger is blue, but his hair is red.
The cow is green.
The cat is orange.
The dog is yellow.
The bear is red.
The fish is green.

Untitled
Meli U.

I can see police. I can see a moon. I can see parties.

Untitled
Luis M.

Chair, how old are you? Chair, why are you
so big? Chair, you could be my friend. I have
some other friends. Chair, do you eat? Chair do
you walk? Chair, do you sleep?

The Desk
Janet C.

The desk has four legs.
And the books are his food.
And where I write is his head.
And the feet are his eyes.

Book/Pencil
Jody R.

Pencil, I'm expecting you.
Yesterday it was my party.

Untitled
Bladimir L.

I see my TV and radio.
I hear music and parties.
I think of school and ghosts.

The Lying Animals
Steven V.

The red eyes with dragon,
The blue eyes with dragon.
The bee is blue.
The dog is orange.
The people are green.
The water is red.

Untitled
Kevin O. P.

My super power is to make plan to
Speed from trouble and speed from bad boys.
I always have a plan.

Haiku
Eva G.

Winter is boring. The chimney is
hot. Now the night is hot. I got very
very hot. Winter is boring.

Untitled
Lexy C.

Shark shark attacks a man
with no eyes The shark is white
with no sense of humor. It
attacks without warning.

Poem
Orlando L.

The butterfly goes to a flower and drinks nectar.
Next, it puts pollen on its feet and goes to other flowers. After, it puts
the pollen down on the flower.
Lastly, the flower starts growing.

Untitled
Codie G.

My mom eats plums. I don't like plums.
I don't eat plums. Plums are yucky
and gooey. I tasted it before. It tasted
yucky. I hate plums. I don't like
to eat yucky plums. I don't like
it. Plums will make me sick.

Haiku
Emiliano V.

Hail!
The size of minivans
Crushing pieces of cars!

Poem
Kaitlin L.

I ate some strange pizza and turned into a white tiger. I looked around
the room and I saw a piece of chicken and I ate it and turned into a giant
snake. My cat ate dog food and turned into a monkey.

Untitled
Karla C.

My purple giraffe ate my hamburger.
A red rabbit ate my chicken.
My orange alligator ate my orange.
A pink duck ate my brother and had a big stomach.

The Clown
Charly H.

You're a spirit, how
Did you do that? You know
How I want your information?

Poem
Jessica A.

I can break a
tree in half.
I can lift
up a car. I can
carry a big
house. I can carry
400 desks
in only one hand,
some in the
other hand.

Untitled
Darrius O.

The
Tree
In
The
My
Sister
A boy

Haiku
Kayla W.

Tap-tap
My mom's
Car door got stuck

Collage Poem
Jaelyn R.

Earth neighbor
On last
U.S.S. Macon:
A cloak of fog
On Assignment

338

Untitled
Karla R.

Glue, you have a big body
but a tiny, orange head.
Where're your arms and legs?
I guess you don't have
any at all, and you have
a white, fat neck.
Glue, what you so weird?

Untitled
Malik A.

A green Snoopy came to the house
and played baseball and broke a
window. The baseball fell in the yogurt.

Lie Poem
Arely S.

The blue elephant ate my pizza.
The green polar bear at my pasta.
The pink rabbit ate my yogurt.
The orange finch ate my ham.

Untitled
Andrea O.

My ruler is thin and straight. In only
has one eye. I feel sorry for it.

Poem
Jacky D.

A blue rabbit
jumped in my
room and
ate my
water bottle.

Lie Poem
Marc C.

I ate pizza and watched a blue tiger play hockey.
The tiger was playing with a red
Monkey with a hotdog. A black rhino threw
A hamburger-shaped bed at the tiger.
A blue bird was eating green ice cream.

Untitled
Luis C.

I can go in the sky.
I can go to Texas without running.
I can beat up four men at once.
I can go to New Mexico by my body.
I can climb one big tree.

Haiku
Maritza R.

The snow is
falling like autumn
leaves.

Collage Poem
Josue R. and Eric O.

Dear One Drinker, Hello again.
Pride jaguar you need energizer
"Yes, Sir!" Ghost Cat.

The Fan
Sara I.

Why do you
cool us off? You have
teeth. And a tail. Why
does your tail go into
the wall? You are trapped
in those bars. You always
dress up in black and white, but why?

Oh Ravens!!
Michael C.

Oh Ravens, ravens, ravens,
You look like a burning
Green bird in the sky.
Oh ravens where did you
Come from? What makes
You attractive in thy eyes.
What makes you so
Incredibly skilled? Some
People say you're nothing,
But I do not. I wonder,
Wonder so much.

Big Sailfish
Peter N.

They go fast
like cheetahs
but they can swim past you.
Its nose is like
a needle ripping through.

Too Much Work!
Jorge A.

Head! I did the
work you told me.
I tried to figure
out where to go.

My cells gave up,
I failed you. Can
you forgive me?

I have returned fresh
and ready. I hope you
still forgive me.

This will arrive
when it does, or
I failed you once
more. Brain!

The Noisy Rain Again
Mark A.

I was sleeping in my new trailer
the rain blew through
the open window
it was hitting the roof
like it was playing the drums
it started hitting the roof harder
and faster
then it stopped
I will never forget that

Super Speed
Anthony J.

I would run 100 laps in 10 seconds.
I could run on water.
I could run on hot lava.
I could run upside down and
1,000 miles in 1 minute. I can
never die and I can lift you up to the sky.

Untitled
Eduardo M.

Why do thee go out in the night?
When did thy decide to go
out in the night? Bat, why do you go into
caves, why thee why? How did
thee learn to fly? What
is wrong with staying in
the day? Thee is nice to
stay in day. Why do thy use
sound to find your prey? Why do thee not
stay in day? Why do thee be
black all day?

Haiku
Jose I.

There's enough snow out-
side that we can have
a snowball fight.

Untitled
Jocelyne M.

The orange shark danced on land.
The purple goose went to the buffet to eat shrimp.
The yellow zebra kicked a squirrel at the nursing
    home.
The pink monkey went to Miami driving a convertible.
A blue donkey lived in a mansion.
A red cow yelled at me at school.

Untitled
Gladis M.

The big red
wheel jumps around
the yellow sun.

My Dog's All Alone
Kassandra F.

My dog is all alone.
The computer bill
is high. Why it's
high, I don't know,
but I think the
dog is using it, a lot!

Haiku
Dimitri R.

The ocean
freezes I, I
fall in, I am paralyzed
I and I sink.

Untitled
Loan K.

A wolf in Alaska running on
the snow, running and running,
trying to find the Lunar
Flower that glows as bright
as the moon, looking for
Paradise, the place they all

said was a legend. The place
full of true happiness like
any wolf would want. The
last Lunar Flower is not
what is seems. It is alive
but it's not in its true
form. Only a wolf with a
desire for freedom may
enter the doors of Paradise.

Ocean and Moon
Kierra C.

Dear Ocean, you should
try talking to your friend, Mr. Moon.
he's nice. The moon is a
nice man. Ocean, you two
should be good friends,
you can see each other at night.

Wind
Jazmine C.

Blizzard go
by see
wind fly

Untitled
Antonio N.

My dog is fat and he is blue and he has been deported to Mexico but
the fat dog can't find his way home, but he sets on the ground, then on
the pond, but the pond can't carry him because he was too fat and blue,
and can't speak Spanish. 2 guys are talking to him, but say nothing. He
only barks, barks, barks.

The Big Mistake
Uriel B.

I once pulled out
a chair for my
cousin so I could
be a gentleman
and when she
sat down I pulled

344

it farther
and she fell to
the ground
next thing you
know I'm the
one on the
ground.

Untitled
Marshauna B.

The yellow duck licked my dog and ran to Africa.

Untitled
Juana R.

here call me
another memo day
give me my chips
at midnight

My Glue
Aaron E.-F.

My glue is loyal.
It sticks to me
When I am in trouble. It sticks
Up for me.
It is alive!

Untitled
Brian Q.

When I sleep in my room in the night I see the sun rising when it's very
late. I get up and get a glass of water, then see a man standing outside.
I go back to bed and dream about the moon turning into a skull.

Fish
Jasmin B.

Fish fish swimming
in the pond with
icicles all over

Collage Poem
Maribel C.

Dolphins work at
State lunch in 1992 at Fish Kingdom

Untitled
Marco H.

Salsa no hi what
A moon say moo see ya
The cows say doom
Go wake up the
Cartoon

Collage Poem
Rodney T.

Fearless cowboy shared Fuji brain
With Rodney
We build a dream, one robot at a time.

AMBROSE PLAMONDON ELEMENTARY
Principal: Dr. Yvonne Austin
Teachers: Ms. Christopher, 4th, Mr. Maciulis, 6th, Ms. Novak, 4th/5th

Ray Bianchi, Poet in Residence

Ray, a native of suburban Chicago, educated at the University of Iowa, spent most of the 1990's living and working in Latin America first as a volunteer in a men's prison and later in international business. His poetry has appeared in *Red River Review, Near South, Antennae, The Economist, Tin Lustre Mobile, Poesia e Cultura, Kenyon Review, Moria, Fiera di Lingue* and many other journals. His first book *Circular Descent* from Blaze Voxx Press was published in 2004. It was nominated for the Pushcart Prize. Ray is also Publisher at Field Press: a poetry book press based in Chicago. This is Ray's second year at Plamondon Elementary.

Mexico
Juan A.

In Mexico you don't
have to go to school.
You can pop fireworks
or just drink pop on a hot day

You can stay home all
day. Go to the store or
play all day. You can
go to watch bullfights

I wish I lived in
Mexico. Sometimes its
boring but mostly
fun all day

You visit new places
or catch some rays
Play games and sports
all day. Its truly fun.

Deaf
Anayeli R.

I am a deaf girl
I can't hear nothing

I'd love to hear but
there is no use

I would do everything
normal kids could do

but I am different in one
thing; I can't hear

I can't hear the birds
singing outside

I wish I could hear
for only five minutes a day

348

Untitled
Elsa R.

How are they like
are they mean, are they grouchy?
do they get mad alot are they lousy?
How do they act? are they noisy?

Maybe their nice
or they are helpful
are they thrustful?

Some are good.
Some are nice,
some are always in a good mood
some are mean and always grouchy

The neighbors are all different
nobody is the same
who knows how they are?
You only know how they are
until you meet them.

Tomorrow
Karina V.

Today is filled with anger filled with hidden hate. Scared of being outcast
afraid of a common fate.
Today is filled with tragedies which no one has two faces. Nightmares
turn real tonight is full of rage. There is
also violence in the air. Alot of children are rude cause no one at home
cares. Tonight I lay my head down and anger never stops. But tomorrow
everything will change. A chance to build my spirit heart and ideas.
Ideas that are true tomorrow I will wake up strong because of my pride. I
know I fought with all. My heart two keep the dream alive

My Summer
Desaray B.

My Summer is hot
My summer is cold
My Summer is warm
Most importantly my birthday
is in the summer and
I will be taking me a vacation
for my birthday and that my summer is going to be

Someone
Lisbeth

Someone that
I will like to
know someone
I will never
know someone in my life

Love is
Jasmine G.

Love is you
Love is me
our love is meant to be
love is kind

it takes a made up mind
I do believe God above
set you down for
me to love...

If you should die
before me I would not
have a complete life
without you

But if I should die
before you I'll wait
on heaven steps for you
that is what love is babe

Untitled
Daisy G.

My cousin is like my sister
my cousin is like a friend
we always hang around
over and over again

I think she is trustful
I think she is very fun
I've always loved her like a sister
I've always loved her as a friend

350

We always talk together
we always help each other
and that is how we understand
each other.

Our friendship will never end
as that I am sure of
because we've been there for each other
since were were little kids or rather little friends

My Friends
Jesus V.

My friendship with my friend is
the best thing I have
even when they end
but when they end a new one begins

my friends are fun
and they are funny.
some are smart
but some are just dumb

When I take a taest
I always thing I will fail.
But then I realize
my friends are behind me
so I just do my best

So when I ask them
they play soccer with me
they make me laugh
but they can see
that they are my friends
so that makes me happy

hat
Eric

the person knocking on the
door the chimes making sounds
and hearing cards passing ny
When

Five AM late in the afternoon 5:56 PM in the evening

On the second floor of the apartment, in the porch and
on the highway.

Why
Someone is dead; ghosts are passing by into the house, the
ambulence is rushing by.

Untitled
Virginia P.

Who are you? I see into your eyes and see you mad and tired person
screaming everytime.

Who are you? Why are you mad? What happened in your day. I wonder
who you are?

are you really who I think you are? or are you someone else instead?

Why are you always mad? You are always throwing things around. I
wonder who you are?

Untitled
Vince E.

Angel is my friend
I don't know much
about him should be

I know he likes football
and that he is tall
sometimes he is funny
and his ears are like a bunny

Angel likes to eat
and has big feet
he likes hot dogs on a bun

My Grandma
Griselda U.

Her eyes are like
a rainbow in the sky
when the shadow of
her face shows on,
water she looks
bright as the star.

She went to the store to get an apple
but was not so red as her heart

I wish I liked
Rafael C.

I wish I liked the bees. I wish I liked the light. If something don't hit me I
think I am going to die.
I hate the dark. I saw something going on in the part. I am going to get a
pet, I want a Lynx that's going to be hard to get. I wish I liked the sunset,
I wish I liked the moon.

I saw a girl with a broom.

Good Morning
Jessica G.

The sun peeks through my window
making my eyes twitch
another day of walking
another day of new beginning
But today is very different
summer is no more.
As I set my feet upon the floor
My head is rushing around once more.
Teachers, friends and cafeteria mess.
Do not worry for I'm not feeling resent
but true excitement and nerviousness
I shuffle to my dresser
and pull out my new shirt. My new jeans pants and hair bands. Make
going back more fun.I can smell the waffles baking and hear the orange
juice poured.

El Maestro
Joseline C.

El Maestro es muy bueno en poesia a me gusta esa clase con amor y
agonia es la clase mas bonita que tenida en mi vida el maestro es
guero y bueno en poesia. Yo tengo razon en mi corazon el maestro me
a ensenada a escubrir bien las poesias que yo no sabia.

The End of the World
Oscar M.

Five or ten horses will be upon us devouring each and everything in its path one will make us destroy each other but the only way to stop the tragedy the only way to stop the tragedy is to change our ways and see what crises wants us to do stop the violemce stop the wind destroying the trees, the animals and mother nature the wind will turn into a swirling dying soul all of this is true. Let it be so for God tells us so. The end is near snow is falling down from the sky onto Mexico unexpectedly, people dying of diseases, falling snow since December till March what has the world become to discover these tragedies.

Love-
Jasmine F.

Love is what you want love is what you plead love is what you for when you are in need

Love is what you for when you are in bed love is what you hope for when the one you love is dead

Love is what you cry for every single night when the one you like hates you and is ready to fight

How do people go on in life without love well I guess they get it from the one lives above.

Animals
Juan S.

I love animals but the one animals of all the animals is a cat. Cats are loved by humans and they come is all different colors, Cats are the one animal I love, I have a friend names Leon he is a gone I Have not seen him for 7 years.

Untitled
Martha M.

I wish I liked...

I wish I liked to play, I wish I liked green, but I don't but I like... my teacher I like cookies I wish I had a baby brother.

what is red .... read is my heart red is my favorite color red is a butterfly and red is my face when it is cold outside red is the color of my lips

what is blue… blue is the color of the ocean, blue is the color of the
heavenly star blue is the color of the sky from afar.

Grandfather
Margie P.

My grandfather I remember that he always used to take me to the store
but he cant no more because he died and I miss him allot but I can't do
nothing about it he is dead. When I go to my granddad's house I still
think her is still there. His birthday past and my mom and grandma cried
and they made me cry too.

The Quiet Kid
Diana S.

The boy
lives with me
he never talks
he never looks
at me because
he is blind
he never goes inside
I just look at him or look away
I just remember him still standing
there

Tomorrow
Karina V.

Today is filled with anger filled with hidden hate. Scared of being outcast
afraid of common fate. Today is filled with tragedies which no one has
two face. Nightmares turn read tonight is full of rage, there is also
violence in the air allot of Children are rude because no one at home
cares tonight I lay my head down and anger never stops but tomorrow
everything will change.

A chance to build my spirit hear and ideas ideas that are true tomorrow I
will wake up strong because of my pride I know I fought with all my
heart two keep the dream alive

WILLIAM H. PRESCOTT ELEMENTARY
Principal: Avelino Martinez
Teachers: Ms. Buttle, 4th, Ms. Hines, 5th, Ms. Jacobs, 3rd

Allison Liefer, Poet in Residence

Allison Liefer studied creative writing at Northwestern University and received her M.F.A. from the University of Michigan. A published poet, she has worked in publishing and has taught writing courses at several universities in both Michigan and Chicago.

I Want to Be
Room 306 Class Poem

I want to be an Honor Roll student because I like school
so I can be Number One in my class.
I want to be fast but not so fast that everybody on my football
team seems slow.
I want to be cute but not so cute that everyone will like me.
I want to be tough but not so tough that everyone seems weak.

I want to be fast but not so fast that
a jet seems slow.
I want to be
fast but not
so fast that when
I get in the bed
my mama will be
beating my butt.
I want to be water but not too watery
that when I'm swimming or drinking water
people can't see me.
I want to be strong but not so
strong that Eddy seems weak.
I want to be a jet flyer
but not so fast because
I would crash into a building.

I want to be rich
but not so rich that I waste
all my money.
I want to be fast
but not so fast that a Dodge Viper
feels slow.
I want to be big, but not so big
that people can't see me.
I want to be smart
But not so smart I can't think.

I want to be a star
But not that dark or light. I want to glow.
I want to be red but not so red
that I will mess up the world.

I want to be fast but not so fast that
I pass everything by.
I want to be a comic book writer
so I can read and share my comics.
I want to be a basketball

player that could make 50
baskets in one day.

I want to be orange but not so orange
I become a tangerine and someone
bites into me and my juice falls
everywhere.

Untitled
Apple S.

I touch my mom's nice earrings.
I see my mom going to sleep.
I feel like I am growing up.
I taste like I am eating candy.
I hear a boy singing a song.

Taking Picture
Estrella V.

People
smile
to
camera
everything
turns
white
flash
come
everybody
look pretty
for picture
and we
see
picture
hang
in
room
we
remember
when
we
were
little

Untitled
Jose C.

Song is the rhythm
and the beat
it makes me dance
I hear everywhere
in the kitchen
in my car
in my house

Sadness is a Gloomy Child
Evelyn G.

a sad frown
a child crying on the floor
a tornado destroying homes
a bad toothache
if you don't get your favorite ice cream
if you don't get your favorite job
when your stomach hurts
when you're scared
when someone dies
when you lose a game
when you lose your best friend
when you lose your teddy bear
when you lose your mom in the mall
when you get into trouble
when you are miserable
when your best friend doesn't invite you
for people that don't have money or food
when your big brother hits you
when you fall off your bed
when you cut yourself
when you have to leave
when you are by yourself

Sun, Sun, Big & Yellow
Dyanne P.

The little girl with nice brown hair
was dancing at the beach.
Three young boys said want to come to Mexico
There will be cookies
but she didn't care.
Five ladies said come with us to have
a better life in Australia. But the little girl did

359

not listen. Her friend said let's go on a
ride to Africa. But the little girl said I have
a family that loves me. Her mom said Let's
go to school so you can learn. But I want to
stay here said the little girl.

Arbole Poem
Agustin V.

Come to space with me mom.
There we will jump from planet to planet
and see maybe the moon is made of cheese.
Come to the North Pole titi with me
There we will meet the penguins and feed them.
Come to Puerto Rico with me cousin
There we will go to the beach and play ball.
Come to Six Flags Great America brother.
There we will go on big rides.
Come to Wisconsin with me uncle.
there we will go on big water rides.
Come to a big indoor water palace other uncle
There we will go on big slides.

A No Poem Song
Angelica C.

Sour quit playing in Mexico.
A crowd cheering at a cat.
It's playing a car song at a
wedding. It's very cool to have a
car crowd cheering. It's a piano and
a crowd playing a pencil.
The music is going slow and a
little fast. Jessica is playing
a truck. Taccara is beating on
a book. It's so sour and
sweet. A cat running and eating
at the same time. A man sings
a happy song. I love piano
playing a no song poem.

Memory Calendar
Jamal P.

I remember my green and yellow parakeet.
I remember my brother's death in the army.

I remember my old friends Jaime
and Tony.
I remember my german sheperd dog
Lucky.
I remember my visit to Guatemala.
I remember my fish seedy.
I remember my grandmother.

Chicago
Reina H.

Children
hide
in
covers
and
go
outside

Untitled
Randy S.

cold winter days
here I stand
in the wind
cool as ice
and breezy
go to play
outside

Untitled
Taccara E.

A group
of people
playing
ball.

throwing
it back
and front

in the sky.

My Building
Cadijah S.

The building is clean
by brooms and mops.
None are small and
None are big.
With metal door knobs
Mirrors for walls.
People are not dreaming
about snakes and cats.
An old bus driver smoking
Up a storm.
Big kitchens and small pots.

A bad day
Iesha R.

I had a bad day
Water splashed on top of me
And I got dirty

Untitled
Moises E.

Sun sets on my back
Water sparkles on my hands
Ocean far and near

My Mom & Dad
Lamon D.

Mom by my side
Dad helps with my homework
Plus they both love me

I Want to Be
Room 307 Class Poem

I want to be fast
because I want to go
to the next dimension
and see the world
tomorrow.
I want to be strong but not that strong

that my muscles will break.
I want to be fast faster than a racing car
so I can race to Florida. Sometimes I want to
be faster so then I can race somebody and win money.
I want to fly because I could see the skyscrapers.
I want to be in the future
because I want to see my family's
future and my future.
I want to be fast
because then I will get a trophy.

I want to be a puppy so no one can find me.
I want to be an angel so I can be with my family that has died.
I want to be tall because I can drive and go to the mall and go hang with
my friends and go see a movie.
I want to be like a bird so I can fly and go see people from the sky.
I want to be a pie but not to eat.
I want to be an airplane so I can go really fast to Florida
Not so fast I don't know where I'm going.

I want to be big big as a mountain so that everything I see is small.
I want to be small so small that I'm smaller than an ant, beetle,
bumblebee and as small as a piece of paper.
I want to be a pilgrim because in Thanksgiving I could have a party and
invite the Indians.

We want to be old but not that old that we grow big toenails.
We want to be a friend a friend that is kind. But not kind that everyone
fights for me and gets in my mind.
We want to be fast so we could see the future and see what is going to
happen to everybody.
We want to be invisible so we can do jokes on our brothers.
We want to be fast but not that fast that we fall off of earth. We want to
be Tweety to be able to fly.
And that's what we want to be.

My 8 Sentences
Lizette P.

I hear people talking each other.
I could hear birds singing.
You can hear the dentist talking. You could hear dogs
barking. You could hear cats
Meowling. I could not hear people
talking in the store to each other.
I could hear people talking in
the dance. I could hear the world.
Each other.

I Like To Look At the City
Evelin G.

city
big
city
late
city
with
a
mall
city
with
cars
city
with
people.

I Hope and Wish...
Stefanie E.

I hope and wish
that I was tall so I
can reach up and take the
clouds.

I hope and wish I was small to swim
in the puddles when it is raining.

Untitled
Daniel R.

Come to Mars, mom.
There will be volcanos,
acid rain, rocks to look at,
lava, and red sky.

Come With Me
Arneal T.

My friend was in the house looking
glum and sad he was really mad because
he couldn't go outside so I said come
to the beach, my friend for we will have
fun and we can lie covered sand under the
hot sun.

Come to...
Juanita C.

Come to the stars Grandma
so you could float but remember
to bring astronaut suit because
there's no air and you will
see the big star guess what
it is it is the sun the big
yellow sun then you will be
on the air seeing the beautiful
planets and the stars and
you will see that the stars
will glow so bright you would
can step on them because
there will be so hot and
the sun will be more and
more and more hot then ever
that if you are in the air
the sun be so hot that
is going to burn you and me

Acrostic
Guadalupe U.

City with places to go.
High hills to climb.
Icy streets that make you fall.
Circus with clowns that make you laugh.
Art to see great drawings.
Going fun places like parks and zoos.
Out in the snow playing.

Chicago
Eunice D.

Cat and dogs
howling prowling
I like the howling and prowling in
Chicago
and other animals
going home to their
owners

The Book Club
Moneejon S.

We read a book. We

Had this look. We

Went to the library. We

read a book called
Wild Cherry. We left the
Library and went back to our homes.

And we read some poems.

My Dream
Giovanni A.

I have a dream I was happy
I was thinking of color green and
yellow. Green and yellow
that is a flower and a sun.

Tiger
Nathan B.

The tiger is not like a bear when it growls
or it sound is not like a meow. It's not
like an ant because it is too small
and the tiger is big and tall. It's not like a bird
or the birds chirp. It's not a fish that
swims in the water and the tiger does not
like to get bothered.

Untitled
Alexis G.

An exhausted night
from working at my hard job
then sleep quietly

Untitled
Linda B.

I love the sky. It smells
like fresh air. I taste but
It taste like air.

366

Untitled
Eunice D.

The moon looks
Right at me if
I were the stars.

My Aunt
Dzhane T.

My aunt died on
December 29, 2004.
When she died I got a chance to
touch her.

Untitled
Tony G.

Sumo wrestler
Fighting against each other
Suddenly one falls

Untitled
Kiana F.

A ballet dancing
in the ocean
There's a march
in Mexico
I see kites
I hear poems
I hear loud music
I see spring rain
dancers flying dogs
barking

Memory Calendar
Room 304 Class Poem

I remember getting my first cat and dog.
I remember that I grabbed a snake and put it on my arm.
I remember going to vacation in Oregon and I touched a snake.
I remember the first time I slid and splashed into the water in Mexico.
I remember playing basketball in spring and summer.

367

I remember watching The Lion the Witch and the Wardrobe.
I remember in the summer I went swimming with my family.
I remember I caught a big spider.
I remember my first time doing a 360 on my skateboard.

I remember playing video games.
I want to describe myself like my big sister.
I want to describe myself as friendly.
I want to know how do I look if I dress like a clown.
I am much too smart but not enough.

I am too much like my sister but not enough.
I remember riding my bike in winter without snow.
I remember my dog bit me, I kicked him.
I remember when I saw the lion roar.
I remember that I used to sit out in the back
   yard with my grandpa. He used to
   plant cucumbers and tomatoes.
I remember when I played basketball.

I want to be able to make the best spaghetti.
I wish to make myself invisible.
I remember the waves were higher than me.

I am...
Patricia G.

I am a happy girl with my friends and family like a happy bug.

I am much too scared like a thunderstorm that is scary.

I want my parents because they protect me but not when I'm in trouble.

I wish I had a dog but not a dog that bites but when a robber robs my house then it could bite.

I want to describe myself like the ocean but not to salty.

Untitled
Nico S.

I am much too smart, but not too dumb

I want to do nothing. I don't know why.

I wish to go right back to bed

I want to describe myself like my father, so that I can go to war whenever he does.

Sadness
Luis L.

A boy lost in the ocean
swimming feeling the sea turtles
and fish passing by him tasting
the salt water.

Untitled
Luis G.

Death lives in the hottest light.
All day death will be like a room without escaping.
Death wears a red suit with a big cane.
Death looks like the hottest place in the world.
I said to death I will always keep running so it don't catch me.
Death said he would always be there.
I could tell death was like a place without imagination.

Untitled
Antwon H.

Death lives far far far in the South.
All day, Death looks at people.
Death wears a suit and
Death looks like his face is blue or black.
I said to Death do you like to talk to people.
Death said Get out of my house.
I could tell, Death was mad at me.

Untitled
Michael V.

Cops
Hitting
I said you're under
Citizen's arrest
Asking for another chance let me
Go the cops are
Observing the person

Untitled
Ronald S.

nico & me
run
play
laugh

Untitled
Ericka N.

Pretty puppies running in the wind
across floor plants crashing dirty
paws puppy prints across the floor

Untitled
Luis G.

the day goes
fast I could
hardly smell it

t.v.
Somaira Q.

loud t.v.
people listening and talking
on the news people killing

Ninja Movie
Julio D.

haa, pow, boom, slash, crash
big screen, bright colors, ninja
karate movie

Cold Coffee
Diana C.

Cold cold cold cold coffee
going around
with his salt in
the top.
Boring going around
the hall and people
walking by the
ocean
People dying
Fun cool out
side.
Cold cold cold coffee
trees going around
the hills
sad, boring, fun
nothing around
nothing instead of
me, myself, and I

Untitled
Summer M.

Long long heavy violin
Sad unhappy Cinderella Mouse
and the Prince Graveyards are
like books Grey and Black
like a Cave slow Hurt
Gold fish Goodbye Crying
Stone

CASIMIR PULASKI FINE ARTS ACADEMY
Principal: Leanor Karl
Teachers: Ms. Diaz, 8th, Ms. Leland, 8th, Ms. Tischler, 8th

Paige Warren, Poet in Residence

Alyson Paige Warren has a B.A. from Michigan State University in English and is currently a Master of Fine Arts in Creative Writing graduate student at the School of the Art Institute of Chicago. Paige has taught in such programs as the High Jump program at the Latin School of Chicago and guest lectured at Indiana University and Grand Valley State University. Her work has been featured in the *Red Cedar Review* and multiple poetry readings, as well as winning both the John Cash and Oldenburg poetry awards.

Untitled
Alexis R.

He worked at a McDonald's not far from here. Once he walks in
McDonald's there are a bunch of hungry customers with grease all over
their mouths and ketchup on their shirts. He is a cashier, he sells fat
people what they want. Some of them do not order one Big Mac but two
Big Macs. He hates the smell of grease.

His dream is to work at Subway, watching healthy people eating healthy
subs. He likes the smell of fresh salad and breads. His favorite meal is
the Chicken Teriyaki.

The Truth Hurts
Amaryllis O.

I remember I was in my room.
I was only two and all I heard was a smack.
Even though I was young
I just told myself what the hell was that?
I jumped off the bed and went to the living room.
All my dad said was I will be leaving soon.
I then saw my mom lying on the sofa with her hands on her face
and hot tears running down her innocent face.
I went up to her and said it's ok mommy, don't cry.
Then my mom told me my brother might come out blind.
All I did that day was cry.
'Till this day I always remember that.
But, the most important thing I remember is abuse in a marriage
is not a joke, it's a fact.

Untitled
Anthony M.

When I woke up I was on the couch. The dark
room was cold, the sky through the white roof.
I knew something, I could do nothing but see. And as I watched, all the
street lights from outside and
bright to see everything, a fire burning through the
roof to stare outside.

Untitled
Anthony S.

I remember when my first bike was stolen.
I remember when U.S. caught Sadam Hussein.

I remember when I jumped off a two story building into a huge pile of snow.

I remember when my brother fought with Max in the morning.

I remember when I won my first trophy in baseball. It wasn't first.

I remember when I thought a drive through car wash was an octopus.

I remember when I first went paintball shooting.

I remember when Clinton was president.

I remember when our twin towers fell.

I remember when I went to Six Flags.

I remember when I fell in the shower.

I remember when Peter accidentally cursed.

I remember when my mom used to cook everyday.

I remember when I earned $1,000 in a D.J. concert.

I remember I went to Hawaii.

I remember when I got bitten by a mosquito in Hawaii that was the size of a Chapstick.

And I will always remember people who ask for money.

Silly-Day
Antonio A.

I went dog with my runs skateboarding. I
jump to silly flip. I blogged most of the time. I
ran it the last time. I nursed home to rest my
sillys. When I woke up, I was outside with my
skateboard, doing silly flip. I was sleepboarding.

Love in 111
Bobby R.

There we sat in the same room
our seats next to each other.
I knew she liked me
and she knew I liked her.
We sat in back of everyone in class.
She passed me a note.
I opened it slowly
and read: " I think you're cute."
So I sent it back to her and it said
"I think you're cute, too."
As time passed, slowly we began to connect.
I asked her out and she said yes.
Love had us holding hands and we did not care.
At the end of the day, we were saying goodbye.
When I gave her a hug, she kissed me on the cheek.
It was unexpected at first, so I kissed her back.
I was going for her cheek and missed and got her lips.

She was in shock and so was I. It was a moment of love
and we were both really sure.

Victor Diaz/Carlos Ortiz
Carlos O.

Victor Dias
He used to be in Clemente High School.
            playing baseball and doing his work. He
            tries hard in his game all the time.
            But his dream is to play in the major leagues
for the Chicago Cubs. He keeps on playing baseball to make his dream
come true.

Carlos Ortiz
Right now he is in school sitting
on his chair doing his work. That is all he
doesn't want to do right now.
He wants to go to High School and College
and then go to the Minor Leagues
and then to the Majors and play for the Chicago Cubs.

Untitled
Carmelita V.

Drifting into a sleep of never waking up.
Never seeing your family, friends.
Drifting off into a sleep of never waking up.

Untitled
Cassie W.

They aren't paying attention. They just keep on ignoring authority. They
are criminals. Masterminds of mischief. When they get caught, they are
sent free.
They go back to doing what they do best.

Their dreams are to get away and never be caught.
But it's impossible. They can't get away, that's why it's a dream.

Untitled
Christopher J.

On a summer day walking with thin shorts and a shirt a thundercloud
appeared.

If only I would have noticed it there would have been nothing to fear.
But thunder and rain drizzled upon the earth.
The earth motionless like a body in a hearse.
I was a sponge absorbing h2o.
    I was feeling bad if only y'all knew.
I ran quickly to a house, rung the doorbell but no one came out.
A car pulled up glistening black.
It was my Mom with my brother in the back.
I was waiting and waiting for the day to end.
I was crying but the water on my face was blending in. She asked me what happened, I didn't know what to say I told her the quickest thing, which was "okay".

Unititled
Idaia S. G.

I remember being told about my long gone biological father.
I also remember the time my mama
gave my dog away for the sake of its own life.
I can never forget my first anonymous crush.
I was anonymous, not my crush.
I'll never forget the day I got out of special ed
and had many struggles to overcome ahead.
How can I forget how I almost lost my friend who was a neighbor and a best friend.
    I remember the first time my mom left me at pre-k and how she fed me raisin bread with butter before she left for work.
    I remember begin scared for the first time in my life. I was scared because my mom had an abusive husband.
    I remember the first time I went to summer school and how at the end of the first day the teacher said "I'll pass all of you. At least, those of you I can."
    I remember the "Beautiful Let Down" from Switch Foot a Cali rock band. The whole record reminded me of how I got my first broken heart.
    I remember the first time I got into my first fist fight. Someone was trying to pick on my big cousin when I was in first grade. I swung, they swung but that was only how the fight begun.
    I remember the last day I saw my grandpops before he died.

Inside
Jasmine J.

I used to go inside. A private School for the Religious. Though I'm not it. Inside a lovely cathedral summoned by blood red. They start to sing, which takes for hours. I just stare at the mosaics. Then to the column wish I wasn't here.

376

I dream I am older where I create games
that make those wannabe scary lame. I'm in Japan
with a sketch book at hand. Just drawing whatever comes to mind,
sitting by the window, drinking a cup of tea. Seeing a reflection of my
own novel that I have written in Japanese. I close my eyes just to hear
that noise and smell. The sound of the rain dropping off the leaves. The
sweet smell of flowers getting wet.

I remember
Jasmine J.

I remember my wild style. I remember water guns of every size.
I remember swing on tires with my friends alongside.
I remember my mom's sweet voice that lulled me to sleep.
I remember the bed that springs show from playing up and down on.
I remember a life-sized Barbie doll that made me sigh.
I remember the warm sun on my face while I lay down.
I remember my first flips I did on the sidewalk.
I remember the black dog that licked my face.
I remember always laughing when my cousin sleeps.
I remember my mom's lap when I jump on and lay to sleep.
I remember my Tweety costume that I wore on Halloween.
I remember my birthday cake. I remember presents.
I remember the breeze that blew my ponytails.
I remember the cute boy that I danced with.
I remember my favorite friend who became my twin.
I remember that I dream.
I remember my hair that I wore down all day.
I remember the uncle that I put to rest.
I remember my dreams. I remember my sister who died that turned
sixteen.
I remember that I remember never to oversleep.

Untitled
Jean Carlos R.

He plays video games. He plays for hours. He wastes the whole day
with his eyes glued to the TV. All day you can call his name and he will
never respond.
He wants to go play some basketball.
He wants to be outside. He wants to see his friends. He wants to go
look for a girlfriend.
But the game has taken advantage of him.

The Never Bothered Book
Jeremiah S.

He left   she came.
The books sit there everyday
and rust as we get older.
He fights and knocks him out.
But the books sit there.
I talk about him and they laugh
but the books sit there.
She sees him hurt and cry
but the books sit there.

Untitled
Jessica M.

I remember when I was young and my godfather
made a bike for me from pieces of other bikes.
I loved that bike, I would ride it day and night
if I could.
I also remember the day my stepdad brought home a dog, but it had 2
go back the next day.
I remember when we found a ferret in the streets.
I loved it bcuz it didn't hurt me.
I remember so many things in my life that I wish I could tell you them all,
but there isn't enough time for me bcuz I still have a life to live.

Chicago
Jesus M.

Chicago beautiful like a woman.
Not scary like a monster.
Chicago is fun like the carnivals, happy like
when you get money and see your family.
Chicago quiet like a mouse.
Chicago is a city to have joy and fun.
Chicago is calm like iguana.
Chicago not a mess like a kid who did a mess all over the place.
Chicago not mad like a bully.

Untitled
Jonathan B.

I once had an eggie named dogie. I threw dogie at the bus. It covered
the windows and wheels. I missed it so much I bought a doggie and
named it eggie. So I went to the parky and saw some narkys. I picked
up eggie and threw it at the narkys. Bet you don't know what happened
next.

378

Untitled
Jonathan R.

I remember
I remember you driving
I remember the car stopping
I remember me following you out the car
I don't know why I remember, but I still remember
I remember it was dark outside
I remember you going away
I remember you left and I couldn't find you
I do I remember so much
But I don't remember me waking up!

Untitled
Juan R.

I gave you my heart without knowing how.
You were there for me like oxygen for water.
I am with you every day.
I'm your hair gel you put on.
I put you aside but don't know where.
I look for you day and night.
When you're not with me it's like a person with no air.
You were tall like a tree.
You laughed more then a hyena.
I miss you when I don't know.
I try to speak but my voice is low.

Untitled
Juan R.

He had to go, racing past the red traffic lights, not caring for tickets but
for a loved one.

Her eyes filled with anger, blood over the leather seats. Faster,
faster, he thinks, go to the place faster, faster. His foot hammers the
break, screech, the car made. He almost flew off a cliff. He reverses, but
stops. Looks at the blood, the woman. Suddenly he forgets what's
happening. He blacks out. The woman screams his name, then realizes
he's out, cries for help. The woman had little strength but made it to the
man. She hit him as hard as she could, but as hard as she could was
like a pen thrown by a 2 year old.

He woke up 10 minutes later, looked at the car. He saw the
woman, breathing slowly, almost
asleep. He screamed: "No! Why did I rush? Why, the cliff…"Then he
drifts away.

Faster, faster. Police have caught the sight, the flash, the blue and red, but he doesn't stop. Faster. Road block the police have created. Twice he thought: "I'll never save her." He just looks and goes around them. More cops come. He's almost there but he crashes into another car. He never made it.

I remember
Julian C.

I remember watching people play sports
and me trying to emulate them.
I remember getting taller and everyone
saying now you're taller than me.
I remember lounging out with my best friend, my grandfather
I remember sitting at home playing my Nintendo 64
I remember my first kiss that my girl stole.
I remember watching my brother
play baseball with his friends in my backyard.
I remember watching my sister take her first steps,
and how my mom told me "Jay, hold the camera right."
I remember watching my grandma dress me up to go to church
I remember living with my friend and throwing water balloons on people
from the roof of our house.
I remember watching my mom as she had grease bubbles on her face
because her best friend burned her out of jealousy
I remember when God gave my mother back her face.
I remember my grandfather's funeral, when I lost my best friend.
I remember going to visit my father in Stateville penitentiary.
I remember remembering to write this poem, there's more, but I'm still
trying to remember

Stocker to Singer
Ladiron H.

Stacking cans, putting prices here and there.
"Excuse me, do you know how much this costs?"
That's the question I hear everyday. I want to say "No, go find it
yourself." But I can't because that's my job.

That's where my life is, but not my heart. My life is on the stage, singing
until I can't any more.
All those faces looking at me, smiles from here to there. My heart is in
front of the screams
and the loud live music. That's where my heart is, but not my life.

Untitled
Marilu G.

The life there is so free you can ride horses
on the streets.
Does little store bell ring
ring from the school?
Little kids running, buying candy.
The women hanging their clothes to dry.
Men coming to work. Kissing their wives.
Women serving their food.
Little kid, playing soccer, basketball, volleyball.
The night has come. Everybody is asleep.
The beautiful Guerro.

Candy Shop
Joshua B.

He used to work in a candy shop. He likes his job.
He had a kiss fantasy. A place full of candy in every
spot. He would come home with a bag full of candies. He wrapped one,
he wrapped the other. Packed them in boxes and bags. The other boys
shift them to stores.

His dream is to one day be able to step his foot in a
pro court and play for the Chicago Bulls. Every night he pictures himself
playing ball. He just had to
believe. His dream came true.

New Year
Tomii G.

He used to work at Mickey D's. Don't get me wrong, he loved the fries
and cheese. The money was o.k. but what should he do? Get laid off or
work late?
This job, there's something new every year. A new burger that's full of
fat and cheer. When he walks out the door he looks at Ronald and says:
"Man, Ronald, should I stay here another day?"

His dream is to work as a star and follow the actors before him. All days
a year, no break.
Someday, it will happen.

Untitled
Tomii G.

I remember when I knew I could dance, smile, clap my hands.
I remember when I first tasted rice pudding.
I remember when I used to cry when my mom would say goodbye.
I remember I used to stare at the blind girl sitting in the chair.
I remember when I first went to Deep River Water Park.
I remember when I went to New York, Mississippi, Arkansas, Missouri, Florida, Ohio, IOIC, North Carolina.
I remember those fun days I used to have before my friends died in a fire that lasted to 12:00.
I remember when the world was so tight and so nice and so right.
I remember everything 'till this day, this is Tonii signing away.

Who am I?
Tracey T.

I have been a dark gray cloud with rain falling down.
I have been a changing dice that has never been thrown.
I have been an icicle that has fallen to the ground.
I have tried many colors but only one fits me best.
I have been the one in a corner with a book to read.
I have always been a snowflake that is the first one to fall.
Who am I?
I am the one with the honors
I am the one who stands up for the small guy
I am a hero that is not seen,
but I am also a friend in need.

Her Mistake
Yuriana F.

She is at the grocery store, in the baby section,
buying all the things that she might need for her baby.
She is miserable because the guy that got her pregnant left her all alone. Now she has to go through this by herself. Her mom is so upset with her, she hates her so much. She doesn't even want to see her. She dreams that she could go back in time and fix her mistake. She wants her mom's respect back.
But it's too late. She realizes that it's impossible for her to do that.

PHILIP ROGERS ELEMENTARY SCHOOL
Principal: Joel Bakrins
Teachers: Ms. Airo, 5th, Ms. Jackson, 4th, Ms. Schoenfeld, 6th

Adam Novy, Poet in Residence

Adam Novy is an Assistant Professor at The School of the Art Institute of Chicago, where he received his M.F.A. in 1998. His work as appeared in *Verse, Quarterly West,* and *American Letters and Commentary.* This is his second year with *Hands on Stanzas.*

Wolves
Melissa E.

As the wolves came running
The caribou ran out of sight.

The moon appeared
The wolves came out and howled

The paw of the wolf
On the snow
Snowflakes fell
The wolves slept

As their prey moves
So must the wolves

The wolves' eyes
Glow yellow

As night approached
So did the wolves

The wolves gazed
Upon the horizon

Untitled
Brentan W.

Along the trees
The fastest being
Was the fox.

The fox ran into the river
And the river carried him away.

A river and a squirrel are one.
A river and a fox and a tree
Are one.
I am not sure which to pick
The sparking river
The long, tall, snow-covered tree
 Or the fox, running.

Haiku
Ada D.

Winter days
      Snowflakes glisten and
Ask us to save them from the sun

Sun
Adrian M.

The sun is going down
The villagers get cold

The rain
Sounds like bullets

The food is cooking
Coming alive.

Haiku
Mohammed H.

The snow is falling
      And the village is flooded
With a white blanket

Poem
Madalina B.

Learn about words from the words
And about sentences from the sentences.

Poem
Madalina B.

The man in the red jacket
Was neither a plumber or an ordinary man
Like a lizard that passes
For an amphibian at one time
And a frog at another

Haiku
Brenten W.

Winter snow
White as clouds
Speaking to each other

Rabbit running
        Camouflaged from the wolf
Thanks to the snow

Run along the riverbank
        Little fox
But carefully, carefully

Haiku
Raphaella T.

Snow is falling
        And the houses are stiff
With ice

Haiku
Alex T.

Worm almighty,
        Defeat the sparrow
And the robin!

Haiku
Andrea S.

The chipmunk steals my old fair nut.
He's running away, away!
I've lost my little old days!

Haiku
Paige D.

The computer
        Gives me advice
About writing

Haiku
Mohammed H.

The fly
        Can't land
On the blade of a knife

Haiku
Edessa D.

I am surrounded
        By many people
Yet I feel alone

A legend
Ada D.

Make 100 paper cranes
Give them to a sick person
And they'll feel better

Poem
Melissa E.

Green turned to brown
And orange
And orange turned to white

The green grass glistened
Because of the dew.
The dew glistened
Because of the sun.

Haiku
Shahneil C.

One time,
My computer was a cheetah.
Now it's a turtle.

Haiku
Corey F.

The star
Shines, but
So far away

The black cat
        Passes
Nothing happens

Haiku
Zohra R.

Even in Chicago
        Hearing the bird
I long for Chicago

Haiku
Miso K.

Clicking and crawling
        Hopping and jumping
A cricket wanders in the grass

Amber
Melissa E.

The piece of Amber becomes invisible if you place it on the sun.
Amazingly, no one's tried it—I wonder why. However, if you swallow
Amber and step on the sun, you won't be invisible. Then you put on
Amber earrings and look in the mirror—you see nothing. Why is this so?
Because you are the sun.

Poem
Edessa D.

If you swallow jade, then your hair would turn jade. You will lose sight of
jade if you throw it in the grass. If an insect's body was jade in the
grass, then it will be protected from predators. Hold jade in your hand
and you will have no connection with your nerves. If you put a jade
anklet on, you will transform into the grass.

Poem
Madalina B.

The violet becomes transparent through the packs of flowers. If you take a transparent flower, you will also become transparent. Be aware of the transparentness of the color violet, because if you rip one petal from the violet flower you will no longer be transparent, and all the bees will sting you. If you sew a transparent violet color on a painting, then you must press lightly, or you will never see another transparent flower.

Blue, A Mystical Color
Brenten W.

Blue, a color of sorrow and water. The color blue would dry beneath the sun. It would turn to blue steam that would create another blue. The blue would drift into the air, it would follow the trail of other blues. The blue would multiply, make other blues. The blues would come together to make a sea of blue. It would attract animals to its grasp. The animals would give one touch and become slaves of the blue. The animals, when they die, will transform into another sea of blue and travel together to find the next blue ready for the journey that awaits itself. They will travel together to make their own sea of blue.

Poem
Hirangi P.

Oh!
Mother Earth, why won't you speak to me! I stand outside just for you,
but I just hear leaves crackling windsblowing carsmoving
and you won't say anything!

Poem
Mary T.

Oh!
Eraser! You get smaller and smaller every day.
I use you once,
You're half the size!
I sue you twice,
You're just a speck of pink on my desk!

Spirit of the Staircase
Miso K.

Oh Spirit of the Staircase,
Why did you take away my idea?
Oh! I can't remember my idea,
I just know it was a good one.
Why can't you impress me
Like that monkey over there?

Poem
Brenten W.

Dog!
You have powerful traits.
Claws like blades.
Agility of a cheetah.

You should fear nothing!
Why hide behind a tree?
What has become of you?

Shall you lie there
Like a cowardly squirrel?
You must not fear anything!

Black
Samuel R.

If you put black on a dead person, it will disappear. If you put black on a
grave and it is still visible, the person within is still alive. If you put black
on, you can see what is to come in the next life. If you put on black and
you cannot see, you are dead. This is why the grim wear black.

Knife
Brentan W.

It resembles the bark
of a large tree
the longness, straightness, and toughness.

The shape of
New York

As the beaches
Stay and are
Calm and move at night.

Spoon
Vicky T.

You look like a person's face
But with no eyes

You have no feet
To walk with

You are shiny but too blind
To see anything.

Piece of Paper
Paige D.

Become a piece of paper.
I want to be paper
Not a box or a book.
Paper is the way for
Me.

Always getting thrown away.
Or ripped to pieces.
Little kids crumbling it up.

White, black, blue, green.
Maybe pink.
So many colors,
So many meanings.

Black Olive
Hirangi P.

A black olive looks like an eyeball.
It looks like black chewed gum.
It looks like bad, nasty cavities in your teeth.
It looks like a black bouncing ball.

Sestina
Ada D,

Sitting in the bank, he was clueless
Of what to draw. So he withdrew money
To buy a paint brush
And some inspirational paint.

But he still had some money
Left. He felt clueless.
Should he buy another bucket of paint,
And another small brush?

Not knowing what to do, being clueless,
He splattered some paint
On the canvas, and, using a small brush
To mix the colors, it turned out to be money!

He's not clueless
anymore! He took some more paint
and another brush,
he splattered it everywhere, and out came a drawing of money.

Sestina
Michaela L.

Just think
Of your dreams
Of your friendship
How it hurts
When you have faith.

It hurts
When you think
Of faith
And your friendship[
Splits up in your dreams

Your faith has its own dreams
And controls your friendship.
Its also hurts
When you think.

My friendship
can't dream
but it can think
when my heart hurts
and says "it's faith."

My dreams
And what I think
Is faith
Are my friendship
When it hurts.

392

The Girl and Objects
Raphaella T.

There was a girl named Bicky
She loved to eat cheese.
She would wash her hands with soap.
Her hair was struck by lightning.
She's hate to take a shower in the rain,
Instead she liked to dance.

The soap was as thin as lightning,
So lightning always struck the soap.
She loves to play in the rain,
But inside, she hates to dance.
She had a grandma named Bicky
Who hated eating cheese.

The cheese looked like soap.
The soap was like cheese.
The rain loved the lightning,
The lightning loved the soap.
Bicky loved to dance
Bicky loved her grandma Bicky.

Sestina
Andreea S.

I never knew you had a shoe.
Did you search in the attic
For your freaky ghost?
Did you find paper this summer
Or lovely spring?

Do you always lose your shoe?
In the attic
It was spring
While in the basement it was summer.
Did you draw on paper
The mysterious ghost?

I saw you trying to draw on paper!
You are really the evil ghost
Who hides in the attic
In summer and sweet spring.
Hey, I found your shoe!

On a beautiful summer
Day let's search for your shoe.On an ugly spring
Day let's spit on your paper.

Paper Crane
Jasmine V.

I made a paper crane
And let it fly
Peacefully and gently
With the breezy wind.

Bird
Jasmine V.

Up high in the sky
There is a wounded bird coming
Down as it is shot.

Sestina
Devin N.

A dog was on Pluto
And a fish was on Mars
In the future
Possibly the past
Was it a painting or was it real?

The thing is, it's real
Not a painting
A dog was on Pluto
And a fish was on Mars
But is it the future
Or was it the past?

It was the past
Not the future
But someday we will see it real
A dog on Pluto?
A fish on Mars?
It sounds like a painting.

Or was it real?
Was a fish on Mars
Was a dog on Pluto?
Was it a painting?
Is it the past
Or future?

394

Untitled
Iqra R.

Everything lay still
In the snow
Except the rabbit

Dark and quiet
Everything moving
The rabbit lay still

The rabbit
Is white as snow
And quiet
While everything is moving
Everything lay quiet and still
An owl hooting.

Untitled
Shanique M.

Take down the eyes
So it won't see what you're doing.
Open up the inside.
if there's light, close your eyes,
And place it in a sky of dark clouds.

When you find the shores of blood
fill your cup.
Next time you get cut, you'll have extra.

Quickly, and with courage,
search for its heart.
You'll need to run through
Far and scary woods
And listen hard
To hear it whisper.

SHIELDS ELEMENTARY SCHOOL
Principal: Rita C. Gardner
Teachers: Ms. Dennehy, Ms. Farrell, Ms. Fialkowski, Ms. Graefen, Mr. Heredia and Ms. Hughesdon, 5th; Mr. Kaszynski, Ms. Koclanis, and Ms. McCormick, 3rd

Larry O. Dean, Poet in Residence

Larry O. Dean was born and raised in Flint, Michigan. He has worked with Academy Award-winning filmmaker, Michael Moore, been widely published in the alternative press, and also worked as a cartoonist. He attended the University of Michigan at Flint and Ann Arbor, during which time he won three Hopwood Awards for his poetry. In addition to writing, he is a singer and songwriter, working both solo as well as with several pop bands, including Post Office, The Me Decade, and currently, The Injured Parties. After living in San Francisco for over a decade, and despite current rampant gentrification, he makes his home in Chicago. See www.larryodean.com for more information.

"This year at Shields I was privileged to work with both 3rd and 5th graders and some excellent teachers. We studied such poets as Carl Sandburg, Gary Soto, Lola Haskins, Mark Turpin, Adélia Prado, Pablo Neruda, Kenneth Rexroth, David Ignatow, Billy Collins, James Tate, Robert Creeley, Randall Jarrell, William Carlos Williams, Delmore Schwartz, William Stafford, Denise Levertov and Kenneth Patchen, writing poems on such diverse ideas as what we see every day, odes, Halloween, history, hands, colors, obligations, memories, special places, weather, dreams, music, windows, apologies, and becoming something new. We also composed class poems inspired by Walt Whitman's 'Song Of Myself,' creating a biographical tapestry for each room. These 'Songs Of Ourselves' are below, followed by a representational lot of individual student poems. I regret not having more room for the many beautiful poems written by my Shields students."

Songs Of Ourselves
Ms. Farrell's Class, Room 405

I'm a vegetarian.
I like Fridays.
My pet's name is Oso.
I hate beef.
Dogs are the best.
I like to hang out with my friends.
My name is Guadalupe Roque Rodriguez.
I find the dolphin an interesting creature.
I was born in Illinois in 1994.
I hate soccer.
I am a football player.
I was born in Los Angeles, California.
So many people want and admire my hair.
I go for Chicago Fire & America, those are soccer teams.
My favorite holiday is Christmas.
I care about my family.
I like dodge ball.
I hate fish.
I was born on July 17, 1993.
My favorite player in football is Randy Moss.
My name is Gabriele Loredo Michelle Garcia Rodriguez Banda.
It's hard to control the soccer ball when you first try.
I love math.
I love skateboarding better than anybody.
I'm an MVP for baseball.
My favorite subject is science.
I hate cats.
I am very athletic.
I don't even like broccoli.

Ms. Hughesdon's Class, Room 407

I hate pizza because it has a lot of cheese.
My name is Daniel Cuevas.
The best teacher in the world is my favorite ... Ms. Hughesdon.
I was born 8/13/94.
My favorite subject is reading.
My mother's name is Delia.
Cats are the animals I hate the most, with their creepy eyes.
I help people cross the street.
My ball is red.
My favorite two cars are the Ferrari and the Rolls Royce.
I was born in a hospital in front of a park.
My parents named me Jessica.
I hate when they kill animals.

I love stuffed crust sausage pizza.
My favorite baseball player is Sammy Sosa.
I dyed my hair blond on 12/11/04.
I don't like snakes and snails because they both are slippery.
I remember when a bird came in our classroom.
My favorite thing is math.
I have six sisters.
I like chicken nuggets.
I hate fish you eat & fish that swim.
I like machines.
I hate girls that bother me.
I was named after 6 presidents, 1 town, 1 river and I signed the Declaration 7 times.
I was born 1993.

Ms. Dennehy's Class, Room 403

I am scared of spiders.
I never had the chicken pox.
When I say no way, they do the opposite.
I got my name from my dad and uncle.
Someone who's funny is my dad, because he makes a joke out of everything and you never know when he's serious.
I like enchiladas with crema and salsa verde.
I love Slipknot and Korn.
I hate heights.
I am scared of the movie, Leprechaun, because it looks like his body is inside out.
I love when my dog howls when he wants to go to the bathroom.
I like cheesy, big hamburgers.
I'm the only Jacquelyn in the whole family.
I have two rings.
I hate my name because it sounds like a little kid.
I love the view of snow falling.
I dislike beans because they taste funny.
I like to dance.
I love my mom, she always takes us to Buffet City.
I laugh very, very weird & funny.
I hate green vegetables.
Both of my parents are from Mexico.
I hate the cold wind, hitting me in the face, it feels like I have not a face at all.
My favorite kind of dog is a bulldog. They are very loyal to their owner.
My nickname is Nini.
I like Math because the questions are hard.
My favorite sport is basketball. I'm good at it.
I love my family.
I like tortas.

My favorite show is The Simpsons because they make me laugh all day.
I hate waiting for a surprise.

Mr. Kaszynski's Class, Room 205

My favorite sports are ballet, jazz, tap, hip-hop, and baseball.
My favorite food is mac and cheese.
I hate to play with glass stuff.
I like dinosaurs.
I like playing with my nieces.
My middle name is Flower.
I hate doing my chores.
My favorite sport is basketball.
I like presents.
My favorite game is Topple.
I like to go to the movie theater to see different movies.
I like school because we get to go to gym.
My best four friends are Andres, Gerardo, Ramon and Orlando.
I'm named after my dad.
I like to go to parties and see my whole family.
I like the snake in the class because it is fun to see when it eats.
I hate homework because you need to write with your hands and it
hurts.
My mom likes me.
I like when Santa Claus comes.
I believe in Santa Claus.
I hate sausage pizza.
I'd like to have some brothers and play with them.
My name is Michelle Rodriguez.
I hate to sleep.
I like people that respect me because I respect them back.
I like colors to see.
My cat's name is Cookie because she likes cookies.
My favorite place is Navy Pier.
I like the thick crust.

Ms. McCormick's Class, Room 214

I like burritos with lots of salsa.
Chocolate used to be my life.
I like pizza from Pizza Hut.
My name is Crystal Reyes.
I like dolphins.
I like to ride my bike because it's fun.
I hate my two sisters because they yell in my ears.
My favorite book is called Amazing Spider-Man.

Every summer I go to the park.
I am 9 years old.
My name is Naomi Hernandez but they call me Nome.
I like to play soccer.
I love to put on make-up.
I like no I don't like it I love pizza pepperoni.
I think I was named after Michael Jordan.
I'm 8 years old May 14th is my birthday.
My favorite color is red.
I'm named after a famous composer.
We went to Alabama to see my aunt.
I like WWE.
My favorite color is blue, like the sky.
And sometimes I can be nosy.
My mom and dad's names are Ana & Enrique.
I love cheese pizza.
What I like about afterschool is going on the Internet.
I was named after my dad.
I don't have a dog, I have a cat.
My favorite planet is Pluto.
I like to spend time with my family.

Ms. Koclanis' Class, Room 001

My name starts with the letter Y.
I like to visit Haunted Trails.
I hate my cat.
Our whole family goes to Six Flags on the fourth of July!
My favorite thing is a CD player.
I like math.
I like to play with my Yu-Gi-Oh cards.
I like to swim almost.
I like stuffed animals. I hate bugs.
My favorite color is pink.
And I also like knock knock jokes.
I hate dentists.
My other place to visit is Mississippi.
My name is Karla Leon Esther.
My favorite sport is paint balling.
I like math because I like to add and subtract.
Cats like licking me.
I like to draw cartoons.
I hate math!
I like to do poems about my dog. And I hate math.
My favorite pet is a hamster.
I like chili peppers.
My age is 8 years old.
My friend is Kenny.

The food that I hate is spinach.
Sometimes I get mad with my sister.
I like writing.
My favorite thing is to go to Shields School.
My favorite classroom is 001.
I hate cookies.
My bird's name is Kiko.

Ms. Fialkowski's Class, Room 402

I like dogs with curly hair.
Two of my brothers are named from their dad.
My favorite sport is basketball.
The color I like least is purple.
I like to play sports.
My house is haunted.
I'm from here, the U.S.A. but my mom and dad are from Mexico.
My name means looking at both sides of the story.
I want a dog.
I like to sk8.
I hate the color red.
My birthday is on October 1.
I like tamales but I hate cats. And when I smell, I remember my mom
making tamales.
My great, great, great uncle fought for Mexico and died a long time ago.
My favorite food is spaghetti.
I'm 10 years old.
I hate not being noticed, I'm like a ghost, invisible, not alive.
Someone likes guitars.
My name is Christopher Escobedo.
My favorite place is the comic and cards shop.
My favorite video game is Godzilla Saves the Earth.
I was named from my dad.
What I like about myself is I can run really fast.
My family is huge.
I like Smackdown.
I like making music and sounds like 15" speakers, the brand Kicker
Competition.
What I like is dancing, and playing sports.
People get confused from my name.
I don't like to do homework.
I like wrestling and action movies.

Ms. Graefen's Class, Room 404

My name means the littlest son.
The hospital I was born in was Saint Anthony Hospital.

My four nicknames are Shadow, JB, Gio and JoBunny.
My favorite food isn't onions or spinach but it is spaghetti.
I like to play with my cousins but I hate it when they start fighting.
I love the mall.
I like presents because I could get them on my birthday or Christmas.
When I was 8 years old I went to Mexico.
My name is Samuel Pantoja.
My favorite teacher is Ms. Graefen because she makes our brain be more smarter.
I like architecture, I want to be one when I grow up. I want to go to college, get my diploma, become an architect and a few years later I will like to see the light.
I hate cats. They're ugly and dirty.
I was born in Illinois.
I don't like fish.
My favorite night is New Years Eve.
I was born on May 13 1994 on a Friday.
My favorite word is Good.
I like to ride my bike.
I have one sister.
I hate pizza when it doesn't have sauce but when it has hot sauce and ketchup, mmm ... delicious.
I like fish sticks, they're really good.
My favorite thing is art and I like to read a lot and I hate math.
I am a girl, I was born in the United States.
When I call my cousin Josephy he calls me Michelley.
I like to see much TV.
I was born on 12-3-93.
I'm very stubborn.

Mr. Heredia's Class, Room 414

My mom is named Gloria.
My life is weird, cool, wonderful.
I wish I had a mini motorcycle.
I don't have a middle name.
My favorite pet is a dog.
My least favorite sport is soccer because it's a little hard.
My favorite chips are hot chips.
My cousin's name is Mike.
I don't like to wear a uniform to school.
My mom named me because of a book.
I come from Spain, Mexico & America.
I hate myself for killing my bunny.
If I'm in poetry I have tons of ideas so many it's toxic to my brain.
My favorite car is the Nissan Skyline.
My name means diamond.
I suck in reading.

I like all my pets. My favorite is my tarantula, and snake.
My best friend's name is Karen.
Mi favorita cosa es la bicicleta.
I like to eat pizza.
I hate when my brain is not working.
My favorite soda is Dr. Pepper.
The colors I hate are green and purple.
My mom's name is Esperanza, which means hope.
My favorite desert is cake.
The best party I went to was my friend's. It was a pool party.
My favorite favorite place is Ixtapan de la Sal.

Butterfly
Jennifer A.

If I was someone at the age of
nine I'll be a butterfly but I don't
know why? Maybe I could help people
that I see cry. At least people
don't think that I'm butter because
instead of making people cry. So they
would tell me where's that puny
butterfly?

Witches
Emilio A.

This is a witch. It is in
the middle of the moon.

Feel, Touch and Grab
Ruby A.

As I'm in my class room
or house I write, think, and work.
When I work, I think, when I think
I write. When I'm in a store I
reach, grab, feel, and touch. I can
touch a pencil, I can feel my bird.

The Music Reminds Me Of
Carlos A.

The music reminds me of a
person that is crazy. And this is
a very dangerous music.

When I Touch My Pencil And Really Write
Teresa A.

When I touch my pencil and really write.
It comes through my mind really fast.
Oh! How I do just right.

Oh! What despairs me, other poems they write.
How nice and wonderful they are.
Don't think.
These things are good to write.

Ode To My Family
Arlene A.

Going somewhere every day,
Having fun and going to play.

Getting in trouble with my dad,
That's me, oops my bad.

Cleaning the floor using a mop,
Likes to stop and go shop,
That's my mom, she loves to shop.
He's a little boy who likes soccer,
Believe me, he's a shocker!
That's my 9-year-old brother.

He is a big man tall and glad,
Sometimes he's happy and mad,
Yeah! That's my dad!

Soccer
Sandra A.

I like it there
because I get to
exercise. I get
to play more
sports which
is great. I
think that place
is where I
take my worries
out of my
school.

Zoo
Daisy A.

My favorite place is
a zoo in summer
because we can take
some pictures of
the flowers that
bloom. It's a very nice
place to take pictures.
With a sunny day ready
to go!

I can go there noon
or night. I always
think of a zoo with
flowers named
daisy and buttercup.
And plants too. It is
a nice, sunny place
to take outdoor photos.

Dream
Andy A.

I had a dream that I
was a person who kept
eating eating and eating
then one day I wanted
to go to the store but
I couldn't fit through the
door. I was stuck there
for years and got skinny.

Seeing Trees In The Air
Jessica A.

Seeing trees in the air. Hearing apples
fall. I pick them up they feel so rough
they taste so juicy when I bite.

I'm Sorry
Enrique A.

I'm sorry
for breaking
your glass duck

I know
how much
you like it

but I
could not
control the ball

When That Was Done She Gave Fudge Some Socks
Jennifer A.

When that was done she gave
Fudge some socks.
Then my mother raised her
voice 'cause I gave my cat
my brother's goldfish.
"No, I'm sorry, Fudge," Dr. Brown said,
"it's still not as good as Peter's shoe."
Then I woke up and picked my nose and
then I went back to sleep.

Texas
Javier B.

Texas is my best place to stay. They
have cowboys riding on
horses. It's like a dream world. You
can go anywhere is Texas.

I See The Cars With Different Colors
Maximiliano B.

I see the cars with different
colors. I hear the horns beeping
at each other. I smell the
smoke from the cars' mufflers.
I feel the cars as I cross
the street to get to school.

Ode To My Family
Crystal B.

They help me with my problems,
They make me feel alright,

406

They're very special to me,
I couldn't live without them.

They're the best in the world,
They're always on my side,
They make me feel special,
They give me all I want. (Most of the time.)

They always make me feel good inside,
They're the best in the world,
I couldn't live without them.

The Piano Is Shaped Like A Rectangle
Heidy B.

The piano is shaped like a rectangle. The keys are
gold. And it sounds sad.

Dancing, running and jumping, and moving a lot.

Playing with my little sister.

Flowers: the smell of roses opening
and growing.

Listening to music.

Old Ceiling
Gabriela B.

Oh, old ceiling,
don't fall down.
We still want you
so water bombs
won't fall on our heads.

If you do
you'll hurt us
with your body
and legs.

Red
Jose C.

Red is like a rose dipped in red. Red is
dark, light and any other form. Red is my
favorite color. Hearts are red. Red are
lips. Red is a garden of roses. My cheeks
turn red when I run a lot.

I Go To The Park With My Dad
Ramon C.

I go to the park with my dad we play
a little ball he teaches me some moves.

I'm In The Rain Forest
Seraphina C.

I'm in the rain forest.
It's very calm.
Hearing the rain and
feeling the humidity
makes me think of paradise. Nice and silent.
I could almost taste the air and water.
There are trees and plants everywhere.

I Would Be The Wind
Jennifer C.

I would be the wind. Because
you can go fast, slow. Then high
and low. And close to everything.
Be pushing myself everywhere
but no one will see me. I would
be as invisible as a ghost. I could
go up to the beautiful sky and
swish swash and see the sky. Move
left and right. Go to Europe pushing
myself. Then land home.

Blue
Alejandro C.

Blue: the sky is blue and so is
my shirt. The blue stands out like
a big doughnut in a cup
of coffee.

My Room Is A Good Place
Liliana C.

My room is a good place, where I
could feel comfortable, do whatever I want,
where I don't get into trouble. In my
room I could do whatever I want,
watch TV, sleep, jump on the bed and I don't
get into trouble. That's where I feel comfortable.
In my room.

Two Little Apples
Justice C.

I looked at a tree and two
apples were staring at me. They looked
very good so I shook the tree. An
apple came down, I heard it
thump. It felt very smooth.
It smelled juicy so I ate that
juicy apple.
It was yummy! Yummy!

Look Out The Window!
Dagoberto C.

I look out the window
I see the nice blue sky.
I look out the window I
see a nice small bird, but
when it finally lands I say
oh my god it is huge!

If I Could Be Anything
Susana C.

If I could be anything I would be
a dog that lives in the zoo. If I could
be anything I would be a nurse
that lives in the zoo. If I could be
anything I would be an orange
that lives in a tree.

Dull Day
Maria C.

It was
a dull day
like always
my list
was full

I could not have
at least one
the rest to
have some fun

It was the
lousiest day
I wish it
was the
funnest not
the lousiest

The Window
Janett C.

I see people that look like ants.
I see houses tiny enough for an
ant.
The window is so small
I could barely fit my had through the
window.
Looking through the window made
my head & stomach hurt. I felt like
throwing up!
I'll never forget that day on
the airplane!

The Song
Asusena C.

The song makes me happy,
excited and surprised. The song
makes you happy, not sad.
When you have music, go
and dance with your partner.
Guitars have loud sounds. Make
your own band, you can even
be a singer.

410

The Dark Street
Dylan C.

I can't see anything.
It is so dark.
It's really foggy.
I see light ahead.
There's a ghost
in the car
and there's more
in the back.
There are ghosts
walking the streets.
I see ghosts through
the windows
in the houses.

If I Could Be Spring
Ruby C.

If I could be spring
I will smell the flowers
and look at the butterflies.
Also, look at the colors of the
flowers like color pink, light or
babyblue and some other colors.
But the thing I like most is
everybody outside, butterflies
all around also making me so
happy.

I See A Wide Face
Alejandro C.

I see a wide face touching
my tank. I try to swim away, once
I get far I crash on the
window. When I get my food
I swim up and eat it. It tastes
like shrimp. I can't really smell
because I have gills. Still the
water is really clean and it's like
breathing. I can hear my cleaner
pour clean water and bubbles. I
feel happy to live in my fish tank.

Snow!!!
Ariana C.

Snow is white, cold, frozen
cars, schools closed, everybody
is glad, everybody is playing
outside, throwing snowballs.
We wear scarves, gloves, hats,
jackets, boots. We're off to
play, we yell, "Snowball fight!!!"
Let's go drink hot cocoa
after that.

Gray Is Steel, Hard And Gray
Diego C.

Gray is steel, hard and gray.
White is the color I see every
day. Black is a color I see every
nighttime. Blue is the Atlantic
Ocean. Green is the grass. Red
is an apple rolling up and down.

Winter
Daniel C.

The day is white not
even white mice can be seen
in the snow. Kids sledding on the
snow. Cars slipping and slopping.
Kids wet with white.
I fall and get mad because
I get hit in the face with
a snowball from my dad.

I Like Poetry
Jorge D.

I like poetry, it makes me feel
successful with what I do. It makes
me feel like I'm really in the idea
or picture. It makes me feel like I'm
alive. But sometimes it
just makes me sigh.

When I Go Out For Candy
Kassandra D.

When I go out for
candy, I always see
witches and monsters

I never knew that
monsters and witches
ate candy

Just Some Blue More
Yiczel D.

Just some blue
more. It's really weird
or could cause someone
to break their neck. Thank
you for pointing me
out. Nobody knows what
will happen to you
when you die. The
creature reached the spiky
metal gate. This felt very
fortunate indeed.

New York
Raymond D.

I feel the hard sidewalk
when I walk to places. I hear
the cars passing and honking
horns. I smell the dirty sky
full of smoke. I also smell
the delicious food from
McDonald's. I see seagulls
and pigeons eating pieces of bread
at the harbor. I can taste the
crackers I am eating when I
take a break.

Country
Christopher E.

Getting up in the country.
The music blows to the wild.

413

Country music,
soft in the trees.
Cars in the streets.
Crying and singing.
Living in the guitar
or water through
the singers.
Turning on the light.

I Would Want To Be A Monkey
Ashley E.

I would want to be a monkey
and I will have a party with-
out permission and we knocked down
the house with a truck.

The Carpenters
Yesenia F.

Instead of
working they are lying
around, talking
and laughing
and telling jokes.
All of a sudden
they start working.
No wonder,
the boss is coming!

My Favorite Place
David F.

My favorite place I like to go to
is my cousin's house. It's fun in the
summer because we get in the pool.
Sometimes we play soccer.

I Remember
Yaneliz F.

I remember when I was
eight years old. We went to
Alabama and the city Rosabel.
We saw something like

414

Niagara Falls but littler.
In Spanish it is called
"Cascada."

When I Write A Poem
Jessica F.

When I write a poem I want it
to make sense. When I write I want
it to be funny. When I write I want it
to rhyme. When I finish writing a poem
I hope people like it.

I Can See My Dog Fetch A Ball
Claudia F.

I can see my dog fetch a ball.
When I feel him he is cuddly.
After taking a bath he smells
sweet. When he hears me yelling
for him he runs.

Noise
Erick F.

The baby is asleep.
Makes me think of peace and harmony,
when I'm on the sofa trying
to sleep. I fall in a
careless pit of delight. The
baby wails in fear
and I feel like I'm
in a prison full of
screeching monkeys. When
I go to put him in
bed the sound of him
snoring makes me feel like
I'm in the middle of the
stampede of life and death.
But when I leave the
room I feel like I'm
in a forest of thunder
and loud noise. My brother
was throwing a party. The
baby wakes up. I feel
like I'm in a pit of laughing

and troublesome hyenas.
When I try to sleep, the noise
spins in my head. When
it's over my brother plays
loud games. He is screaming,
the baby is crying and no one can
stop it!

White Is The Color Of My Dog
Geovanny F.

White is the color of my dog
that I see every morning. White feels
fluffy like my dog, Snowball. Like water
that runs down my hands and goes
through my fingers.

Green Smells Like Grass
Javier F.

Green smells like grass
Green looks like Ms. K's behavior chart
Green tastes like a lime
Green sounds like a lawn mower
Green feels like money in my hand

I See The Sky
Miguel F.

I see the sky
I see birds flying
I see my house
My house looks small
Most of the houses are made of bricks.

My Place
Elideth G.

My favorite place is China
Buffet. I like it because it is
nice and very fancy. I also
like it for my whole
family. I usually go
only on Sundays only.

Every Day
Karen G.

Construction workers,
working on a building.

Hammers pounding hard
on nails

Hearing loud noises

Seeing kids running around
playing with each other on
the sidewalk

There's always things
happening every day.

Music Is About Strong Feelings
Sergio G.

The music is about strong feelings.
I think of the color blue
when I hear jazz. It has
lots of emotion. When the
trumpet is loud I think of
screaming. I think of a dark
place. I see dogs that are
not barking but listening.

Once I Had A Dream
Jessica G.

Once I had a
dream. A lucky dream I
suppose. I dreamed that
I was playing the lottery and
then I found out that
I won $100,000,000!!! I was
the richest person in
the world!!! I woke up I
didn't see any cars,
houses, pool, anything! So
it was just a dream. I wish
it would come true. I still
told myself no fancy dresses.

My 6th Birthday
Yesenia G.

I
remember.
It was
my 6th birthday.
My family threw me
a surprise party. They
also celebrated my sister's
birthday with mine. It was
a fun party. Two cakes were on
the table, lots of balloons in my backyard.
My sister and I went inside of our
house. We went outside again and loud
voices said, "Surprise!" I was happy.
My sister was happy too.

My Dream
Juan G.

I had a dream that I was
sleeping, then I woke up and everything
was upside down. Then I went
to the table and it was up-
side down. Then I went and
saw my parents, they were upside
down. Then I realized that I was
the one upside down. Then
I fell down and hit my head.

When I Closed My Eyes
Cesar G.

When I closed my eyes
it felt like I was playing
the music.

When I closed my eyes
the second time I felt
like I was dancing.

When I closed my eyes
the third time I saw that
they were clapping for my
music.

418

Monsters
Edward G.

Kids walking down the street.
Some have teeth that can bite;
others have claws to scratch.
They have furry costumes
and long bloody knives;
lots have a sword;
but all of the kids
like to get the candy
while the real monsters don't;
they have no taste for candy,
they have a taste for blood.
Monsters aren't so dandy,
all everyone needs is a piece of candy.

If I Were A Rottweiler
Jaime G.

If I were a Rottweiler
I would be biting anyone for no reason.
A snack there and there. Barking
and scaring people and fighting dogs.
Or I will be a hockey player.

Getting hit by a puck a
few times. Winning games and
fighting people. Losing once losing twice.
The rest winning and winning.

Grandma
James G.

When school is over my grandma's always
there. She's in the street in the car,
she drives me home with my bro.
When I go home I have to do my
homework, while my grandma's doing
lottery tickets.

The Dream
Omar G.

I dreamt that my brother was bigger than me
and he could do my homework for me.

I could watch TV all night. And he was
15 years old. It felt real. And he was
nice and cool.

I'm A Raven, Soaring Through The Sky
Jessica G.

I'm a raven, soaring through the sky
I can feel the wind thrashing by.
I can taste the air when I open my
mouth, I can hear myself talk through and
through. I can see the trees down below. As I
reach the ground I fall fast asleep and
I listen to the crickets chirping.

Using My Hands All Day Long
Elizabeth G.

Using my hands all day long,
coloring and cutting,
gluing and drawing.
Doing poems and stories,
everybody working very hard,
so quiet that you can hear the
clock ticking all day long.

Yellow Is The Color Of The Sunshine
Daisy H.

Yellow is the color of
the sunshine. It reminds me
of The Simpsons. Yellow is my
favorite color, it is bright and
pretty. It feels like butter
and looks like the sun.

Ode To My Poems
Freddy H.

It's an ode to all the poems I
make that makes me smile when
I write, makes me happy when
I am sad, or when everybody
likes the poems that I make. And
every time I make poems it

fills me with joy and happiness.
Oh my poems make me so
happy. I wish to never stop
with my poems.

Like & Hate
Isamar H.

I like my hands & I hate
them. I wish I did not have
them. I hate that they are too loud,
they never stop they just go. They
talk a lot. When I write I
write too much but my hands talk
too much, they never stop, I hate
them. I wish I did not have them
because I do altogether too much
work. I like them because they're
mine. I'm glad I have them
because I'm able to eat, I
like them. I hate my hands
& I like them.

The Playground
Naomi H.

I go to school, I see the playground.
It is yellow and purple. It is big.
In the morning they tell you to
please get out before the bell rings.

I'm Sorry
Brandon H.

I'm sorry for fighting with
the dog. But she bit me in
the toe.

My Room
Alyssa I.

I have a room that's like my 2nd home
it's a place where I can be alone
My stuff is there
sometimes it's everywhere

My room is messy
when I have to clean it I am fussy
I like it 'cause it's a place where I
can be
To be there I am happy

I'm Sorry, Miguel
Andres J.

for using your Game Boy Advanced
SP when you were at the
store. I'm sorry for losing your
game of Spider-Man 2, it was
a boring game anyway. So
I'm very sorry, brother.
I will never do that again.
I will try to find it in the
house where I lost it.

My Clock
Sandra J.

Every morning he wakes me up.
Every time he comes in he
starts to meow.

He wakes me up at 6:30 am.
He is always hungry so I have
to serve him.

I got used to him. Now
he is like my clock.

The Board
Maria J.

The board is always
white
white as steam
white as paper

The teachers always
write on them
they write every single
day except Sat. and Sun.
White as a refrigerator
the board is always
tired

My Bee
Lizbeth L.

My bee, yellow and
black, so cute and
hairy. I would like to
be like my bee.
Because I could
fly, eat honey from
flowers, it's so fun.
And to poke people.
I will chase
people all over the
place.

What Happened
Victor L.

I remember when I was seven years old
I went to my aunt's house
where we were celebrating Thanksgiving.
Then my brother fell down.
I was laughing at him.
Then when I turned around
I hit myself on the door
and I fell down on the floor.
Everybody was laughing.
I was embarrassed.
My forehead was red.

4 Of My 5 Senses Are All Mixed Up!
Karen L.

4 of my 5 senses are all
mixed up. I hear with my nose
I smell with my ear. My senses
are so mixed up! I see with
my mouth and taste with my
eyes. The only sense that is not
mixed up are my hands.

In Spring It Rains
Karla L.

In spring it rains, beautiful
flowers grow, blooms

and roses. The next
morning you will see
green grass and you
will finally see leaves
on the trees! The weather
will change to 60 degrees.
Kids will go to the park,
ride their bikes and have
a cookout. Some people will
go downtown and
shop for spring clothes.

Fish In A Dish
Miguel L.

Mom, I don't want
this fish. It looks like a
potato. I bet it will taste
like the worst fish in this
dish. Do I have to eat
it? It smells like garbage.
It looks like the lunch
lady's face. I can even
hear its ugliness in my
ear. Mom, I feel like the
fish in the dish.

I Remember When I Went To Buy
Cristian L.

I remember when I went to buy
my Timberland boots and after we
went to buy pizza at Domino's.
When I got home I put on
my boots and went outside.

Snow Is White Snow Is Fun
Giovanni L.

Snow is white snow is fun
build a snowman but don't
put on his scarf too tight.

I Want To Be ... When I Grow Up
Michelle L.

When I grow up I
want to be a lot of
stuff, I just can't
decide!
It's hard.
There are a lot of
things I like!

A teacher,
a soccer player,
a writer,
a singer
(extra).

I just can't
decide.

Blues The Clues
Gabriela L.

Weather makes me sad &
happy. I like the rain, I love the
snow. I grab a ball of snow, it makes
me wonder where does the snow come
from? Who makes it? Does it taste like salt?
I want to know. The clouds make
forms, I tried to see things up there.
The hours take too long. Why, why can't I
go up there so my wonders would go
away with the wind and the
rain and the sadness. Please go away.

Blue
Ashley L.

Blue's the color of the great, high sky.
When you pass the blue, blue water, you ask why.
Take a bite out of a blueberry.
Feel the color's sadness.
Blue, blue, blue.
Nobody can take eyes off it.
Think of it when you pass the oceans and lakes.
Blue jeans match with anything.
Can other colors do that?

Pink, green and yellow are his/her enemies.
Be careful of blue tornadoes.
Ask yourself, "If you don't like blue,
you don't like water."
Many blue colors await you.
Don't make them wait.

Creepy House
Viridiana L.

Passing by the house
with bloody walls and shadows.
Frankenstein peeking out the window.
The crying of a cat on the roof.
Demons flying about.
Zombies walking around
with bloody shirts.
This house holds secrets.

I Would Be
Denis M.

I would be
a bee flying in
the sky or flying
flower by flower.

I could fly inside
or outside the flower
because I'm little and
I could go anywhere I
want because I want
to go there.

I could be in a
rose or a daisy
because I have
bee friends

And we go somewhere
we like to
go.

Halloween
Jasmine M.

As we knock on the door
we say trick or treat.
We get our goodies and
take off our identities.
We eat eyes one by one.
We leave the rest of the
eyes and go on to the
bones.

The Family Necklace
Kevin M.

The family necklace, passed down from
generations. But who wore it first?
From past to present, the history
of it. Who made it and who is
wearing it? There are a lot of things to
learn. And now I have it. I have
to pass it on to the next generation.
The tradition is in my hands.

The Wind Is Blowing So, So Hard
Adriana M.

The wind is blowing so, so hard
while dogs pass by and start to
bark. I was just four years old and
I lost my first tooth. My mom
took me to the movies and
she went straight to the ticket
booth. My mom started crying.
She had a box of tissue.
The my brother and I
fought and he said, "Girl,
you have an issue."

Home
Kevin M.

I can never forget my
home. I can use the phone.
I like a home with a phone.
I like shrimp. And soup.

If I Could Be Anything
Alexiss M.

If I could be anything
I would be a teacher.
Because I get to work with
kids. Work in a classroom.
It will be very fun.
I will give homework. Five days a week, on holidays, and
vacations I will not give homework.

I Walked In The Rain, I Saw Raindrops Splashing
Christopher M.

I walked in the rain, I saw raindrops splashing
on the dried cement. I held my tongue to taste
the rain, I felt rain hitting my face. I heard the
rain hitting the fence and I finally went
to school.

The Beautiful Bunny
Jessica M.

I love my bunny. I play with
her, and she plays with me. She is
very beautiful. She likes to be nice.
She sleeps in my bed or in a box.
She likes carrots. I give her my toys,
she plays with them; she plays with my
friends. She has babies and she
likes to help me with my homework.
She is colored white.

Poetry
Melissa M.

Six letters symbolize meanings. When I
think of poetry this is what I think
about: P is for peaceful, O is for over-
look, E is for everlasting, T is for
trying to make words come to life,
R is for reading, Y is for your own
meaning.

I See A Dog That Is Lost
Victor M.

I see a dog that is lost.
He's all brown with a black
spot on he nose. He's tasting
a large bone and drinking
water off the floor. He feels
sad and happy at the same
time. He hears a voice
calling. The dog says he's
here.

Hands
Nora M.

Hands, hands,
you get me tired.
I always write
with my hands.
I clean, write, and
I play with my
hands. But you
still get me tired.
Hands, hands, you get
on my nerves because
I always do stuff
with you. Hands, hands,
leave me alone.

I Could Be Anything
Maritza M.

I could be a feather, I could
be a good friend, I could
be a marshmallow, a
fruit, a kiwi & a berry, fruits
& juice. A stick & a
broom.

Ode To The Cellular
Marcos M.

I play games on the
cellular, I like it
a lot, and maybe I
will bring it in one day.

I have the cellular
at my house and I
hide it because my
brothers or sisters will grab
it.

Sorry
Gabriela M.

For letting you down if I will stay
for summer school,

I know it will be your 15-year
birthday (in Mexico)

but I know that when a cat traps
a mouse, you stay down.

I Want To Be A Monkey Because I Could
Luz M.

I want to be a monkey because I could
jump everywhere. And I could be in the jungle.
And see my friend animals.

History
Luis M.

I wonder about history.
History is all around you.
I wonder if my house used to be
a movie star's.
I wonder if it was a
president's, or a guy's from the
war.

My Window
Abraham M.

My window, I look out
the window. My living room
window. Where I watch the
street and cars. I see
people riding bikes, skateboarding

and just walking and
saying goodbye. But it feels
like it's two worlds
beside us.

I Try To Do My Best
Lea M.

I try to do my best
making up poems. I want
my poem to be funny or
they can also be true. I
try to think but some-
times my brain gets
locked in a big great
dungeon, locked up so tight
that I can't think. I want
my poem to be funny and
try but sometimes I want
my poem to not be
true.

Ode To Pickles
Salvador M.

I like pickles. I see the jar
with pickles all green and wet.
I feel them in my tummy, all swirly
inside, tasting sour and salty
like the pickles I taste.

Every Day I See My Family Waking Me
Alan M.

Every day I see my family waking me
up in the morning. I eat my breakfast,
I brush my teeth and I'm set to go.

Every Day The School
Gricelda M.

Every day the school
on the corner,
a lot of kids in and
outside school.

Homework after school,
faces of fifth and fourth
grade teachers.

Kids talking, writing, and
listening.
Faces of construction workers
by my room 405.
It is just people everyday.

Clouds
Karen M.

Are clouds from smoke?
Or, are they from air?
Where did clouds come from?
And how were they formed?
Are all of them different?
Or are all of them similar?
My brother says they're made in
a factory.
I say they're made of rain.
I really want to know.
Can't anyone tell me now?

Favorite Places
Luz M.

I once had a place that was
special to me. I sat on it.
I wrote on it. It was special it was the
beach. I found sea shells floating
in the water. Crabs hiding in their
shells. Sand so soft as cream. Trees
so big as the sky. Big planes up
in the sky. Stars around me.

Last Summer I Went Fishing
Ivan M.

Last summer I went fishing and I
got the biggest fish. It was fun and cool.
I always went on Sunday. I fell
in the water when my line got tangled
in another line. It feels great
when the fish bites.

I See An Apple, It Looks Shiny
Ruby M.

I see an apple. It looks shiny.
When I bite it it tastes juicy.
When I touch it it feels hard.
If there is a worm I hear it
say hi.

My Dream
Luz N.

I dreamt we were asleep at school
and it is wartime. When we woke
up a funny bear was dancing
all day because he was
scared about the war.

Ode To School
Nidia N.

It helps me learn, it's fun, it's big.
I meet friends there, to hang out
with. The experiments are a little
hard, yet fun to do. Even though
I have to wake up early I still
like to go to my very cool and
fun school. When Saturday is
almost near, that's not cool.
I wish I could stay from Monday to Sunday
right at school. The homework is the
best part of going there. I don't
mean to sound like a nerd but I'm
just a kid who loves school. School
RULES!!

The Cold Comes To Chicago
Fernando Ojeda

The cold came by rain
the rain came by the lake
the rain on the lake evaporates
then the wind comes with rain.
It gets cold. The snow
comes from rain, cold and wind.
The snow covers the city and
that's the cold that comes
to Chicago.

Nasty Witch
Margarita Ortiz

I see a nasty witch, she
stares at me. I run away
but she follows me. She chases
me and throws spit at me!

Poet's Obligation
Esther Pacheco

When I write food poems,
I feel hungry.
I imagine the food,
I smell the food,
I feel the food soft,
I hear my mom calling me to eat.
I like to write food poems
because I get hungry.
Food poems!

I Like Snow
Marisol Pacheco

I like snow. When it is
December my mom tells
us to go outside and make
angels. She takes pictures
and we do snow fights. I like
snow we can play with it.

On My Way To School
Daniel Padilla

On my way to school
I see people walking behind
me. I hear and see cars
passing by. I always see
the tamales girl selling
on the corner. I see
a lot of kids on line.

Poetry
Jasmine Palomar

Poetry is running through light,
running through freedom,
running through light,
tell me how you like your rhythm.
Rhyming, funny, sad or exciting,
you tell me 'cause I like them
all.

Snowing Cats And Dogs
Samuel Pantoja

When it is snowing cats and dogs all
the kids go crazy. They go outside,
they have a cats and dogs fight.
Making a cats and dogs snowman
the parents go crazy. It's snowing
cats and dogs and having cats and
dogs snow days it will be cool.

Winter (Snow)
Jesus Patino

I always see
the sky. When it st-
arts to snow, I wait
until it gets high.
I always play sno-
w ball fights. When
we are done I
fall in the snow
and do angels. I
do a lot of angels.
Winter is my favorite
season of all because
I get to play a lot.

Halloween
Jose Patino

Once a year is Halloween
when ghosts and goblins and witches
are seen. They screech and scream
around the nation, the rest of the
year, they're on vacation.

It Makes Me Feel
Oscar Patino

It makes me feel
warm inside with horses in
my mind. I feel the dust
on my back, the song repeats
over and over.
The man riding the bull
in circles, the guy
screams in happiness,
the guitar makes me
feel like I'm in a
rodeo. The horse stares
at me, saying ride me.

With My Hands
Miguel Peña

With my hands I play while
mom is cooking dinner.

With my hands I write while
my little sister makes
a mess.

With my hands I help my
dad, carrying the toolbox while
my dad drills the wood.

With your hands you
can play, cook, write, help, drill, and
even make a mess.

My Room
Pedro Perez

I come from school
And sit in my bed
I turn on my TV
but fall asleep
And when I wake up
I look around
and see my room
so calm and quietly
I see my TV on
so I just go back to sleep

436

Colors
Nelly Piña

Red is like the smell of a rose.
Red is like the fresh fruit of a
mango. It is also like the shape of
a heart. Red is cool, red is like
the sun, shining through the
sky.

My Hands
Yesenia Popoca

With my hands,
I do a lot of things.
I write with my hands
I use my hands to move.

My hands are not that big,
but they aren't too small either.
On my hands I have nails,
my nails are polished white.
On my hands I have rings too.

Ode To Art
Andrea Pulido

I love to paint,
It's like seeing a saint,
You feel the color,
Your favorite like no other.

And when you color,
You can feel the wonder,
I love all kinds of art,
I say this from my heart.

Mexico
Alejandro Ramirez

Mexico. It's hot and dry
the time really may fly.
It's also busy but hot
always. I don't want to
go back to the school
hallways.

437

Blue Is Great
Efren Ramirez

Blue is a nice color.
I have a brother named Blue.
Blue smells like blue tulips.
Blue looks like skyblue.
Blue tastes like blueberries.
Blue sounds like a friendly color.
Blue is my favorite brother.

When A Pizza Is Hot
Mario Ramirez

When a pizza is hot it's
yummy, when it is cold
it is gummy.

I Remember I Was Little
Jessica Ramos

I remember I was little
I was three years old.
It was two days before my baptism.
I broke my right hand!
I cried a lot because my hand hurt.
My parents didn't know my hand was broken
They found out after my baptism.
Now I write with my left hand.

Ode To My Fish
Leobardo Ramos

I can see my fish swimming.
I see them in the sea.
I wish to swim along with them,
They swim away when I tap on the glass,
The speed they swim,
Oh how beautiful they look.
I can see them jumping,
But then I see them being eaten,
I can't imagine a life without
fish.
So I wish to swim with them
before they go away.
Their scales shine along with the water,

They make a rainbow streaming down
the stream.
The splashes from their jumps,
They make a pattern with their color.
I wish to swim along with them.

Teacher
Crystal Reyes

I want to be a good girl
when I grow up. I am going
to be a teacher. I will be
nice to the students. We will
have art. Play games, read a
story. And Reader's Theater.
I could be red, blue,
green.

Colors
Omar Reyes

Colors are everywhere,
your shirt, jeans, everything has
colors. Colors are shy, colors are
happy. They're also dull or mean.
Colors are cool and dumb. They're
smart and some are crazy.
Some are rockers and some artists.
But my favorite color is red.
Red is my favorite color.

A Weird Dream
Chante Reyna

I had a dream. In school I was so not normal.
I was late and my teacher was my sister and
Ms. Dennehy was my sister. We were in Australia
and the only thing I could understand, the
door next to me was in Chicago. Weird because
a weird tree started to sing, "So not cool OW!!!"
The chair started hitting me, I need a doctor.

Black
Giovanni Rios

Black doesn't put a smile on
your face. Black makes you mad
and furious. Black reminds you
of an old raisin. Black
just fell off the tree
or a soda called RC
or Pepsi. Black like gothic
kids walking down the street.

Music
Marisela Rios

It was a summer night
and it was raining. I saw you
on the beach. The beat of the
rain sounded like the cry
of a baby. I realized you
were sad because you thought
you would never see me again.

The Library
Naomi Rios

The place I like to come
and go to is the library. At the
library it is quiet. You can't hear a sound.
I like to read at the library.
I really like the Jake books. And the
poetry books. I read ten books a day.
At home I have my own library.
It is big and has five bookshelves.

Crazy Poem
Cristian Rodriguez

I was playing soccer when I saw
this crazy ball. It was named
To See The Ball Of Dough Double
Size. And the moist dough was
a good place to play. In ancient
times the best way to keep the
ball from molding was to keep it
dry.

In A Box I Found
Mariela Rodriguez

In a box I found thrown
away I saw driven nails
a hammer and another five things.
I wonder who used it?

I Wonder Who Was Here
Michelle Rodriguez

I wonder who sat at my desk when I
was in second grade. I think it was a girl.
If only I knew who sat at my desk!
I dream that the girl likes to play
baseball. Then we could play together.
Maybe she lived in my house. Maybe
she has two sisters and two brothers
like me.

I've Broken The Plate
Roberto Rodriguez

I've broken the
plate that was
in the dining room

and which cost
you a lot of money
for that plate

Forgive me
I'll make it up to
you I'll find a job.

Experience
Liliana Roman

I experience myself in a
blizzard. There's a tree covered
with snow. I felt like an Eskimo.
A snow route had mountains
of ice.

The Lunar Eclipse
Marcel Roman

The eclipse comes.
Walking along, with my
eyes, I look up,
nothing happens.
The moon being covered
by a dark presence, says
look up but don't look down.
I am standing on air,
the moon closer, closer,
but remember what goes
up goes down.

My Favorite Place To Go
Jennifer Romero

My favorite place to go is Enchanted
Castle. Michelle and I like to race.
We eat pizza, we play games.
We like to chase everyone
around. We use the dragon roller
coaster, we play in the arcade.
We play inside, we play
inside. We talk and walk. We
play and laugh, we dance and
sing, we sit and drink. We ride
home chatting. We
go out running.

Rhythm
Elizabeth Salgado

The rhythm of the air makes
me feel at home. It makes me feel
concentrated. When I am focused real
hard on something it makes me feel
calm and not to think so hard, to
feel the rhythm of the music. They
both make me feel accomplished.

It Reminds Me Of A Song
Romel Salinas

It reminds me of a song like
a rock song with a fancy truck
with people inside hearing a
song like the one I am hearing.
Some people are really
goofy in there, swinging their
long hair and going crazy
with a guitar, drums, piano and
there are some people dancing.
It sounds like it was played
on December 10, 1879 and it
makes people crazy, with funky
clothing and with funky shoes.

My Place
Gerardo Sanchez

I always wanted to
go to an island
all by myself with my favorite
food, now that's where I
want to go. I could have
my own beach. But I would
have my friends come over
and I will have so much
much fun. And that's my
place I want to be it's
called your favorite place.

I Use My Hands To Eat Spaghetti
Marcos Santiago

I use my hands to eat spaghetti
My hands brush my teeth
I need my hands to turn pages
My hands help write my homework

Sorry
Erika Silva

I'm sorry
teacher. I
don't mean
to shout out.

443

I probably
should never
shout out.
But I know stuff.

Forgive me. But
it's not my
fault. You ask questions
& I have answers.

Yo Me Recuerdo Que Cuando
Karina Silva

Yo me recuerdo que cuando
yo estaba dormida y vea mi
ropa chiquita y cuando me
desperte voy a mirar mi
ropa y la miro grande
y le digo a mi mama lo
que soñe.

Oh! What Memories
Jacquelyn Soto

A morning walking to school.
The fog floating in the air.
My friend and I telling jokes.
The air blows softly down.
A group crossing the street.
The street lights on,
the teenagers crossing the street.

Alphabet
Brittney Stanford

Who invented the alphabet?
Did the person have more letters than 26?

What if that person was not born?
Would another person have made it up?

Where would we be without the alphabet?
Was there more than one person who invented the
alphabet?

I Hear The Drums
Jose Tapia

I hear the
drums more than a
guitar. I like how it's
mixed but I also
hear the drum like
my heart pounding and
pounding, like when the blood
spreads the music does too.

Snow Snow Snow
Yesenia Teran

Snow snow snow
I wish it was summer.
So much snow. Wish it
would melt.
I wanted a snow fight
but I guess it melted.

Ode To Ice Cream
Veronica Tolentino

Ice cream, ice cream
how I like it. The
way it drips from
top to bottom.

In the summer
I buy a lot, but
oh oh here comes
the winter.

When I buy it
it's so frozen and
cold I have to
wait until it cools.

When it's cool it
melts in the sun, but
oops it's melting too
much I better get
a cup.

Here comes winter
and no more ice cream.
The end has come but
there's still a summer
coming every year.

Halloween
Jonatan Torres

Everyone is putting on
costumes and egg bombing houses
and trick or treating. Boo. Kids
dressed like ghosts. Every party
kind of scary.

Memories
Jorge Torres

My memory in Wisconsin.
I remember that I moved,
we had no house,
we slept in the car.
We went to explore,
I found a park,
near it was a house,
we bought it.
At school,
the milk was in a bag.
I tried to put the straw in
but as I tried a kid said no,
you need to hold the top.
And that was my first friend.

Black
Yvonnes Torres

Black sounds like a black cat. Black
smells like a web. Black looks like a
dark room. Black feels like a spider.
Black tastes like junk.

When I Write Poems
Vaneza Tovar

When I write poems, I like how
they sound. I like how they are. I like

446

what they say. I like what they are
about. I like how the teacher says
them. And I also like how I say them.

Today Is Another Summer Day
Edgar Trejo

Today is another summer day & people
are running. You could even say drummers are crying.
The sun is sparkling. The water is stopping.
The rain will stay up in the clouds & won't
come down. Until next spring.

I Go To The Flea Market
Angelica Tuetla

I go to the flea market
I see tiny turtles
They cost $10.00

The Sea
Mary Ulloa

The sea is my favorite
place. The blue water and
the sky. The sand. Lots
of sun is out, really
hot.

The sea, so beautiful,
so quiet. But I hear the
kids screaming in the water
because they are having
fun.

The sea so bright. In
the morning it is hot. In the
evening it gets cool, but in
the night it gets cold.

I like the sea. I want
to go again. I just
can't wait until summer
is here. It is so fun in
the summer.

The Blues Stays When You Are Sad
Diego Valenzuela

The blues stays when you are sad.

You listen to yourself weep because of
needy requirements.

The tense and mad that have nothing listen
to people having good times while you're poor
outside.

Feeling cool, cold air. Unfortunate to not be
happy when you had it all. Tense, you
will go mad.

Bruises On Her Hands
Dalia Jasmin Vasquez

Bruises on her hands
& people stare as they
watch her cry on
her back this is my
fault oh sorry we were
just playing how did I
hit so hard!

Being A Dog
Yesenia Vega

I feel the cool
breeze in the freezing
pool.

I smell the food
in the kitchen room
my tummy growls like
a mad lion.

Tasting the food
in the kitchen room,
feeling hunger every
second.

Seeing the food
coming toward me.

SHIELDS ELEMENTARY SCHOOL
Principal: Rita C. Gardner
Teachers: Ms. Marfise, 3rd, Ms. Michel, 5th, Ms. Salcedo, 3rd, Ms. Vazzana, 3rd, Ms. Vilchis, 3rd, Ms. Wiegers, 3rd

Allison Liefer, Poet in Residence

Allison Liefer studied creative writing at Northwestern University and received her M.F.A. from the University of Michigan. A published poet, she has worked in publishing and has taught writing courses at several universities in both Michigan and Chicago.

Memory Calendar
Room 202 Class Poem

I remember about going to the circus and I saw a lion that jumped
into a hoop that was on fire.
I remember that in 2004 with Mrs. Morales we went to a
field trip and we saw dolphins doing tricks.
I remember a field trip
to see Cinderella.
I remember when it was Christmas. I remember when I opened my
present.

I remember going to Mexico.
I remember chickens, birds, dogs, cows and horses.
I heard the dog barking, a fox,
a cat, bee, mice too.
I like hamsters I have my room all full of hamsters.
I remember my dog.

I remember that it was summer and we swam in the pool.
I want to be invisible because my mom and dad wouldn't find me
to go to the check up.
I remember my birthday party
strawberry cake the donkey piñata when
they broke the piñata the candy was falling on the ground and prizes.
I remember when I played musical chairs.
I remember about Christmas that I went to my cousin's house to have a
party.

I remember when I went to Ohio
and I saw too much snow and I touched the
snow and we played snowball fight.
I remember Christmas with my family in my cousin's house
I got a Mrs. Pac Man video game and ate a big chicken.

In Texas I remember when in school it was
recess time. I remember my birthday in Texas.
Then it was church time we were singing each
person looked at a book to sing.
I remember everything about Mendora and
I love going there because it's beautiful
Mendora and Chicago and I love the two places.

Poem
Zaira Quinones

Sweet is like you love some one.
It's so sweet like a turkey.

Sweet is like Valentines day.
Sweet is like eating candy all
the day. Sweet is like love.
Sweet is like you love your family.
Sweet is like no fighting with people.
Sweet is like have a lot of friends.
Sweet is like a cake of chocolate.
Sweet is like a lot of love.

Untitled
Michelle Quintana

Come to my house please can you go and if you go my mom is going to bring roses to the house. And there are going to go the girls and me. And clowns in my house and there is going to be ice cream and that is your favorite ice cream chocolate too. There are not going to be parents just my mom. And that's why I want you to go to my house please go to my house.

Untitled
Juan Najera

Miguel come to my house and we play computers we do experiments and we do things like stories and we paint pictures like dinosaurs and we play and we eat cake.

Memory Calendar
Yesica Aramburo

I remember the spring, flowers, butterflies and the sun.
I remember the spring joy.
I remember the spring when I got wet with my sisters and brothers.
I remember the springs lady bugs.
I remember the flower and roses in the spring.
I remember the rainbows so bright.
I remember the trees so bright.
I remember the water so hot.
I remember the insects.
I remember Mexico's foods and Mexico's pozadas.

Memory Calendar
Karina Bucio

I remember riding a horse at Texas there
were some cows, a dog, and a chicken. When the

chicken layed some eggs my brother and me
were going to get the eggs.

In Texas I remember when in school it was
recess time. I remember my birthday in Texas.
Then it was church time we were singing each
people looked at a book to sing.

Then it was my sister's birthday it was
fun because we played Bingo and I win the game.

Memory Calendar
Miguel Rodriguez

I remember studying the multiplication tables.
I remember celebrating the new year.
I remember about my birthday, the cake.
I remember Christmas food, presents with family.
I remember new 3 day of school.
I remember going to a field trip in 2 grade.
I remember the horses in Mexico.
I remember going to the dentist.
I remember going to the circus.

Untitled
Tanya Sanchez

A fish jumping
Way in the deep ocean
Jumping jumping where it is deep.

Untitled
Rosa Rodriguez

The snow is
Falling that
Looks like ice-cream.

The snow is
falling like little
white seeds.

Untitled
Maria Guzman

My little brother he
thinks he is
flying all around the world

I Want to Be
Room 201 Class Poem

I want to be water so that people can swim in me all day long.
I want to be a good student because I talk too much.
I want to be a living-dead that flies and scares people.
I want to be a reaper so I can make people live and die.

I want to be a horse because they run fast.
I want to be a Christmas tree because on Christmas they decorate me
pretty.
In the night I would grab a star to touch.
Also, when people go to the stores in their cars, the people won't know
that I am inside their cars.
I want to be invisible to sneak into places to eat and scare people.

I want to be president of the U.S.A. but not to be bossy.
I want to be a bat so I can drink blood.
If I was a superhero I could save people. When people are in a house
on fire I will go in and save lives.
I want to be my dog because I won't go to school. I will stay home all the
time. I will go to sleep all day. I will feel how my dog feels.

I want to be fast, I want to be so fast that lightning is slow, so no bullet
can hit me.
I want to be invisible but not for long. Then people will not be able to see
me.
I want to be a pilot so I could fly in an airplane, so I could see the clouds
up high.
Sometimes I want to be small but not so small that somebody could
step on me.
I want to be Zero with a flame sword and run like the wind, but not so
fast that I would run past people.

I want to be fat, but not that fat. Then I could fly like a balloon. I could be
a green balloon and go to the zoo with a kid who buys me.
I want to be fast but not so fast that I can't slow down or I can't sit on a
chair. But I could win races.
I want to be faster than lightning. I can be like a train. I want to beat
everybody at racing.

I want to have lots of attention, but not enough attention that I would feel embarrassed that people would hear or see my mistakes.
I want to be a bee so I could go from rose to rose. And I would be feeling the rose. I would be getting honey from rose to rose.

My Five Senses
Julian Alquisiras

I felt a hand waking me up.
I smell coffee at the morning.
I herd a radio on at the morning.
I see a car at the morning.
I tasted coffee at the morning.
I felt the hot glass at the morning.
I smell out side.
I heard a car turning on.
I see people in cars.
I tasted bread at the morning.

Fall
Rene Salas

I see colorful leaves
I feel the cold wind in my face
I hear the wind whistling
I smell a pie baking inside
I taste that pie and it is good
then in my yard
I hear my neighbor's dog bark
I see the trunk of a tree
I smell the engine of the car
I taste a pear from our tree
I feel tired and go inside

Happiness
Janet Garduno

I am happy with my dog and I will always be I will be happy forever and I will be
the happiest girl with my dog and my sister will be happy with me and my dog and
her dog too as we will be always and I will be the happiest girl with my sister that is all
I will be for the rest of my life.

The Orange
Daniella Torres

The orange that
my sister left on
the table looks
so good and tender

I forgot to ask
because how good it
looked so I ate it

I told her forgive me,
forgive me but how good
it looked I counldn't
wait so I ate it.
Forgive me!

I want to be
Janneth Diaz

I want to be a butterfly
because I'm going to be colorful.
And I want to feel the fresh air.
And I want to fly so I could feel the fresh air.
I want to be a bee so I could
go to rose to rose.
And I would be feeling the rose.
And I would be getting honey from rose to rose.

Poem
Mireya Maldonado

I want to be invisible
so I can go through doors
and walls. Wherever I go
I can go through. Also
in the night I can glow
and I can scar people.

I want to fly to see
birds, and airplanes also
to see stars in the night.
But when it rains I'll go
on top of the clouds.

Invitation to Wendy
Diana Vasquez

Come to the zoo. We would see a lot of animals like lions, tigers, and bears. But best of all we will see dolphins. So will you come with me?

Death
Ivan Gil

Death lives in the rainforest in
the tallest tree. Death looks like a
monkey with horns. Death wears metal around
him. Death feels anger for the other monkeys.
All day Death eats meat. I said to death, "why
are you mean." Death said, "because I don't
have any friends." I could tell death is a
monster.

Untitled
Jonathan Diaz

I remember going to Texas I saw my family.
I remember my family from Texas.
I remember my bird when I was in Texas.
I remember my Dad come with me to Texas.
I remember my dad and me and my brother come to Texas.
I remember come back to the house I saw a reindeer.
I remember going to my house we went to see my family.
I remember going to sleep because I was tired.

Love
Wendy Ramirez

Love is like a heart
Only Love is not a heart. Love
is like a flower only it is not a
flower. Love wears pretty dresses
all the time. Love feels soft when
he is touching my hand. All day
my heart jumps up and down when
Love is here. One day I said
to love why are you here.
Well I had come to play with
you Love came to say. You could
tell Love was nice not bad or
mean. Love was only here to
play. With me!

Community
Erick Blanco

One time I went to my dad's work and
he has a whole bunch of friends where
he works is very, very cold. It's like
in a refrigerator but colder. My
Dad always has to chop up meat.
And it's very hard work. But I helped
my dad and we got the work finished.

Untitled
Brian Garduno

We swim like dolphins all the way to the
bottom We jump and splash in the water
We dive from the deep We turn in circles

Untitled
Alejandro Gutierrez

There are 2 apples in the tree.
Two fall down on the ground
And get dirty. We wash them in the sink.

Untitled
Jose Escamilla

I am going to the beach tomorrow
I'm afraid I am going to drown
Throwing myself in the water.

A NOT Poem
Vania Gonzalez

I went to the hospital with my
favorite birthday dress. I looked at
the window I saw the zoo and
there was a trained dolphin jumping
in the water. Then I bumped my
head and I dreamed I was being
rich.

459

Untitled
Eduardo Ruvalcaba

A building with lots of
windows very tall and
two elevators goes fast
up a lot of people looking
out and seeing the city

a bird flying up
in the sky with blue
feathers going to his nest
to feed its children

I dreamed I was
flying like the bird

I Want to Be
Room 002 Class Poem

I want to be a super star
I want to be very smart
I want to be a net
I want to be a sun to melt the universe
I want to be small

I want to be an Alderwoman to make my community a better place, like
by picking up the garbage.
I want to be in a soccer team to hit all the balls and make a goal.
I want to be a strong person, but not so strong that I could carry a
building.
I want to be a famous A.C. Milan soccer player so the cheerleaders
could cheer for me and I'll score all the goals. I want to be a guinea pig
so I could be cute and fluffy and be free in the forest.

I wish I could be strong, but not so strong I carry something that weighs
infinity.
I want to be a girl that passes through fire. To grab the fire, and sleep on
fire. To help people. To play with fire. Even to save my family if my
house is on fire.
I want to be a big T-Rex so I can destroy buildings.
I want to be small, but not so small that no one would see me.

I want to be small like a bug to sneak up to my sister's room and steal
her stuff, but not so small that my mom can't see me and smashes me.
I want to be tall, but not so tall that everything looks small.
I want to be stretchable but not so stretchable that I can go to the
moon.

460

I want to be smart, but not so smart that my head will burst.
I want to be 12 so I can be tall.

I want to be a teacher so I can teach kids.
I want to be the smartest kid in the whole school, but not so smart that I
will lose my friends.
I want to be in school because I get to learn.
I want to be a game. I want to be a genius.
I want to be the craziest maniac, but not so crazy that I'll lose my
friends.

I wish I can be invisible, but not too invisible.
I want to be a genius, to know everything from the past history, like
mummies, pyramids, magic, genies, and how everything started.
I want to be a superstar, so I can give people my autograph and dress
like a rock star.
I want to ride in a limo, walk down the red rug.
I want to be little, but not so little that a tiny germ could be a giant to me.
I want to be a black pencil, so someone cool wrote with me the
Declaration of Independence and they put me on a jet to Egypt.

A Poem This Morning
Dessiray Trevizo

yesterday I tasted pumpkin seeds
yesterday I tasted lots of candies
yesterday I tasted pizza when we ate

yesterday I touched lots of candy
yesterday I touched lots of pumpkin
seeds when my mom got mad that
I made a mess.

yesterday I heard lots of music in houses.
yesterday I heard people having a barbe Q outside

yesterday I heard people saying trick or treat.

yesterday I heard people singing
saying trick or treat

Tonight
Robert Gontarz

Tonight I'm going to taste spicy Mexican rice.
Tonight I'm going to smell good food.
Tonight I'm going to see a funny movie.

Tonight I'm going to hear people laugh loudly
Tonight I'm going to feel very happy.

Untitled
Seleny Albor

Joy is playing with my friends.
Joy is playing with my baby sister
Joy is having fun.
Joy is reading a book.
Joy is seeing the flowers growing.
Joy is seeing the time changing to summer.

Airplane
Daniel Rodriguez

long
fast
white
sky
clouds

Dragon
Caesar Campos

Wings
large
teeth
tail
gold
sharp
nails
cool

Untitled
Janina Sanchez

I want to be a rabbit that could to hip hop. I want to be a bird that could
fly in the sky. I want to be a teacher so I could teach them so they could
be smart.
I want to be a doctor to help people. I want to be a butterfly so I could fly
through the sky all the way high in the sky. I want to be a guinea pig so I
could be so cute and fluffy. I want to be a frog so I could live in the
pond. I want to be a rainbow be all around the sky. I want to be a
panther be real fast. I want to be a singer so I could sing pretty and
dance pretty. I want to be a book so they could learn lots of things from
me. I tell people to care for everyone not just themselves.

462

Untitled
Edgar Gonzalez

I want to be black but not so black that black people hate me.
I want to be a boat sailing in the sea.
I want to be a jet flying fast as lightning.
I want to be cool.
But not so cool that everyone wants to hang out with me.
I want to be a pencil writing the Declaration of Independence.

Untitled
Joselino Guerrero

Plant plant
pink and green

A little boy
picking flowers for
his mother. Along
came a cowboy
with red and blue
clothes and hand-
some hat. "Come with
me to the bar
with me, Cabyero!"
The boy kept on
picking which he
had ear plugs
on his ears. A
few minutes
later came a
bull rock 'n
roller. come to
the farm to
throw rocks at
the bull. But
the boy could
not hear
he had ear plugs
on his ears. so
he went home.

Untitled
Alondra Andrade

Fear lives in the deep
blue sea.

Fear looks like a bear.

All day, Fear takes a
bath.

I said to Fear
be quiet.

I could tell fear was
mad at me.

Untitled
Jacqueline Padilla

Love lives in a big house.
Love looks like hearts.
love wears a suit.
All day, love walked his dog.
I said to love "hello!"
Love said "I beg your pardon."
I could tell love was a worker.

Untitled
Crystal Perez

Fear lives in our heart.

All day Fear is all around me.

Fear looks like a monster or a dark room.

I said to Fear I am not going to let you
win the happiness.

Fear said I will let you go.

Memory Calendar
Ruben Bernal

I remember when I found a big scorpion
I remember when I found a small plant
I remember when I found a ring in the dirt

Untitled
Laura Casimiro

      I remember when
       I had a mom I
remember when I was
in death I remember
when I wail about
my mom.

                I remember
                when I was
                gloomy when
                my mom left
                me when I was
                so little even
                I still miss her
                I does not matter
                I was about one month
                year old.

I remember when
I was cute I remember
when I was wee miniature minute
microscopic slight Love looks
happiness Loveness.

Untitled
Josue Acuna

Cranky city
Home for people
City of Chicago
A better place than new York
Good place
Only place with Sears Tower

Classroom
Stephanie Rodriguez

We are children. We are smart. We are
study. We are cool than other schools.
We memorize poem. We seats in
groups. We got two nice
teachers. We will soon go to
4th grade.

Untitled
Evelyn Avalos

balloons play
dancing in the hard music
outside go be crazy

Untitled
Janet Morales

sun light
going in lines
with dust inside

Untitled
Ruby Guzman

Alexsander My brother
is a cry baby He has
brown hair his skin is white

Untitled
Angel Artega

My mind is empty
I feel empty in my mind
Nothing in my mind

Untitled
Jose Lemus

A hotel is big and fancy
It has pretty rooms and soft sheets
the scent of it is fresh flowers
and the aroma of spaghetti

Black and White Bear
Janet Morales

The black and white bear swings and plays in
the park. He can't dance in a disco. He goes to
read books in the green jungle. Also he writes
poems about his life and living in a jungle. He
talks and talks about his world

being able to talk and being able to do things like humans. Also he goes to third grade and studies a lot.

Poem: A dream
Laura Casimiro

My grandpa took care of me
He gave me food
He gave me candy
He gave me toys and much more
But now he is in the sky he still
takes care of me. He watches me.
And soon or later I would be with
him in the sky and then I will
watch him.

I Want to Be
Room B15 Class Poem

I want to be green like Hulk because I can scare people that hate me and I can throw them far.
I want to be invisible but not so invisible that people can't see me.
I want to be fast but not so fast that I could scare people.
I like dogs because they can have puppies.

I want to be invisible but not so invisible that I can't see myself in the mirror and nobody can see me.
I want to be fast but not so fast that a race car, cheetah, and lightning seem slow.
I want to fly because when I see the birds it makes me want to fly.
I want to be big so I can play with my cousin.
I want to be fast like a cheetah because I don't want to be late for anything.
I want to be smart but not so smart that my brain is full of information and I can't remember things about me.

I want to be flying because I could go to Mexico to see my Grandpa and my Grandma.
I want to be fast but not so fast that nobody can see me run.
I want to be small but not so small that nobody can step on me.
I want to be invisible but not so invisible that they can't see me.
I want to be spider man for I could climb buildings and spin webs.
I want to be a fire fighter so I could stop the burning houses.

I want to be a bird so I can fly to the Sears Tower.

I want to be bigger than the Sears Tower so I can go to school in one step.
I want to be invisible so nobody can see me.
I want to be a superhero so I will be strong and help people.
I want to be a hero like Superman so that I can help people.
I want to be invisible but not gone.

I want to be tall but not so tall that houses look small.
Sometimes I want to be white but not so white that I could camouflage into the wall and no one could see me.
I want to be a smart boy so that I could create seventeen inventions in one day.
I want to be fast but not so fast that I will crash into a car and that I will miss a bus.
I want to be strong but not so strong that I can carry a car.
I want to be fast as a cheetah because if I don't people will kill me. Then I could eat other animals.

I want to be an artist to paint and make beautiful pictures so I could have money to buy a beautiful house so we can be really warm.
I want to be tall but not so tall I can't fit in my house.
I want to be strong but not so strong that I break a window while playing baseball.
I want to be smart but not so smart that I have nothing to learn.
I want to be a big rocket and carry astronauts.

Untitled
Mario Rivera

The leaves fall off the trees.
They feel soft.
They smell like trees.
They might taste like water.
They sound like the air.
Leaves feed the trees water and then
they fly from the trees.

The Most Wonderful Lake is Gone
Alan Santillan

Come back sweet
lake come back
wonderful lake
come back to
the empty
hole where the
dried up lake
disappeared

468

Untitled
Maximo Gamberale

I am
sorry
I have stepped
on your plant
I will make it
up to you I
will build
a seed for you.
Among your plant
lives the life of
death but I
will make it
up to you an
apple tree.

Eggs
Gabriela Garcia

I'm sorry for
eating your eggs
for breakfast but
they were so
delicious and better
than my eggs
and I forgot
the salt sorry
friend

Untitled
Madelyn Gonzalez

Death sounds like a skeleton
in a black cape. With glowing
red eyes. With a sigh shaped
like a knife. Death lives in
a cave. It lives on fire. Deep
in the Desert.

Untitled
Alejandro De La Cruz

Love lives inside of us.
Love looks like kiss your mom.

Love wears light and happiness.
All day Love is with me.
I said to Love you bring joy to me.
Love said to me you bring joy to me too.
I could tell Love was with me the
whole time.

Untitled
Victoria Rodriguez

Come friend we will go to the moon
to play with your dog.

Come brother we will go to
Mars to play soccer.

Come Mom we will go to
Cookieland to cook cookies.

Come dad we will go to
Jupiter.

Untitled
Gabriel Urquiza

Come to the moon father,
so we can fight aliens,
and to see how dark is over there,
Also we can float,
and see holes,
and see the earth.

Untitled
Salomon Navarro

I want to be invisible but not so invisible that I
will be gone forever and everybody will never see my
face again.

I want to be so fast that I will be faster than a
car, and don't have to ride the bus anymore.

I want to be weak but not so weak and can't
put my own foot on the stairs.

I want to be smart like a scientist and explore the
planets in the solar system, and look at the sun
and see if it's a star.

Untitled
Itzel Garcia

I remember going to Mexico
and eating cake at a party.

I remember playing hop-
scotch with my cousins.

I remember breaking a
piñata at a Christmas party.

I remember running to
school.

I remember climbing
a big tree.

I remember getting
candy at my house.

I remember hugging
my Grandma.

Memory Calendar
Blanca Cisneros

I remember going to Wisconsin to the pools
I remember playing at the water park
I remember going to Brookfield Zoo catching chipmunks
I remember going camping in the grange
I remember throwing fireworks at night
I remember planting flowers in my garden
I remember balloons hanging in my backyard at my birthday.
I remember breaking the piñata and throwing confetti
I remember going to my aunt's house and playing with my cousin.
I remember watching the stars by a telescope

Untitled
Ray Soto

Chicago is beautiful. So beautiful you can see
Houses all around. You can see
Ice in the winter. in the summer you can do
Cannonballs in the pool.
At night you could see some of the stars.
Go to Chicago it is very fun. In
October you could trick or treat.

471

The Two Brothers
Ismael Laboy

We laugh a lot. We
love a lot. We
have fun. We
play a lot. We

like our friends. We
like our food. Me
and my brother we
like each other.

Untitled
Hector Arellano

The sun is lighting
up. It shining in
the city.

Untitled
Clint Hernandez

the city was big
the city was cold
you could smell food in the city

Untitled
Rebeca Martinez

Tall, old Grandpa
he put alcohol on
my brother's hurt foot.

About a dog
Miguel Angel Ramos

A dog that bites
and a dog that plays
goes to sleep

I Want to Be
Room 104 Class Poem

I want to make fireworks for everybody in the world
and for the poor people in earth and for my family, my cousins and my
aunt.
I want to fly in the sky so I can go to the house of my friend.
I can invite my best friend to fly and go to the store and be invisible.
I want to be an angel because I could fly around and see
the other angels up in the sky and have wings
and have a white dress and white shoes.
I want to be a teacher so I can learn much because I like to play
teacher.

I want to be an astronaut so I can see
the beautiful planets. Because I will be on a space ship.
I want to be a ball so they could hit me.
I want to be a parrot so I can be many colors because I can fly.
I want to be a fish so I can discover all the things that are in the ocean.
Because maybe I can find shells to collect them.
Sometimes I want to be a toy and a triangle so other people could play
with me.

I want to be fast so I can catch the robbers when they are in the car or
in a motorcycle.
I want to be fast because when I play tag no one will tag me.
I want to be big but not so big because I can have a real car and I can
run the car.
I want to be small so I can go to space because I want to see the galaxy
and to see the sun shining and to float in space.

I want to be a singer. Why? Because I like to sing. I like to hear different
music and rock and roll, pop, and more. That's all.
I like to be invisible so I can go to school at night so I can read more
books.
And that I could fly so I could go high to the moon.
I want to be a cloud so I could see everything in the whole wide world.
I want to be invisible so I can go anywhere I want to. I can sneak in the
store and in the school.
I want to be an astronaut so I can see the planets because I could land
on the planets and see if the moon
is made out of cheese if it's made out of cheese I will eat it.
I want to be invisible because no one could see me at night when I'm at
school.

Untitled
Alejandro Duran

Memory is candy and juice at Halloween.
Memory is pizza and soda at pizza hut.
Memory is toys and food at the store.
Memory is turkeys at Thanksgiving.
Memory is roller coaster at Six flags.
Memory is food and presents at Christmas.

Untitled
Cesar Hernandez

I have broke
your car
that you like
I am very
sorry
but I didn't
mean to do it.
but my little
brother when
we were crossing
the street he
dropped it in
the street

Memory Calendar
Erica Hernandez

I remember going to Mexico.
I remember when I had friends.
I remember the first day of school.
I remember when I got a baby sister.
I remember when I learn to ride.
I remember going with my cousin to six flags great america.
I remember when I got glasses.
I remember my first day to the doctor.
I remember when I learn to talk.
I remember when I learn to walk.
I remember when I noticed my family.
I remember when my mom cut my hair.
I remember when I stop using Pampers.
I remember when I went to six flags and for first time I got to the Viper.
I remember when I learn to ride a bike.
I remember when I lost my first tooth.
I remember when I learn to draw.

Untitled
Diana Muñoz

Maricarmen ven ala luna,
Maricarmen vamos a jugar
vamos a la luna.

My Basketball Team
Maria Cervantes

We like to pass the ball to
our friends. We like to win. We throw
the ball. We score some times.
We lost but we don't care
because we know we can win them the next time

Untitled
Miguel Quiñonez

I dream I dream I was in a haunted house the house is
Haunted with ghost are different ghost
Are vampire and The houses
Scary and The ghost They can be
Everyone and They are scary
And they are powerful They are
Not people do not go to a haunted
Houses and They are strange things
If you die you are going to
Be a ghost.

Untitled
Gabriela Martinez

My dog is not big
As the tree, he
Don't drive a
Car, he don't
To call like the
People, he could
Not fly, he
Could not
Go to school

Dinosaur
Rigoberto De Alba

big
scary
fast
large

Untitled
Yesenia Pimentel

I taste the
soup it was warm
and I was cold

Untitled
Edgar Carrillo

Un perro es tavan en una casita comeno
Comino des pasito en su casita comeno comino
Des pasito.

Untitled
Beatriz Cervantes

Dad take me downtown
the river was not blue it was
green Why?

Untitled
Paola Reyes

Yesterday was raining
I could not sleep because
the storms.

Last Night and This Morning
Room 401 Branch Class Poem

I saw a big plane
I touched my hamster when I got up
I heard my bird singing
I saw my brothers eating breakfast
I smelled a tree

476

I saw a baseball game on TV
I touched the glass to drink my juice
I saw my mom sitting in bed
I tasted cereal for breakfast
I tasted the candy
I heard the wind whistling in my ears
I tasted a rainbow
I saw a fluffy white dog barking at a mailman because he threw a paper inside the
        house
I saw my mom making breakfast in the kitchen
Yesterday I heard my mom singing
I saw a bird through my living room window
I tasted the hot dog on the train
I couldn't complain
I saw some kids trick or treating on Halloween night
I saw beautiful roses that were very red
I felt my red fish when I cleaned his bowl
I heard my bunny eating his carrot in his cage
I heard my dog barking
I saw kids playing with a black and white ball at the park
I touched my dog's soft and puffy fur

In My Life
Michelle Ventura

I felt my heart beating.
I didn't know what to do.
I saw a rainbow this morning I
thought I was dreaming guess I was
not. I smelled the flowers through
the sky. I tasted my self living. I
heard bird twuitwl. I felt happy.

Poem
Yahara Martinez

Sweetness is -- like
tasting a peach in the
country side with a full
smile.

Joy is -- having a party with
all your friends in there
house dressed nice.

memory is -- thinking of
your family in a wedding
seeing all the great
fun it was that day.

Sadness is -- a girl with
a frown wearing a dress
in a park sitting on the
ground because she
fell off a swing.

Poem
Cristina Cruz

Sadness is tears dripping down a baby's cheek
with eyes as the color of the ocean
with tears the color of glass
with sweetness and joy
like the leaves falling in fall
warm and soft
like the wind blowing on the trees
when the memory comes back
with sweetness and sadness at the
same time

The grass hopper
Noel Tellez

ho grass
hopper so
green

I wish you would
come back
with your
cool colors

your wings are
yellow and
I miss you
so much so please
come back old green
grasshopper

Flower
Iliana Gonzalez

Along
the
bright
green
grass

soft
and
yellow
petals

under
the
sun

lives
the
brightest
flower

Untitled
Elias Gutierrez

Sorry for not inviting you
to my party and not telling
you and forgetting all
the fun you didn't have.

My Happiness
Denise Munoz

I am happier than ever
I want to celebrate my happiness
I am too happy but not enough
I want to fly up in the sky
I wish to be a bird to fly and enjoy my happiness
I have never been so happy
It is hard to compare when I am sad
I have this joy inside I can't take it out
I don't want to be sad and mad
I want to remain the way
I am right now
I can't explain my joy and happiness

Untitled
Jennifer Valdez

I wish to be an angel.
So I could fly.
And so I can fly fast to the sky.
I wish to be smart but not too smart.
I'm nice but not too nice.
I will like to fly away.
But not always.
I wish wish wish to be a very
good angel and go everywhere I
want to go.

Love Is
Omar Vega

Love lives in a kingdom love
looks like a fire love wears
red clothes love is taking
naps I told love what
do you do and it said
I am burning up inside love
was burning red.

Excitement
Fidel Trejo

Excitement looks like a tall boy
with spiky hair. He jumps up and
down every day every hour every
minute every second. He jumps to
get coffee every hour. He lives in
a big brick house. He has a swimming
pool and he jumps up and down in it
and it's full with coffee.

Untitled
Juan Carlos Mendoza

Anger lives in a house with gates

Anger looks like an angel with red
hair, blue eyes
Anger wears T Shirts

All day, anger yells

I said to anger get over it

anger said no

I could tell anger was mad at me

Feelings
Group Poem

Sadness is tears dripping down
a baby's cheek. Love looks like joy
and full of surprises and fun. Joy is a
mom and a little girl hugging each other
in the garden. Anger can't explain what
he feels inside. Joy is a girl skipping
in a field full of flowers with roses,
indigo, and tulips. Sadness is like a
baby angel crying.

Untitled
Cristal Zavala

Come Carlos
Come to the great fields
But Carlos can't not hear.

Carlos come to the magic world.
But Carlos can't not hear.

Carlos come to star world.
But Carlos can't hear from
all the way of that hill.

Carlos come to town
But Carlos it is too far and
can't hear.

Cleaners
Victor Mata

We clean Late. We
fix straight. We

Take Breaks. We
go back. We

ride safe. We
get home. We

come back. We
get to work.

My Not Poem
Esther Meza

My house is not a smelly
old damp house. My house
does not have a purple,
green, and orange computer.
My house is not dirty with
mud and dust all over the
floors and doors. My house
does not move or fall with
just a sound it is strong
not super weak. My house
is my home and I won't
change it for any other junk home.

Bunnies
Angelica Ortiz

Had you seen
a black and red
bunny that wears
tight blouse and
very tight pants?

he may look
weird and kind
of funny but
really nice inside

You may not
judge him cuz
of his style.
You're going
to have to
deal with
it cuz
he don't
care!

Not Poem
Liliana Arellano

The bakery is
not far like the stars
The old clothes are not
torn or not worn since
I was born. The pandas
from China are not green or
or aqua green like the fish at the
sea. The girl does not dream
of a black sea. But of a blue green
sea.

Untitled
Jesus Torres

A duck coming
out of the water
and scaring a little boy

Untitled
Crystal Torres

My puppy sleeps
With me in the
Cool weather!

Untitled
Mirna Azpera

Tasting dust in the desert
It felt like pebbles
in my mouth

Tai-Chi
Juan M. Guerrero

riding up
a tree. falling,
flipping, seeing
blurry on my
way down.

HANNAH G. SOLOMON ELEMENTARY
Principal: Susan Moy
Teachers: Ms. Goode, 5th, Ms. Jones, 4th, Ms. Liu, 6th

Marvin Tate, Poet in Residence

A widely published poet and performer, Marvin Tate merges poetry with music. He has performed his work at the Wicker Park Poetry Fest, The Knitting Factory (New York City), Old Town School of Folk Music, Nuyorican Poet's Cafe (New York City), Lollapalooza concert, Iowa University, and others.

484

Credit Card Debt
  Sean R.

i have to pay this big bill
i do not know what to do
i think I'm going to run up the hill
if i could get rid of debt
these people are really mean
i hope this suit does not make
me look fat the billers' name
is dean i will go hunt him down
i will get in his sight i will buy
this crown(that's the reason
i'am here in the first place)
we will have a match a fight
i will beat him and now he owes me
oow !

Sleep
Emmy M.

sleep is like black hair
growing from your bed
you're scared it will wrap
you up whenever you sleep
you think of it so you don't
want to fall asleep
legends say that if you don't
think it is true then you become
beyond and then you're dead

Sad Day
Keenen H.

outside
on one knee
looking around to see
what happen
maybe a crash
an injury ?
it's sad
on my porch
i wonder
what happen?
stop the violence
it's not right

Nursing Home
Frank G.

as i passed the new brick nursing home
i heard coughing and perhaps a soccer game
from inside i felt sorry for the old people
they can't enjoy life like us anymore
those that have the strength to walk
are outside looking at an ally cat
they really like visitors

Spelling Bee Blues
Sharif K.

i didn't win
the spelling bee
but that's alright
i did my best
it don't mean I'm a pest
i just didn't win
the spelling bee

i didn't win
the spelling bee
i wish my parents could've seen me
i misspelled THRESHOLD
but i didn't cry
i stood bold

Blues
Jimmy T.

blues are a meaning
blues are a strong breeze of wind
blues go wild often

Spring is Coming
Giovanni P.

ice and snow vanish
teams will be playing baseball
birds are singing now

Melting
Ethan V.

the snow is melting
there is a change in the air
i can see more green

Untitled
Tasha V.

one long boat
    ride
rain, rain
slowing down
the boat ride
is slower the rain
is slower going, going
gone

Time
David D.

every second you move
minutes passing by
like a speeding race car
you can't seem to sooth anyone
you are so far from mankind
stuck in school you wish
you could move faster
that's not cool some people
think you're a disaster
tic toc toc toc toc toc
we can't stop time
you are like a mime
every time you tic we age
you cause so much rage

Weather should be better
Jessica V.

today is gloomy
it's dark outside
th leaves are falling
in a swirl like a ride

i hate this weather
it's not getting any better
i wish someone could change it
to make it much nicer

if only it could be sunny
this is a bother everyone
would be happier if they could
play in nicer weather

Death
Sawson A.

death is
a joyous thing
it brings pain and sorrow
it can bring happiness
it is slow
and time consuming
slow, slow not amusing
but quite confusing
it happens to relatives
and friends it'll never end
it never ends
everyone has to die
no matter what we do
everyone, even me and you
this death, it'll never end
happens to relatives, family
and friends

Time is Clicking Away
Kanchan P.

second by second
time clicks away   sometimes
it goes by   fast   when it slows
i hear the crows
clocks come in different shapes
and sizes YET time stays the same
we can not lock time
time is not to be tamed
clicking away
time goes fast
it's slippery like holding jello
in your bare hands we couldn't STOP
time even if we tried

there the clock stands
clicking second by second
day by day

The Orange
Amera A.

the color orange is bright
nicer than the sky, the water
the night when i see orange
i feel like i can fly
orange makes me feel cool
calm and relaxed
i can hold it in my palm
it can be printed or faxed
it's gracefully but sometimes
it can be hateful the color orange
better than the best

My Violin Class
TashaViets V.

the teacher is talking
to a student am listening
unexpected sounds
a dreaded sound
an unwanted fact
feel the eyes staring
laughter breaking
through their mouths
i' am laughing too
as if i wasn't the one
who farted

Poem
Chelsea V.

walking home
i see a dead possum
going in a different path
the possum was ran over
it's skin is peeled back
bugs flying tasting it's meat
feeling the cool air
your hair moves back
and forth you see rocks

in all sizes you see
your shadow the skin
from the possum
two steps later
you enter my house

Blue
Laith K.

blue is the sea
blue are blue berries
and fairies
blue is the sky
up so high
blue are some eyes
blue berry pie
it's my favorite color blue
i wear blue and so do you
gives you a clue
of what to do
to find my favorite color

My friend's blues
Amber K.

ooo my friends
my cooool
but they are not my friends
oooo that's so sad
once they called you fat
that wasn't so bad
oooooooo
that's my time
with my friends
boo boo boo
okay then
ooooooooooooo

Stranger
Amera A.

we're sitting
on the bench
a stranger comes up
he is preaching
he is tall and scary

i hear the thumping
of his shoes he really has
the blues whisp whisp
hear the swishing of the trees
buzz buzz buzz hear the buzzing
of the beads i have met
a stranger

Untitled
Sharif K.

on a nice cold day
i decided to take a new way home
i want to go home and play
in my room i notice the cold air
blowing a strong breeze
leaves flying on this nice cold day
sweet taste of ice cream truck
drives by i hear a crunching sound
leaves and gas another truck drives by
i finally reached home and ate
delicious food i walked a new way home
on a nice cold day

Downstairs Neighbor
Davidn D.

downstairs neighbor
couldn't hold his liquor
wet his pants like a scared monkey
chalkboard faces attacked him
his mind went crazy wet
his pants again threw up
on his wife got kicked out
the house

Flash Light
Mila S.

the flashlight died
of diabetes and girls
he couldn't handle them
all at once and so he popped
confusion and he weighed too much
and so he died

Flash Light
Hannon H.

the flash light died
ontop of mt. rushmore
saturday march 42, 1842
his mom cried all day
his sister was glad
and partied all day
it died of the chicken pox
before it ate 80,000,000
cherry pies and won second place
at mt. rushmore national pie eating contest
at the funeral everyone cried
except his sister and her cousin
who did everything the sister did

Flash Light
Keenan H.

the flash light died
his wife left him
she used him
and so his heart
was broken
he'd become pitiful
and had an heart attack
i was sad very sad

Skeleton Blues
EthanViet V.

i have the skeleton blues
am falling down
an evil clown pushed me
i' am staring at the clown
with the red nose and blue lips
he's giving me candy
nasty jello this clown
will not stop pushing me down
i have the skeleton blues
it won't let me snooze
skeleton blues
holds me down

A Street
Senit K.

wet
from the rain
dark
spooky and dusty
silent and soundless
moonlight shining down
on me dumpsters and garages
something is falling on me
look around and nothing
is there

Street
Soobin K.

a party is going on
in the streets
the streets are busy
people riding bikes
a parade is present
people buy at the store
a man stands in the middle
of the street wearing a hat with feathers
he looks happy maybe
he has a special gift
this street is always busy

Rose
Rose C.

pretty rose
pretty rose
just like you
pretty rose pretty rose
just like my family
pretty rose pretty rose
just like my friends
my teacher
me
pretty rose

I Have A Dream
Kanwal L.

i have a dream
i have a dream
to see my wings
i want to snooze
not loose I WANT TO fly
high in the sky eat cotton candy
the i go easier to the place
wave at other angels I CAN FLY
my teacher in the sky
show them around
show them my wings
i look so pretty in the sky
than i do on earth
i visit all the planets
am not cold on pluto
am not in a mercury

The Flash Light
Marlon W.

the flash light
died
        of starvation
he also had diabetes
never took his medicine
he once found Ben Laden
with his bright light
getting in girl clothes
and panicked people
mistake him for a mule
and they run

Drunk
Anton G.

the downstairs neighbor
unable to hold his liquer
wet his pants wet as a lake
chalkboard erasers attacked
the yellow panted man
unable to think too dizzy
threw up on his wife she
kicked him out

494

Poem
Ajka K.

the flash light died
he used batteries that
were cheap he suffred
from flash light cancer
in the past he rescued
a team of flash lights
but got scared

The Stranger
Alexandra C.

walking
down
the
steep hill
listen
to the people
kidnapping
my home
is the stranger

Things Around
Matthew

look at everything around
come and explore
there's a lost and found
behind the door
learn new things
there is a fountain
read about a book that has wings
look outside at a mountain
there's a man underneath my bed
a stranger said
someone hit me with a bat
a ball flew at me
i once charged a battery with l-wat
ran and hit a tree

Jealous Poem
Krupa P.

i know why blue berries
are jealous of strawberries
because they have a nice
red color except blue berries
are blue but strawberries taste better
they are different maybe the the seeds
are different
blue berries are jealous
of strawberries because more people
like strawberries better i know why too
i've never seen anyone eating blueberries
when i go to the store with my parents
i think to myself you could think different too

SCHOOL OF ENTREPENEURSHIP AT SOUTH SHORE CAMPUS
Principal: Bill Gerstein
Teacher: Ms. Matti, 11th

Pam Osbey, Poet in Residence

Pam Osbey is an accomplished vocalist, author, and spoken word artist who has been teaching poetry in the Chicago Public Schools for three and a half years. Author of three poetry books and one of the Poetry Center's 2004 Gwendolyn Brooks Poetry Award receipents, she continues to work as a freelance writer focusing on health, business, and self-reflective articles. She has performed at ETA Theatre, South Shore Cultural Center, Center for Inner City Studies, and abroad in Wisconsin, St. Louis, Texas, and New York. She has been has been a featured spoken word artist on Artistfirst, The Reading Circle, Power Talk FM, Higher Ground with Jonathan Overby and "The Peoples Station" in Waterloo, IA. In March 2005 she released her third book of poems entitled, *Black Orchids: a journey to mocha.*

"Being my second year at South Shore, I was delightfully surprised by the diversity in the classroom this past year. We have had our challenges - the block schedule, the learning of new techniques in writing poetic forms like pantoums, free verse, Italian Sonnets, and being exposed to poets like Tupac Shakur, Pablo Neruda, Shang, Alicia Keys, Maya Angelou and others. I want to commend students on not giving up when they were confused about a poem and being able to thoroughly state their point of views in poems. I especially want to thank the entire staff of The School of Entrepreneurship for their partnerships, especially Mr. Gerstein and Ms. Matti for continuing to reinforce the basics of this wonderful program. And the students for their creativity, their drive, their diverse language and being able to use different rhythms, syntax, rhyming, personification, metaphors, and other poetic ways to put their feelings on a page for all to see. Thank you for daring to be different and thinking outside of the box. I wish you nothing but continued exploration of the worlds around you. Let this be your step into a new world that may be your purpose later on in life!"

Poetry is Me Poetry is You
Fourth Period Group Poem

Poetry is me poetry is you.
About deep thoughts and feelings that never come through.
Poetry is knowledge and understanding, emotional, feelings of song and life.
Poetry is feeling poetry is the things that goes in people lives.
Poetry is everyday life, poetry is something you live and die.
With poetry is more than just rhyming, it's something you should feel.
> Poetry is like me missing a shot playing basketball.
> I can't accept failure, but I can keep trying.
Trying to play like poetry getting and every bad thing in life to make an great shot.
What is poetry?
> Poetry is free as the day's fresh air.
> Like a husband and wife's babies bottom bare.
> Like the sun and the moon entwined.
> Like the love of Jesus and the love of his wine.
> Like the sun rises and shines.
I'm poetic and will always be.
> I can feel poetry.
> Poetry is love.
> Poetry is hate.
> Poetry is magic.
> Poetry is a new love.
> Sometimes poetry can be pain.
Like when you lose a best friend.
But to me, poetry is a way to express your feelings and lift you up.
> Poetry is a way to express love.
> Poetry is a way to express your love.

Black Child
by Derell G., Charles W. and George T. III

Some say you're the color of dirt.
Some say you're the color of mud.
Some say you're used as clowns
and we wonder why we can't be understood.

Don't nobody wanna die.
But everybody wanna ball.
But somebody gotta go.
When the killa's get called.

We're all like one.
So let's stand up as a Nation.
Some people different, some with similiar faces.

498

Everyone chasing that same old dream.
Chasing platinum and ice and smoking weed.
But black child stay in your books and
we all know you will succeed.

The City of Greatness
Carl B.

I wish to explore the special very talented streets
of New York.
I want to live in New York and be what it has destined for me.
I want to breathe the gift it has in store for me.
It's also part of my destiny to witness the New York struggle
and emerge from it with New York Greatness.
After I'm trained by New York, surely my face will smile at citizens of
New York from highlights and the side of New York buses.
On my journey to New York, I will prepare myself to be known.
My goal is to set a goal to be a shining start known by not only
New York...
But the rest of the world so New York will prepare
not only me but also the world to be ready to fill my wrath
of Glory, Victory and surely Greatness.

Mississippi, My Home
Niesha R.

I miss the way I wake up to my home
and Mississippi.
Smelling the fresh green country side Mississippi.
My home town just sitting here watching people
walk by.
Kids playing and feeling the hot summer heat.
Older people walking together.
Older people playing their country music.
Some fishing...and the pond.
The big steamy catfish frying on the stove.
Fresh picked greens.
I just sitting here watching the bird fly
by flying south for the winter.
Sitting here watching the tree blow
and the wind just sitting.
Thinking about how it feels to leave the city.
My home town Mississippi!
Just sitting watching the sunset with the
yellow and orange going down.
I can see it now.
When you see it, you can cry, "Mississippi, my home town!"

I Used To Love b
LaTronya W.

Love:
strong affection for another
warm attachment
devotion
admiration

       I used to write poems of
love that how this person had been sent
from above. The way it made me feel
to speak and write of what we had.
Now writing love poems just make me mad.

                Hatred
                Rage
                The feeling of
                Betrayal
                The new found pain
                Sunny days now
                Rain
                I feel the strain
                In my heart

The love poems were specifically wrote for you.
Talking of how you did something you do.
Love is no longer.
Without it, can I grow stronger?
Without...felt strange at first.
Things only got worst.
There were the symptoms plain as day

Depression
Stress
Anxiety
Jealousy
Envy
Jealousness
How could I live without you?
Why did we part?
What happened?
Can I make it right?
Let's do it over from the start.

The more we were apart the better
I become, now I feel...

Joy
Peace
Happiness
No more pain
No more stress
Yes!
I'm blessed
No more strain
                        Depression
                        Confusion

No more
                Jealousy

I'm happy on my own, I found a new one..
It all begins with me.

I Used to Write About Myself
DeMario A.

Myself...myself, young sexy fine.
Tall, built, smart, silly, funny...

                Outgoing..
                Huh, that was
                when myself was nice!

Who writes about myself?
That man whose teachers who have nothing good to say .

                Mean...
                Backstabbing..
                Double-crossing tall.
                Always talking
                                Stupid!
                Not learning.
                Anything fight all the time..

Stayed in jail still on parole
when he gets off nobody knows but
when he do...
                I tell him start writing about
                yourself and move.
                Then everybody will know about
                myself and more...Get it together!

Hood Blues
Jason O.

Everyday is a struggle for everyone that lives here.
The sound of gunshots still ring in my little ear.
Everything ain't all good and we ain't living fine.
It seems some of us commit crimes just to past the time.
Sometimes you get caught in a sticky situation.
And fighting is the only way to resolve the problem your facing.
My whole life I learned the hard way to spot liars.
And it seems like it's usually the ones that's right by you.

Different day...same stuff.
Ain't nothing good in the hood.
I'd run away from it and never come back if I could.
But I can't.
So everyday I just...must survive!
And fight for my life, justice and pride.

Weary Blues: The Stranded One
Chamerlon C.

Driving down the highway one Friday night.
I couldn't help but notice the sad time.
It made me pull over.
That turned out to be a mistake.
As my car died on me, my head started to ache.
The tune kept playing.
I now could find myself relating to it.
I might as well see where this is coming from.
I saw this club at the next exit.
The open door looked inviting.
So I went and found a seat.
Another soulful moan came from the piano keys.

> Ain't going to cry no mo'
> No mo' tears will be shed
> Goin' be easy on myself
> No mo' blood will be bled

As soon as the tune stopped.
So did the darkness of night.
I went to call me a tow truck
to solve this ridiculous plight.

The American Blues
Abdul B.-Y.

The American Blues is full of people who haven't paid their dues.
Nowadays in America, people are created to lose.
Everyday on the news we see another death.
There goes another child's mother or father who they never met.

We're fighting a war, not just in Iraq.
While back in America we're rewarding these political hacks.
The governments worried about Hip Hop Music.
And the way our American people use it.
As an American citizen, I have the blues.
Cause I see our government continues to use.
What I don't understand is that the government has time to complain
about Hip Hop violence.
While they do nothing to stop the death of kind, being nice.
The American Blues are on us cause the government's here.
The jokes on us.

Untitled
Donald G.

There are many thoughts in my head that have yet to be born.
Explored; rewarded by intuition.
My thoughts aren't graded by institutions.
I think on why my love has never come.
Some thought on education.
Were rewarded with elevation.
The thoughts of every wise man and woman run through my head.
I bleed with thoughts of mischief.
Souls of salvation.
Thoughts of reparations.
Caused by my mom's dislike for my Pops.
So I am caused to think of deeper thoughts
that are fought by every white man.
Just let me think...just let me think!

Pen-Ology
Adia J.

I use my pen to get my thoughts through
when times is hard
and when my burdens getting heavier.

My pen is like my life
without it I would be nothing.
I can use my pen to move mountains

and uplift the unliftable.

Without a pen in my life
I would have no thought train.
Things would be leading me in
all types of wrong directions.

With my pen I'm in power.
I'm able to climb the highest tower.
Overcoming all the down falls and
dodging all the blows life throws my way.

U Ripped Us Apart
(dedicated 2 my father & Cancer)
Brittany K.

I wish you wouldn't ever came into our lives.
I wish you would have just let us be.
I wish you would have thought about the affects it would have on us.
I wish you would have chose someone else.

Why couldn't you let him be?
You let him get so helpless to the point
he wouldn't get out of bed.
He didn't even want me to see him.
His own child...
You took my father away from me in a blink of eye.

Cancer is what they say you are.
But to me you are the devil.
How could something take someone's father
without even thinking twice about it.
My father was good to everyone but I guess
you didn't see that, uh?
My father stayed in the hospital for one week and left me.
I didn't even get to say my last goodbyes.
Why couldn't you just let him be?
You know what though..I"m not even going to cry.
For I know you can't help who you are.
Cancer is what you are.
And in my mind, you can be stopped.

It's only up to God.

Like The Rest
Daja N.

Like the soulful cry
of a child in the night
being beaten and broken
out of spite.
Not knowing where life
will take her next.
Hopefully she won't end
up like the rest.
Dancing for dollars on
into the night.
Turning tricks because
her man said it was right.
This poor young girl is throwing
her life away.
Doing everything that
her supposed man says.
Is it her fault that it turned
out this way?
All because no one had nothing to say.
Her father was the reason that she
ran away.
All of this and still nothing
to say.
If he didn't go up to her room that
night.
Do you think this would have
happened out of sight?
Maybe she wouldn't have ran
into that club.
And ended up dancing on the
lap of a thug.
This poor young girl is now two months
pregnant.
Now trying to leave the game, now trying
to end it.
Too late what a shame!
They found her body
floating in the lake.

Too bad all this happened
out of one father's mistake.

The Magic Wand
Branick G.

My wonder, my world.
My little old magic wand.
It's name is "Pen".
He can create many things about me
and/or the world.
Right now, he is already spreading his
magic in this poem.

But I have to say that Pen's true power
 is the ability to create characters, worlds, fantasies.
Drawing is Pen's true power.
His true ability to me.
Me and Pen creates a wonder of drawings and what's not.

Pen and me is a true team.
I would be nothing without Pen.
He is my best friend.
Cartoons is in my mind
all the time, but they all locked up.
My pen pal frees them all.
I love to draw every time
I feel down, angry, bored, or interested.
I grab Pen and get to drawin'.
This is truly a magic wand of power.

Beautiful In My Mind
Theresa B.

Short, dark brown and brown eyes with many pimples.
So what?
I'm beautiful in my own my mind.
In my mind I chose to be tall, dark brown with light
brown eyes and smooth skin. I am beautiful.
My selection is to be a strong but not weak doctor..
To make it through college and not give up and be poisoned.
I am beautiful and strong in my mind and that
is my selection for life.

We Are
Ebony L.

We are black and beautiful.
There are all of so many kind
of people that is African American.

That are beautiful and their own way.
We can make a difference.

There are thousands of Blacks in America.
As we live here and take part in this life
we make a difference on the world.
We have a right to do what we want and when we won't.

We can make a difference.

We are all different.
There are some that get locked up.
There are some that just get killed but everyday we get strong.
And we get born.
There are more than one and two of the us that
is important.

We can make a difference.

The Light Blue Sky
Eric W.

As I look into the light blue sky.
I think of the times I've asked the lord for repentance.
The times I was blind and could not see.
The times when I thought I was too young to be.

To be without the knowledge of heaven and hell.
I sometimes felt stuck in a broken cell.
I now have the wisdom to be where I see.
Up in heaven with God beyond the light blue sky.

In times I lose faith.
But the lord keeps me on the path heading straight.
If I knew I could not make it to spend eternity with him.
I'd sit and cry and whine until the end of time.

And look into the light blue sky.

Because Black Bangers
Dameon W.

Boys be banging black.
Bangers bring bank.
Older blacks be blaming because younger blacks be belligerent.
Blacks be beefing like a barbeque until black bangers start
busting...

Boys turn into men.
Books in book bags turn into bricks in book bags.
Because bank is all boys worried about.
Banging on blocks be bewildering to other blacks
because black on black crime be belligerent.

Say "Thankgiving" Scream it out!
Chanelle M.

Everybody's happy and cheering
with big smiles to come and with a great greeting.
You've just seen Little Tammy in her toddler changes.
Now she's four and going through the Barbie and Barney
stages.
Rolls, turkey, dressing, gravy, and cranberry sauce.
These things that I am grateful for and would be sad
if I lost.
To lose what you love will forever feel great.
So please just be thankful on the Thanksgiving date.
If you can spell it you'll see what the T, and G meaning
in Thanksgiving.
Thanking God is what it's about.
Say "Thanksgiving", scream it out!

Ode to My Granny
Sabrina W.

How much I miss you.
I miss the way we would sit back watch T.V. and relax.
Now I have to talk to you over the phone.
Cause you're long away from home.

You went to Pine Bluff, Arkansas.
Now you're spending all your extra time with
grand dad.
I miss the way you used to say "Bina get yo butt off the corner!"
when it was about Four in the morning.
Me not knowing you was thinking about my safety.
Man, I miss your cooking.
I always used to say that Granny was my best friend till the end
and I really mean it now.
I miss those times we used to just be talking about anything.
You would tell me all the stories that you going..and I would
tell you my day and how I think God sent you to me.
I just want to say I think you're my Angel, Granny.

508

The Secrets
Lakia B.

I have a box in my head that must be closed.
I felt that my life depends on this.
My hopes, dreams, and my goals.
I don't want it to get out to the world.
Cause I'm still a little shy.
I'm only a girl.
As I grow into the woman I want to be.
I could tell you and you can tell me.
The secrets that we hold to secrecy.
I know I will grow out of my shame.
But never will I get rid of all my pain.
So until I give you the key.
You just be you.
While I just be me.
The secrets I kept
I can't let free.

Looking Out The Window
Akeem B.

My life is like an open book.
Sometimes it can be a lot of fun.
Then other times it makes you want to run.
But it is not as bad as it look.
Everything I know I've took.
Though I didn't force with a gun.
But with my tongue.
So don't look at me as a crook.
Everyone learns from their mistakes.
Though some never learn.
But remember this "its" never too late.
So let the past burn.
I hope who's ever reading my Sonnet
Gets one thing from it that, "What you give...is what you get!"

WILLIAM HOWARD TAFT HIGH SCHOOL
Principal: Dr. Arthur Tarvardian
Teacher: Ms. Asvos, Director, Gifted and Talented Program

Daniel Godston, Poet in Residence

Daniel Godston received his M.F.A. at Mills College and his B.A. at the University of Michigan. In addition to teaching through the Poetry Center of Chicago's *Hands on Stanzas* Program, he teaches composition and literature through Columbia College Chicago's English Department, and creative writing and other art forms through the Office of Community Arts Partnership's arts integration program. Daniel also plays the trumpet in a few local jazz ensembles.

Memo
Nichole B.

Memo plus rize equals
memorize.

Memo plus ries equals
memories.

Memories—a big part
of our lives.

Since your first broken leg
or your worst nightmare
they'll always be with you.

No matter where, who, or what you are,
they will haunt you forever.

Bee-You-Tee-Full
Anna C.

Rapunzel, you may say,
had the longest hair of all.
but is that really what you see?

The length is not only what I see,
for length is merely one piece of its beauty
how tough, yet gentle the hair can be,

like a daisy in the morning dew,
hair so golden and full of life, you tip
from the rain that runs from the shower.

It's long and straight from the way it lays,
like the ruler I use in math.
But unlike that ruler you give off a wonderful scent.

The oils that lay atop my head
give off wonderful smells like
when my mother cooks spaghetti.

Like Medusa's hair, the serpents warn you off.
The men stay away, they know that so
much beauty is too much for them to grasp.

So the next time I look in the mirror
I will not take your beauty for granted,
for it is so beautiful I cannot forget it.

Yugoslavia
Carolina C.

I walk toward my apartment
In every place I step
A tear was shed
A drop of blood was shed

I walk toward my apartment
Praying it is still there
Hoping it is still there
Realizing it might be gone

I walk toward my apartment
Hoping that all my possessions are there
Hoping all my daughter's things are there
Hoping everything is untouched

I walk up the steps to my apartment
Hoping I'll get in
I walk toward my apartment
And try to open the door, locked
I walk toward my apartment
And try the key, locked

I walk away from my apartment
Realizing it's gone
I walk away from my apartment
Knowing I can't get in
I walk away from my apartment
Knowing it is stolen

I walk away from my apartment
Knowing it is lost

Death Before Life
Ashley C.

In the murky fluid
my innocent body floating, not
a breath of air had filled my lungs
and it seemed that was the way
you wanted it to stay

Yes, you fed me, led me to a life
you almost ended. I will never forgive you
for what you did on that day
that I saw my life flash before my eyes
even before my life really started

512

I hadn't even felt the air, for the weight
of the world weighed more, and yet
you put mom and dad through so much worry;
you wrapped yourself around me

Waiting for a straight line,
we might as well have cut you then,
left me without a button, for you
had almost killed a life that not had yet lived

Ice in My Veins
Michelle D.

I feel ice flowing through my veins,
freezing my heart, closing me up.
I sit in my darkness, my abyss,
the ice getting closer, crawling up my skin,
freezing my soul, suffocating my heart,
so cold, strong, and hateful. The pain
flows away through my numbed body,
as the ice takes me away from
heartache and into a pain-free land.

Lungs
Andrei D.

One of the largest organs in the human body, you expand every
    time I breathe,
You are shaped like two huge trenches covered with blue and red.
You help me breathe and supply energy that I need.
Without you, I'd be dead, for you take in oxygen and supply
    many things. You supply purple blood cells with oxygen and turn them
    back into live-looking red ones.
You supply our muscles with oxygen so that they have energy.
Surrounded by the heart, stomach, liver, and kidneys, you're the organ
    that stands out the most.
Praise to you, lungs—you work hard each day, and take in 25-30
    inhalations a minute.
Praise to you, lungs—you take in oxygen and then I exhale carbon
    dioxide so plants can grow.
Praise to you, lungs—you keep our bodies going and keep us
    from getting dizzy.
Set inside the ribcage, you are as protected as the heart.
Dear blue-red friend, I'm so afraid of asthma that might make dust
    irritate you.
I'm so afraid of pneumonia that fills your air sacs with infection and
    keeps the air from going to the blood cells so they can rejuvenate.

I'm so afraid of cancer that destroys you from the inside out.
I'm so afraid of tuberculosis that fills people up with blood and makes
  them cough the blood up.
I'm so afraid of drowning—filling you up with water, fatal for both of us.
You do so much for me every day, what no one else does.
You are an organ that is so important you should be hailed as a king.
For you have a power that no human has to keep us going.

Ice Volcano
Huan D.

Ice blasting out, freezing the land.
Cool isn't enough, ice is everywhere.
It's the only thing I see. The world shakes,
It's time to erupt, ice mountain explodes.
All thanks to the ice volcano.

Frozen Water
Elizabeth G.

I hate water. It's not as innocent as it seems.
It can drown you. It freezes over making ice.
Ice is just as bad as water. When it snows
I want to go outside and make it all melt.
When it rains the snow turns into
disgusting slush. I hate it with a passion.

Through My Eyes
Sheila M. G.

I wake up and look around,
thanking God I still have another day of life.
Many people in other places of the country
are being robbed day and night.

When I go to the capital I bring no valuable objects.
For once I brought these beautiful gold earrings,
I turned around and found that my earrings were gone!

It was not fair, life is not fair.
But when you live in places where the only way
to survive is by robbing. What else can you do?

We ask for help, they give us nothing!
The rich could care less for they are safe and sound.
Day by day, night by night, I am alert,
for anything can happen through my eyes.

Green Eyes
Simon H.

you tell a story through your eyes, see inside people
know so many things others don't
because you've seen them through your eyes
live a hundred years with your eyes
your eyes of bright green like limes
or eyes so clear blue like a ghost looking at you
or eyes ringed in kohl looking around at Bourbon Street
or bloodshot eyes as clueless as a child
from crying at how much you know so young
or eyes of bliss when you sing onstage
with closed eyes, or tired eyes from those sleepless nights
or eyes that are always asleep that don't see much at all
or sight through one eye from the alley fight one year
eyes like a camera recording your life
looking at everything around you
you're the size of golf balls but so important
a million little eyes, each has its own story

Trapped Inside
Margaret H.

I feel as if the whole world has crashed.
Screaming, crying, the tragic demise
of children, adults, loved ones, strangers.
Many praying for the spared lives.
I see the people, the hatred of those who
committed such a horrible crime.
The families can no longer come together,
beyond what I could have imagined.
In the spite of terror. my sister has died.
She is here in spirit, in my heart
My mother and father, my grandmother and grandfather.
All pushing me towards her lifeless body.
They tell me to pray. I cry. The tears I shed
for many of those whose lives have been lost.
Screaming, crying, the blood that comes
from the bodies around me, insanity of those
who committed such a horrible crime.
The truth lies beneath it all. My world was once
full of love, laughter, and tears of joy.
Now my world is filled of hatred, crying,
tears of blood. Screaming, crying,
together in this loveless world of mine.

Basketball
Ilir J.

Basketball Basketball Basketball
It is a hard sport
Sweaty and smelly sport
Takes a lot of skill to survive

Very rough sport
So hard but still so fun
Without some skill it's torture
Running down the court is exhilarating

All the work pays off at the end
It is a team effort
Running down the court is a breeze
You work hard to become the MVP

Without a team it's hard
Make as many baskets as you can
MVP is what you want to be
Pass the ball to the open person

Shoot the ball and hope to make a lot of baskets
Win a lot of games to make it to the playoffs
Give the ball to whoever's open
In the playoff win all your games

If you win a lot of games you'll make it to the playoffs,
Win all your games in the playoffs you'll go to the
Championship, so try hard to win in the playoffs
Then you can become a champion

After the playoffs, the championship
Basketball Basketball Basketball
Soon you can be a champion
Basketball, it takes a lot of skill to survive

Dancing Days
Audrey K.

Hours I spend
        practicing for perfection.
You watch me
          but you don't approve.
To you it is pointless,
a distraction from school.
I fall, but all you do

is watch me there.
You tell me to give up
and forget about my dreams.
"You should go to school instead."
That's all you ever tell me.
If I was a bird I'd dance
through the winds
and be free to dance
wherever I wish, forever.
I'll accomplish my dreams and
you're going to have to face it.

Fingers
Timothy N.

Some fingers are big, some are purple. I've got fingers
but they're not purple. Fingers help people do things.
Fingers are not evil. They have nails. Here is a story
about fingers—Ryan was sitting in class. He had fingers,
they were purple. That is my story about fingers,
and this is my poem about fingers.

Nightmares
Catherine N.

I step forward as
The doors open,
Showing me my doom,
No solace here.

The doors open,
I walk inside,
No solace here,
In the dark prison.

I walk inside,
In the black tunnels,
In the dark prison,
To await my fate.

In the black tunnels,
I stand amid demons with glowing eyes.
To await my fate
My soul is consumed by them.

I stand amid demons with glowing eyes.
Razors fill their mouths.
My soul is consumed by them,
The demons that haunt me.

Razors fill their mouths.
Pain and anguish imprison me.
The demons that haunt me
Tear at my spirit, my heart.

Pain and anguish imprison me.
I rattle the bars of my dream-cage as beasts
Tear at my spirit, my heart.
Then I wake up screaming.

I rattle the bars of my dream-cage as beasts
I step forward as
I wake up screaming,
Showing me my doom.

Zyad
Alyssa R.

I'm here with my friends talking, rapping and swearing.
Everything is great. I'm a current exchange student
and love my new family. The only thing I dislike
about this place is Bush.

Everything is great. I really like the people.
I speak 6 languages: Native Moroccan, Arabic,
French, Berber, English (Spanish and Polish from my friends).

I really like the people. I miss my family too.
My favorite animals are pigeons and dogs.
I like the Chapelle show and MTV.

I miss my family too. I'm leaving at the end of the year
and leaving my friends behind, but I will never
forget this truly wonderful time.

Formations
Jim T.

The land is trembling, the volcano erupting.
Mountains are showing off their beauty.
An island is forming, the hills are tall.
The plateau is flat, the mesa dry.

The island draws explorers close
and drives tourists away.
The mountains hide the sun from shining.
These are all the geological formations
of the world that keep us going.

Broken Toes
Richard Y.

In the front room I was playing a good game,
soon found out that I would never
be the same. I called my brother,
he didn't come. So I went running, and this blow
went like lightning, knocked my feet numb.

My foot went up, his came down. When all of this
was over my face was a big frown.
Two toes broken, I was rushed to E.R.
but luckily it wasn't very far. My toes were healed,
I was walking again. My toes could now bend.
I really would have hurt my brother if my toes
hadn't healed. Hard to believe.

So Young, Yet So Old
Julia A.

Old and yet new, this world is strange,
with wide range, very strange.
To old bones the world has been seen
and reseen over and over again, the world
has been changed, reformed over and over again.

Once champion on the ballroom dance floor,
now old and retired, it hurts to see faces so tired.
Very hard to see faces so young.

Old and wearied out, yet still the artist I was.
Now I am a bit repetitive, and now all alone

Old bones breaking away, sorrow seen through
the face that once was. Now only the pain shows,
along with the artist and champion ballroom dancer.

Diaper Dispute
Merita B.

You think that you are so cute
But that is something I must dispute.
You think that face can buy me away
But we have to change you everyday.
You think you can persuade me with those eyes
But here is something very wise.
Don't you even think or try
To use those eyes to sob or cry.
Oh my, Oh my, I can't resist
To laugh when you put up your fists.
Oh no, Oh no, you've missed your chance,
For a sweet little kiss would've put me in your hands.
But you can never ever deny
This is why we love you, my sweetie pie.

Milly
Monika D.

When working in the office on a railroad
I lived my life alone. Born in Italy I lived there till I was 7.
All I remember is the sheep and the grapes, chestnuts,
olives that my family grew. I only went to high school.
The best thing I remember was the church in my hometown.
Then I came here to America I was raised
on the West Side of Chicago and lived the rest on East Side.
I've visited France, England and Austria. Now, I'm here
reading books of history and geography, learning
what I can. Not able to walk and not so young here
in this home alone. None of my family is alive anymore.
I'm here sitting in this chair talking to you. I no longer
work at the office by the railroad.

Beethoven
Rachel D.

My life has come and gone like a bolt of lightning,
yet it seemed too fast, so long. Melodies through my head,
I hummed my tragic songs, hear no evil in my ears.
Yet I can almost hear the drops of my tears. I was bitter
to those who ever cared. Children and such I often scared.
How did this ever come to be? This is not the life I wanted
for myself. I've done well all my life. What good is it
without friends, family, or a wife? If I could have another chance
would I change? Would I throw away all of my rage?

Now as I lay me down to sleep I cannot help but weep.
What I've accomplished I did not expect. I just hope
I've gained your respect. I've written music and it was nice.
All I can give you is this advice: Do not let your work
become your life for it becomes as painful
as the cut of a knife. Though I cannot hear what I say
I promise you that you will thank me one day.

Poem
Aleksandra G.

I am the daughter of an engineer. Born on the South Side
of Chicago, grew up and enjoyed the family farm. I spent days
picking strawberries and digging out potatoes on the farm.
Across the street lived a boy I wished to meet. He was my crush,
my first true love. The one I would remember for years to come.
Then I went off to college and left it all behind. I got married
and started a family all of mine. My children grew up
and my life changed. I came to live here at this facility,
and my adventures have come to an end.

My Arms
Kaitlyn H.

O arms of wonder,
    why are you so needed?
Like a warm blanket
    of love you wrap around others
whom you love. It is you
    who connects my hands
with my torso. Without you
    I cannot hold on. Without you
I'd fall down from above.

Life's Unknowingness
Carissa K.

I am obligated to do things as I've always thought,
to live my life in an unfavorable way,
to have irrational friends who are as unpredictable
as any which way the wind will blow,
to not know the future you can never prepare

for the unknown as well as what you know,
to have a penchant for something
you're not quite as sure as you thought before
but why am I saying such bad things
about life? When you only get one chance—

My Penchant
Weronika K.

El viento swirling around full of love and kisses.
El agua from the sky is peaceful and quiet.
The world is all one. There would be no hate,
just love for everyone, no matter what race
they are, or what their culture is. This is what
my penchant means. But instead there are cruel
and evil wraiths hurting each person, making
them do irrational things. El realidad is painful
and full of loneliness. It is dark and has dismayed me.
I only wish I could change the world into what I see.
I wish I could change it into what my penchant means,
so it could be a peaceful place for you and me.

Emil
Paulina L.

Gardening, cooking, doing woodwork, all fun things to do.
Reading books, writing poems, even more enjoyable.
Traveling, and moving, such fun things. These were the moments.
And getting married was the best moment of my life.
These memories are all almost gone now, every single
one of them. Soon the memory of me will be gone too.

Secrets
Tamas N.

Secrets are everywhere
Everywhere you look
There is a secret
That you don't know about

Everywhere you look
You only see
The outer coating
And not the secrets that lie within

You only see
The things that can be seen
You never try to see
What cannot be seen

The things that can be seen
Are wonderful creations
But the things cannot be seen
Are more wonderful than anyone can imagine

522

"Are wonderful creations"
Many people say that about humans
I say that myself and the reason why
Is because they have the most secrets

Vroom! Vroom!
Curtis N.

Vroom! Vroom! The sounds of a race track.
I have raced all my life, but now I have to only love my dog.
January 27, 1935 will forever be my date of birth.
I was born in Chicago where my heart will always stay.
I went to Columbus High School. Many girlfriends I had,
but none to wed for me.

Vroom! Vroom! Demolition cars were also a love.
I made it out alive didn't I? Daytona was almost won by me.
2nd can be so close yet so far. My career was ended
when my leg wore out. I saw many a big crashes,
but fortunately I didn't crash. My name is and always
will be Ken Gunderson. Vroom! Vroom!

Poem
Sophia S.

I was born in Italy, moved here around when Pearl Harbor
was bombed. I've always loved Gone with the Wind,
will never forget about The Wizard of Oz. The best gift
ever was my wedding band. I treasure it, will love it forever,
but will never forget my 20th birthday. This was
the best day of my life. I love Harry James and Christmas.
Chicago is very different from Italy. Back in the day
everything was handmade. Meeting Al Capone
and having my parents buried next to him is also
a nice thing. That has happened to me, but now I am old
and wrinkly. But I will treasure my moments forever.

The Last Lullaby
Marta S.

I open my eyes to the sound of ChiiKii,
my yellow canary chirping over my head.
His song is peaceful, yet strong, coming out
of his little beak, that seems to be less important.
I look out the window and see traffic down the street.
I spot a bright yellow car, Mama, I think. Yet something

523

catches my eye, a plane, how rare. It glides
over the town. After a minute, a long, silver cylinder
drops down from it. At that moment the world stops.
The only sound available to my ears is a loud Swoosh.
It drops down...going slowly...and hits the ground.
But what comes from it is bigger than expected.
As I see a tsunami of smoke and fire I hear
my canary's last lullaby...

Thomas Edison
John W.

What is this light I see coming from this simple sphere?
It awakens the room when there is no light.
It gives energy to me and everyone else.
It could revolutionize the world, bringing light to all.
Look at what I have made. I have helped the world.

There Were Potatoes
Tegan A.

There were potatoes and I was an onion,
and they were eating toothpaste with such
high curios on their heads. Then the carrots and
the grasshoppers came and joined them.

We Lean Forward
Bonnie A.

As we sit and look
through the window
we see a perfect picture.
We are thinking this
could only be a dream.

As we lean forward
to touch it we blink—
nothing happens.
Is nothing there but
the empty window?

We realize that in life
and after death
you might never
realize your
final destination.

524

Heart
Matthew C.

thump thump bump bump goes the heart
tweet tweet beat beat goes the heart
pumping blood away from it, faster faster,
there it goes, running down the street
where is it going nobody knows
it can play piano lift weights
'cause it's strong, without it I would die
it's smarter than the brain and dumber
than the kidney, it is amazing, you all
have one unless you are a robot

World War I for a Polish Man
Andrew C.

It is now 1918, I have been fighting for 2 years.
You think they would have some respect for a 45-year-old
like me, who has six small kids and let him stay home
and not go to war. But the Austrian army doesn't care.
I have been fighting for them because they rule my country.
I have been in battles all over Europe, but my family
only knows of one, a battle in Italy, bullets and grenades
all over the place. Finally it is over, the battle and the War.
We rejoice as we return to Poland, but then an explosion
almost deafens me. It was a grenade, it injured me
greatly. I was taken to a hospital, and now the war
is over and so is my life.

My Books Are My Soul
Amy D.

Friends!
        At least I think you are...
Why do you do this?
            It's a great book! Why do you mock it?
You don't understand...
                to me these books are very important...
They're a part of me now...
            you laugh at them, you laugh at me...
Remember! We were...
            the best of friends.
Don't make it seem
        to me that you're my enemy.
...I know I shouldn't care
            but it hurts to hear what you say.

When I got home, I collapsed
                        and cried to sleep.
Now do you understand?

The Land of Fog
Jake G.

In the land of fog
all the dogs have made their last bark
all the humans have shed their last tear
all the bodies have made their last twitch

In the land of fog
we couldn't solve our problems easily
all the humans have shed their last tear
they should've known to fear

All the dogs have made their last bark
everyone was lost in the dark
all the bodies have made their last twitch
all the light has faded in the dusk

In the land of the fog
why didn't they just dispute it peacefully
all the humans have shed their last tear
they all knew the end was near

All the dogs have made their last bark
one little spark and the whole world came to an end
all the bodies have made their last twitch
the time for our world has past

Children's Crusade
Colleen H.

It all happened so fast. We were all supposed to
be able to walk across to where the priest told us to go
but it didn't turn out that way. Everything went wrong.
It all started when my mother heard of the crusade.
I was in the yard at the time washing the clothes in the river.
She ran outside to tell me about the crusade.
How all the children would be granted passage
across the Mediterranean Sea. My mother,
being a religious woman, sent me, her only daughter,
on a crusade that was stupid and impossible, to me.
The problem was that once we got to the Sea
when I tried to cross with the priest. I was pulled under

and as the water surrounded me all I could think about
was my mother humming her songs while washing the dishes
and my father with his deep wholesome laugh when my mother
would say something foolish. We were all happy then.
But now the happiness rushed out of me as I took
my last breath. I know my mother would be happy
knowing not only did I die for one of her good
Christian causes but also with all that happiness.

Night Valley
Sylwia K.

The valley is quiet in the morning. But at night
it goes bad. It roars and makes the grass shake
from side to side. It makes the sound of lions,
and you should watch out. Snakes slither close by.
One of them hisses along the roar,
and it is getting closer. The slithering goes away.

We Are the Lost
Caitlin K.

We are the lost, the ones forgotten, and this time
the future is ours. It's in our hands. We're the tear
in your eye, the blood in your veins, the beat of your heart.
We're the sweat on your face, the ones that you chased,
the promise that you made. We're the voice in your head,
the lies that you said, the kids that you pushed away, the lost,
the ones forgotten. We've got nothing to lose, together
we stand up tall, we are one.

I Am Jacob P
Jakub K.

I am Jacob P, otherwise known as the metal devil.
I have the power to physically change metal,
without touching it in any way.

My weakness is that I have only a limited amount of power
to create metallic items. My friend Ivo helps me save
Trichydrex City. His enemies are my enemies.

He has two enemies created by Gly the Dark Mage—
Golden Kill and White Shadow. Ivo has control over paper.
He can make it hard as stone or sharp as a knife.

We chose to keep our identities secret so we don't draw
a big crowd wherever we go. Golden Kill is the fastest draw
in the world but he can only use golden guns or else he's gone.

White Shadow can turn light into shadows but for some reason
he never blocked out the sun. Diav the White Mage created us
for one reason: To protect Trichydrex City.

Diav has sacrificed his life in a dual with Gly which ended
in a double death. I will always take care of Golden Kill
And Ivo takes care of White Shadow.

Isthmus
Demetra K.

The smooth shiny oil moving through the tall never ending silver walls
Slowly the oil makes its way to the other end
A huge log floats above the oil
Going down faster than ever to get to its destination
The huge golden fireball sets, at the end of the isthmus
The whole sky illuminates, the shiny silver walls
The log has now reached the end of the isthmus
Everything suddenly gets darker
The only light left shining on the walls is the fireball's light
Which eventually will extinguish itself to be overcome by night

Laura Ingalls Wilder: Memories
Katie L.

I sit down to write down all of my childhood memories.
I pick up the pencil and search my brain all of the memories
come flooding back to me. It's Christmas day. I'm four,
sitting on my Pa's lap, I can smell the turkey Ma is cooking
and see the smoke from Pa's pipe. it seemed as if it were yesterday.

I write about my daughter, Rose, and her adventures.
She reminds me of myself was I was younger, always
getting into mischief, but having fun doing it. It seems
like a blessing how I can remember, almost all of my past.
I feel happy just thinking about sitting on Pa's lap.
It makes me sad knowing he's not here but I know
he would be proud of where I am today

Watching Seven Short Films by the Lumiere Brothers, Paris, 1904
Laird P.

I will forever remember the accounts of tonight.
It began at the theater in Paris. The seats were packed,
 full and buzzing with excitement. We had been desperately awaiting
this presentation of Motion Pictures. Suddenly the room darkened.
The white screen hanging in theater filled with movement.
The screen was full of moving pictures.
I watched with excitement as the film clips played on.
Soon the fun ended and I returned to my home, but I'll always
remember the magical display of film at the theater.

My Easy-Bake Oven
Casey P.

I do so love my Easy-Bake Oven
But oftentimes it acts like a coven
I try to bake, and bake, and bake, and bake
But all I've accomplished is blown up cake
My care has been given, and all of my time
But my masterpiece cake will never, ever shine
My hope is gone, and my cake is popped
My dream has disappeared, it all has stopped
If I try really hard, I'll bake at the drop of a hat
But if I don't, I will feed that cake to my cat
My love for the easy-bake has slowly drifted
But my love for pie has quickly lifted

The Ocean
Jake P.

The ocean—deep hole all over the world,
full of this wet and salty substance
that we are yet surrounded by.

Through this silky water creatures swim
fast and slick. Without making flaws they whoosh
through the water. The mystery is we know

so little about the fish that swim down further
and further toward the middle
of the dark hole of silky water.

Searching
Katie R.

We are searching, searching for a place to start anew,
a place free for all, a place we can call our own.
We continue to search. There are no maps to assist us,
no known address known to man. Yet our instincts
tell us it's out there, somewhere. Where are you,
place that is calm and peaceful, free of worries and safe
from Mother Nature's curses, place of equality, beauty,
and no social classes? A place where one can only flourish.
We've been searching for an eternity, our hopes diminishing.
spirits dwindling, hearts yearning. We are still searching.
Although our bodies have left us our souls continue
to wander, waiting for the day they find the place.
There they can rest and live forever more.

Bonnie
Lindsey R.

I love to go to the movies with friends.
Every time I go I bring tissues, ready to see The Notebook.
The only colors you see me wearing are
black and blue, which are in my superhero costume.

I use my superhero power to fly so
I can go to Canada and fight The Spring.
The Spring is one of my biggest enemies.
He can use his metal springs to destroy my wings.

Other than saving Canada I love to daydream,
especially about my favorite schools.
Another thing is playing the piano.
It has the most beautiful sound.

It's dinnertime
and for dinner I eat lots of bacon.
When it's Friday I have a big smile.
That's when school is over for the weekend.

Outer Space
Sarah T.

As we look towards the right
Our class begins to take flight
We don't know exactly where to go
But we do know that it's some place unknown
As we head higher and higher
We look around and notice fire

530

We quickly put it out
With time spared to look about
We notice that we've reached our destination
We're on a farm or is it a plantation?
We get out of our spaceship
As we get closer to the prize we also get closer to the tip

Then our teacher asks us to open our eyes
As we all look around we notice a surprise
We have not left our desks at all
We haven't even gone to the other side of the wall
We did learn something today
We learned that imagination does have something to say

CHARLES H. WACKER ELEMENTARY SCHOOL
Principal: Valerie Bratton
Teachers: Ms. Johnson, 5th, Ms. Kyles, 4th, Ms. Robinson, 7th

Pam Osbey, Poet in Residence

Pam Osbey is an accomplished vocalist, author, and spoken word artist who has been teaching poetry in the Chicago Public Schools for three and ½ years.   Author of three poetry books and one of the Poetry Center's 2004 Gwendolyn Brooks Poetry Receipents, she continues to work as a freelance writer focusing on health, business, and self-reflective articles. She has performed at ETA Theatre, South Shore Cultural Center, Center for Inner City Studies, and abroad in Wisconsin, St. Louis, Texas, and New York. She has been has been a featured spoken word artist on Artistfirst, The Reading Circle, Power Talk FM, Higher Ground with Jonathan Overby and "The Peoples Station" in Waterloo, IA. In March 2005 she released her third book of poems entitled, "Black Orchids: a journey to mocha."

"It has been extremely rewarding to spend time with the students at Charles Wacker Elementary School. Upon arrival at the school and seeing the lovely photos of poets like Langston Hughes and Maya Angelou on the wall outside Ms. Kyles classroom was a lot of inspiration. But the best inspiration for me is to help the children delve through their emotions as they try to express themselves as poets who can now write free verse, pantoums, cinquains, haikus, poems about their neighborhoods, what colors they love, how they want to overcome obstacles and even more. They are smart, they are loving, and they are awesome human beings who are now poets who have tools available at their fingertips to show the world their creativity and their poetic souls. I wish them nothing but love and peace and that they continue to explore the worlds around them poetically!"

My Lost World
Marsalis A.

My world is in cold.
   Crying for all who discard.
     I try to get out!
But I cross my arms and cry...
Carefully giving out simple invitation.

But I got tired of love.
   So crossing my heart and cry.
     I waited all the day...
But they just didn't come through.
I stayed in the hole trying.

You, Black Child
Sabrina G.

You, Black Child...
whatever you want to be when you grow up,
be it.

You, Black Child..
Don't let nobody interfere you with someone else.

You, Black Child.
Don't let nobody take your beauty away from you.

You, Black Child.
Tell the haters to get on with their life, Black Child.

I Am
Terrance H.

I am a basketball scoring in a hoop.
I am Tracy McGrady shooting half-court.
I am Ricky Williams running in for the touchdown.
I am the color blue shimmering so bright.
I'm like the voice of Usher singing real smooth and nice.
I am like stairs moving higher and higher.
I am shy like the sun hiding behind a cloud at night.
     I am.
     I am. I am.

I Am
Keyahna C.

I am a black woman who reads her diary.
I am the one who you see when you look out your window at night.
I am the stars, the moon and the darkness at night.
I am the one who will grow up to be what I want.
I am the cubicle that hides inside my body.
I am the rain of tears that keeps joyful hope in your eyes.
I am the one who will write a play one day like many powerful writers...
Charles Dickens, William Shakespeare, etcetera.
I waded through the water like many black slaves.
I am the one who will let nothing stand by me.
I am the one who thinks about myself but mostly
I am me.
I choose to be the one with a Bachelor's Degree.
With a savings bond as high as me.
But mostly I am me.

Bishop
Chanel D.

I don't like my neighborhood because people always fight.
But I have fun with my friends and family.
I touch the trees.
I smell the flowers.
I see people and family.
I run freely on my neighborhood.
I like my neighborhood a little bit because I live 7 blocks away from my
best friend Bridget Hill.
My park is a fun place to be at.
The name of my street is Bishop.
My food places are "Eat & Go".

The Song in My House
Briana B.

There is no quiet moments in my house.
The TV is always on.
My Grandma is always yelling.
My brother is always coming in late.
And I'm always eating.

If my grandma is not yelling at me
to read a book or do my homework then she is
watching the Bulls.

If my brother is not coming in late with the car.
He is sleeping or eating.

And if I'm not eating, I'm watching TV with my
Grandma.

There is always something.
Something going on...in my house.
And I love it.

Song in the Dark
Kyle P.

I sing in the dark pitch in a day light outside..but dark in a way.
I sing a good melody and talk as well.
I'm good outside.
I think I can see as well be my shine, I can rhyme.
Can you shine?
I shine, can you?
With me, you will shine.
I will.
We will both shine...
I will be so bad, maybe be glad!
I am like an apple that will never grow, when rain falls, I fall.

Songs in the Ghetto
Lora W.

Songs in the ghetto, what do I see?
A run down apartment abandoned of people.
Here I come only seven years old with some dingy white shorts and a
nappy big puff ball ponytail.
Church is right around the corner from us...popping five crackers all
year long.
Going to the candy store asking for free candy.
Snotty nosed kids wiping their snot on their shirts.
The warning to all the neighborhood.
Kids that they getting ready to shoot.
Throwing rocks at cars and being called bae bae kids.
Getting arrested and you only ten.
Having the new Jordans, it don't matter.
Getting them dirty right after.
Playing the mud, what do you do?
Try to dig deep to try to find the bottom of the earth never do find it
though.
Cry when you getting your hair washed and getting whoopings for
fighting at school.

535

Walking down the street you see no grass.
Tripping over beer bottles.
That's what I see.
And something else..is my pastor's church in the ghetto.
The only black man with a Lexus parked in front of the church.
Crack heads asking anybody if they got a quarter.
That was the life, sho' was nice.
That's what I saw.
Songs in the ghetto.

I Am
Hope C.

I am a double dutch person.
I am the sound of boing..boing of a basketball.
I am a smart black child.
I am a play watching girl.
I am a traveling girl who likes Wisconsin.
I am a blessed little girl who is spoiled by my grandmother and auntie.
I am a special child who have a lot of clothes.

My Mother
Eddie S.

My mother, she took me to a lot of places and she's a beautiful person to me.
She came to the grass and she went to the driveway.
Her body is shaped like a basketball.
I was nine. And she was mine, driving on the highway.
My mother is a welcomed person.
My mother took me to a lot of places.
My mother is beautiful.
My mother is wonderful.
My mother is love to me.
My mother is a thankful person.

Right On: Violence America
Brittany H.

this country might have
 been beauti
      ful of joy
today.
       now here's a lot
of violence.
      thugs is really taking

over today.
        no say.
        no pay.
day after day.
killing and killing.
        keep on shooting
bad /guys.
        crimes taking over our minds.
stop..don't shoot you, violence America!
this country is so bad I
        wish I'll go blind.

The Basketball Game's Lesson
Frazone A.

When I take it to the hole they know it's
going to go in because we in this thing to win.

It's the last quarter of the game.
I'm acting the same.
We down by five we got 2 minutes on the
clock.

The fool tried to block so
I gave him the shake and threw up the fade.

My coach says "its up to you" and like
Mike I got to change my shoes cause...
They out of the game when I
shoot this three.

I'm gonna be in the hall of fame.

Brother To Brother
Jonathan J.

There's a lot of things going on out here.
We got to stick together.
If nobody wants to be our friends, so what?
That's why we stay together.
Some people ain't got their brothers, but I got you.
If we stay together nothing can tear us through.
We supposed to stick together forever.
Don't let nobody tear us apart.
I was always there from the start.
If we stay together nothing can tear us through.
You got me and I got you.

The Historic Blue
Johnell W.

Slave passed down generation
to generation.
People die.
People raped.
People killed by idiots
of hell like Mussolini,
Adolf Hitler and the assassins of black
leaders and president like John Willie Booth,
assassin of Abraham Lincoln and James Earl
Ray, assassin of Martin Luther King.
The deaths of our black leaders are a resemblance
of blues.

I, Will, Be America
Jade W.

I, am the black, beauty of America,
who stands for her country,
when, trouble comes.
I'm here for my America,
I, am, the center of America,
who stands for the rights,
because, I love my America.
No, I, am America!

I, Too, Can't Be American
Roy B.

I, am, the shadow of America.
They send me in the dark, but I am the light.
I will show America.
I will be in the light tomorrow,
how dare them tell me to go in the shadow
of my creation.

I, too, am America.

Red/White/Blue
David C.

Red is an American color.
Red is my blood which shows my American way.
Red is a rose who lived in the ground.

White is a paper, I write my work on.
White is the snow, I like to play in to make a snowman.

Blue is the ocean that have fish in it.
Blue is the sky, when I look up.
The colors are red, white, blue ...the flag!

Blue, Pink and Purple
Siesha W.

Blue is the color of my friend's jacket.
Blue is like my wall.
   It is Dark Blue, Lite Blue and my
   baby cousin's eyes.

Pink is a pretty flamingo.
Pink is a heart.
   Pink is like my headband.
   Pink is like me.

Purple is my heart.
Purple is my purple outfit with my shoe to match.
Purple is like a purple poster board.

The Song of Peace
Glorielle W.

The song of peace is like listening to palm trees.
The song of peace is like waking up to Blue Jays sing.
The song of peace is like listening to David in the Bible days.
Listening to him play the harp while getting a massage.
The song of peace is like the violin and the chello played in
harmony.
The song of peace.
That's what the song of peace is to me.

Poetry Is
A Fourth Grade Group Poem

Poetry is All of Us
   Poetry is a colorful rainbow.
   Poetry is helping you fly in the sky.
   Poetry is a colorful bird in the sky.
   Poetry is love and happiness.
   Poetry is love of soul and spirit.
Poetry Feels Good to Us.

Poetry makes me feel happy.
Poetry is like a chocolate ice cream.
Poetry is a dream of faith.
Poetry is something that educates us
to learn better in writing.
Poetry is Me.
Poetry is the sun in the sky when I look at it it makes me cry.
Poetry is a rhyme that makes me shy.
Poetry is the clouds in the sky.
Poetry is like inspiration to my soul.
What Do You Think Poetry Is?
Poetry is something that rhymes.
Poetry is sometimes with feelings for others.
Poetry makes me feel good inside or bad.
Poetry lifts me up when I have bad days.
Poetry is something that makes me feel good.
Poetry Is a Time Of Life.
Poetry is everything to us.

Poetry is something that makes you feel good at
what you do.
Poetry is the day light in the sky.
Poetry is like the green.
Like the grass!
Poetry is sunshine in my mind that runs
through all the time.

Poetry Is
A Fifth Grade Group Poem

Poetry is like a beautiful butterfly.
Poetry is like a balloon flying in the sky.
Poetry is an emotional feeling written on paper.
Poetry is like a beautiful bird flying in the sky.
Poetry is my soul.

Poetry is me.
Poetry is a soft cloud.
Poetry is soft as a fluffy pillow.
Poetry is my heart.
Poetry is everything nice.
Poetry is like a day in the park.
Poetry is like me winning a basketball game.
Poetry is like Christmas.
Poetry is like thick clouds in the air.
Poetry is a river flowing down the stream.

For relaxation..
Poetry is like a toy.
Poetry is like a river flowing down the
stream in the spring.
Poetry is soothing just like the
river flow.

Poetry is different things to us.

Poetry to me is like color in words.
Poetry to me is like rhythm and music.
Poetry is beautiful but sometimes is not my thing.
Poetry is my heart and soul.
I am the queen of poetry!

Poetry is like telling how you
really feel.
Poetry is like sunshine on one side
of the street and rainbow on the other.
Poetry is like your expressing
feelings about someone.
And to wrap it all up, poetry
is like sunshine on a cool summer day.
Poetry is love all around town and poetry is
like family.
Last but not least...poetry is like beautiful
colors so beautiful and bright.
Poetry is the best!

Different Colors of Poetry
A Seventh Grade Group Poem

Poetry is like waves in the ocean.
It rises with affection.
Poetry is like parts of speech.
You can express all your thoughts and feelings.
Words..and thoughts, going through your mind.
Nouns, adjectives, and rhymes!
It makes me want to scream and makes
me want to shout.
It's what you eat, think and breathe.
Poetry is in Imagination.
Poetry is like talking to a best friend.
Never being able to get out of a deep conversation.
Poetry is like deep strong love.
What poetry means to us?
It's something that is hard to turn down.
It's like a book for a good friend.

Poetry is your heart and soul.
Poetry is important in many ways.
Poetry makes your body cry out.
It's like Ice Cream, it feels so good.
Poetry is like a new relationship.
Full of excitement and drama.
Makes you cry, laugh, at the same time.
Like Gold, Silver, Chocolate and Vanilla...
All mixed together, that's poetry to me.
Like a parade of different colors, races,
different religions, and different feelings – full of life
and fun and opportunities.
Poetry is a way of life.
May lift your spirits and bring you back down.
Poetry is me.
Poetry.
Poetry.
Poetry.
Different colors of poetry.

A Song In My Body and Soul
Niktya W.

As I slither into my soul.
Its like a big out going bowl.
The tune of my body is cold and hard.
Its so beautiful like a decorated card.

Impossible, can you see it?
I show power but just a little bit.
My soul can fly without any wings.
It takes me many places and I see many things.
So what, my body is wide and outstanding?
But at least I keep my soul and body...
instead of letting it strand.

Why is my soul one of a kind?
But it can see plus use its eyes and it is not blind.
Why is my body weak?
It can find things what it wants to seek.
I am my body and soul.
Cuz I want to be a long pole.
That stretches across the world and builds a beautiful soul.
I am my song in my body and soul.

Game Time
Kevin H.

Shoot ball. Time running out. Try to go pass half-court.
Men own defense trying to steal. Fake the shot, make them jump.
Cross them over. Shoot it! Bounce it!   People screaming.   Now take
the shot. Screaming! Winning. I pop a three. I am in a surprise. I hit it
now. I'm #1! So we won the playoffs. So we did good. It's great!

Song of Drums
Raymond C.

It's the sound of the drums...

Bass.
Symbols.
Snares.
Tenors.
Tom. Toms.
It's the sound of the drums...

The black drummers in my ear.
Oh it's the drumlines and congos.
I love the songs of the drums.
You know how Salem Baptist Church kept me with drums...

I love the songs of the drums.

I Rise
Leodis S.

I rise like a rose bloom
through the month, I rise.
Like a cloudy fog
and floating over the water, I rise.
Like someone who has fallen, I rise.
Like smoke in a burning house, I rise.
Like an airplane when it takes off, I rise.
Like birds flying south for the winter, I rise.
Like a balloon floating softly in the air, I rise.
When I rise high enough I never come back down.

I'll Rise
Doris A.

I didn't want to get up today.
Cause of my bad grades.
But still I rise.
So you may see I am in a bad mood
today.
But ha!
Stay by me and see all the things...you may go through.
But still I rise.
No matter what I may go through.
Through thick and thin, I will rise and please
believe me when I say no matter what you may put
me through.
D.M.A is never putting her head down.
I will have my head up until it's time for me to go away.
So you already know that I will rise and believe me when I say
I will rise. Yep, I'll rise.

I Am
Julian M.

I am a joyful singer who loves music.
I am a boy of journeys who can't be found.
I am the sun who shines over all.
I am a guy of pain but constantly uplifting.
I am a song of rhythm that you could dance to all night.
I am a brother/brotherfriend/shoulder who will pick you up when you fall.
I give all it takes to make it to the top.
I am like no one who loves and won't stop.
I am a songwriter who loves different types of music.
I am an animal of funny who always make you laugh.
I am a person you will see one day on TV.
I am Julian.

WALTER PAYTON COLLEGE PREPARATORY HIGH SCHOOL
Principal: Gail Ward
Teachers: Ms. Murphy, Ms. Imrem

Cecilia Pinto, Poet in Residence

Cecilia Pinto received her B.A. in creative writing from Knox College and her M.F.A. in writing from the School of the Art Institute. Her poetry and prose have appeared in various journals including *Quarter After Eight, Fence* and *Rhino*. She was awarded first prize in Permafrost's 2002 haiku contest and was the winner of the *Esquire Magazine* prize in short fiction in 2000.

It's been an amazing year at Payton. Students rose admirably to the challenge of reading and re-writing Lord Byron as well as impressing me with their heartfelt spoken word and overall commitment to writing. I couldn't ask for better students.

Ode to My Violin
Casey J.

From the quiet dawn
To the depths of the night
You wait for me,
Your serene figure at rest.
You are a well
Waiting to be siphoned,
And when you are your body aches,
And a universe of emotion
Pours out of your soul
And mine.
You are the oak and spruce
In the fragrant moments
After rain,
And the scent of our draws me
Closer.
I am lured to you,
As the most beautiful shell
Finds comfort in the molding caress
Of soft sand on a wet beach.
The vision of those striking strands of silver
Against a backdrop of slender midnight,
And then rich earthiness,
Makes me want to embrace you even more.
You are as magnificent
As the spark that a master artist sees
Ere he is inspired to paint his first masterpiece,
And as secret
As the most hidden part of a glorious blooming flower
Or a clandestine glance.
Your serenades have forever seized my core,
And it means so much more
Because I know it takes both of us
To croon them
So while you slumber
Know that I dream
About when I can once again
take you in my arms
To play.

I see the night sky
Juan M. S.

The sky is bright and full of stars.
The night sky is beautiful.
Maybe there is something really beautiful in the sky

546

Maybe a comet just passed by.
Maybe something else just passed by.
Maybe another plane hit another tower.
It is a beautiful night, a perfect night.

Stopped Motion
Roberto C.

I stopped running when I saw,
A car pass through the stoplight.
The green turning to yellow,
the yellow turning to green.
The car stopping me from going ahead.
The reckless driver who dropped my jaw,
Made me stare in disbelief how he broke the law.
No more motion from my waist to my feet,
Made me feel the driver needed to be beat.
I was so mad, but then the light turned green,
And at that moment, I forgot what I saw,
And continued to run.

Stare Pt. II
Whitnee D.

I know it's wrong to look this long
But I long for you to look at me
If you look in my eyes you'd see a picture book
You'd see how good we could be
Or maybe it's me who should come talk to you, introduce myself
But I wouldn't know what to do with myself being so close
So I sit here glaring and staring at you
Hoping you'll look in my eyes and realize that though
I fantasize about you and me
I know my stare should become a dream come true
The truth is in my eyes and with my stare
So I'll keep staring at you
Until our eyes meet
And our souls greet
Telling you about me.

Untitled
Michael O.

I am waiting for a promised land
So grand, where whites and blacks live with the Taliban.

I want and wait for the world
To open the door
That leads to so much more
Where everyone is equal.

And no one is more equal than another.
But we are family,
And sign with Sisters and Brothers
With love like no other.

Time ticks until the land becomes one where I can be me
Where the U.S. isn't the best, but like the rest.
Where it is really the home of the brave, and land of the free.

Untitled
JanArt W.

Up the road
I can't see my future
I am worried.

I don't know
if I will be here
or gone and buried.

I don't know if my dreams will come true
or will they all go away just like poof...

I can tell you what I wanna be
but skip that
cuz only God knows if my goals is gonna be
a reality
or a fatality, the difference between joy & agony
and I try to think ahead
but Momma always said,
don't count unhatched eggs

I got a lot of dreams in the back of my mind
but I can only live life one day at a time.

Sonnet
Michael F.

Be not with me but always for me
Gaze upon my soul and then paint its worth
Call to the forefront what you can't see
Belong to me, and none other since birth.

Play upon my minds strings
Play with freed fire fingers
One of your sweetest melodies
Until life has stolen voice from singers

Look to the sky as my tears come down
Look to the sea to where desire sinks deeper
Look to the hills and listen for the sound
A slight whisper will whimper weaker

Made for one purpose, and one only
To be with you, or else live lonely.

Mervyn
Susie S.

Mervyn was my grandfather's name; it suggests sophistication and respect, he wasn't particularly either.
He told us that he served in a lot of wars, like the war of 1812 and the Revolutionary War. But that would make him like a million. My mother says not to believe him, he's just teasing. That was a long time ago; he's dead now.
There were mice living under his refrigerator, my mother said we should give him one of our cats, but I think she was joking. I'm assuming he killed them because they're not there anymore. The house is no longer in the family's possession. We get all his mail.
At his funeral there was a board with pictures of him and his family. There were a lot of pictures of us, my cousin told me that was only because my mother was the one that put it together, but actually my aunt did. I don't want anymore pictures of me taken so when I die my family won't be able to make one of those boards.
When I grow into my grandfather I hope to be sophisticated like he wasn't.
When I'm a Mervyn I'm going to be a very reputable old man.

Oreo
Ryan A. S.

Redefinition?
Of What?
Priss? No. Blonde? Maybe.
OREO? That's the one.
So, let me get this straight.
An OREO is someone who is black on the outside, but white on the inside.
Well I guess I'm an "uh-oh" OREO.
Cuz I'm white on the outside, but I'm still black on the inside.

Through and Through.
But what does it mean to be Black?
To speak with good grammar skills?
To respond to words like Tramp and Ho?
I don't think so.
Black.
The blending of all colors.
That's not me.
I'm the blending of many races.
Race.
Please mark your Race/Ethnicity.
African-American, White, Native American or other.
Pick ONE.
Should I deny myself MY culture because you need to know my race?
Should I be classified as something other than MYSELF?
Can you redefine me by the color of my skin?
Can you tell what countries I'm form?
You can try.
Mainly "Black" and Mainly "White"
I guess I'm gray.
That or an OREO is what you want me to be.
Well, I'm not some dinky OREO.
Not a snobby "half-breed" white girl.
Not some black wannabe "ghetto" trash.
I'm not that cookie you dunk in white or chocolate milk.
Screw the OREO.
I'm a MILANO wafer.
I'm above your petty classifications.
You can take your OREOs and kiss my little "Black and "White" butt goodbye.
Because you aren't worthy of my classifications.
People.
Human.
Real.
GONE.

My Mind's Sea
Joi W.

The sea in my mind was thrashing to and from
Thoughts swirling for reasons I did not know.
Waves of distress crashed upon my sanity's shore
And my peace of mind was drowned suddenly to be no more.
The murky foam of pain clouded the water's pure blue hue,
Causing my common sense to be lost beyond view.
The wonderful sunset that once shown its rays upon my sea
Was hidden behind clouds never for me to believe.

Perspective or One Day at Mikva Club
Jacob D.

What stresses you out, and gets you down?
This was the question the teacher laid down

I've got too much homework
said one
tired of being a clerk said another
my parents bother me
said a third
I really hate my little brother

We continued to move around the circle

My friend doesn't understand me
I'm failing math
I feel like my boyfriend
treats me like trash

This went on for awhile
then came the boy with the placid smile

And I'd understood
this world stresses us out far more than it should
I was glad it would be over soon
I mean I had homework to do

Alright, here he goes, beneath a hum

He says:
My cousin got shot yesterday
I know who killed him
and there's nothing I can do.

These words cut right through

I was up now
feeling reflective
all I could say was
this put things in
Perspective.

Emily Calvo, Poet in Residence

As a poet, Calvo teaches poetry at the Young Women's Leadership Charter School in Chicago. Her poetry has been published by the *Oyez Review* (Roosevelt University Press), *Colere* (Coe College, Cedar Rapids, IA) and *Hammers* (Doublestar). In 1999 and 2003, her poetic interests and marketing expertise won her the position of marketing/public relations director for the National Poetry Slam Championship, a national competition between more than 200 poets from 48 cities which was held in Chicago, which attracted local as well as national media attention from *60 Minutes* and *The New York Times*.

A full-time, freelance writer and published author, Calvo and her co-author's first book, *How to Succeed in Advertising When All You Have Is Talent* (NTC Publishing, 1994) featured interviews with 13 of the country's top advertising creative and was used in numerous universities. Her second book, *25 Words or Less... How to Write Like a Pro to Find That Special Someone Through Personal Ads* (NTC/Contemporary Books, 1998), applies the principles of advertising to help single people use the personals more effectively. Other recent titles include *First Comes Love*, and gift books that include *Thought-A-Day Mothers, Thought-A-Day Daughters* and *Scooby-Doo Look & Find* (Publications International, Ltd.). Calvo has a B.A. in Industrial Psychology from Mundelein College of Loyola University in Chicago.

Reminiscence
Caress B.

Remnants of childhood are drifting away.
My memories consist of
b-days, beatdowns, and new,
very new becomings.

Bubbles from the bathtub
tickling my nose, make such
a funny sound once contacted.

I was as happy as a new
born baby, but like a mouse in a hole.

I am put together with all kinds of joy that my
mother inhales as I become more mature.
I am the blue sapphire that
wraps this Sagittarius.

Democracy/Hypocrisy
Kate S.

Democracy is nothing
    But an illusion
A comforting word
In a world of confusion.

From where we stand
In a torrent of despair
We look to democracy
A government who will care.

Founded on hope
Paired with freedom
Focused on people
A glorified idea
That cannot work,
Will not work,
And still, we believe.

It's So Hard...
Seville S.

My blood rushed through my veins
like rushing water
on a stormy night
As tears flowed down my eyes.

A loud silence surrounded me
like a million man army
Everything is moving in slow motion
like a calm and smooth ocean.

Hearing the words that I didn't want
to be true
I try to deny them
As I look at the person
I wasn't ready to say "goodbye."

My Life
Myeesha P.

The Ghetto is where I'm from.
Hood reds and gang lights.
Hearing shots though the night.
Crying because of a dangerous life.
That is right.
I've gotta get through the lights.
Pushing through waves, breathing in fire.
I'm doing good, I have
dreams and desires to succeed in life.
See, I don't know what people
see when they look at me.
Nice, a live healthy growing tree.
No one really knows the true me.
What I've been through, what I've seen.
I guess I've been lying
by not telling at all.

Cool and Confused
Nekita T.

T-bees, white 'tees, K-Swiss
The catch of the mist
She sees herself an image of distress
Keep Keepin' Korrect
These nigga'z can't bring me down
State and Lake, Belmont Avenue
What 'eva you got she already knew
I step up to keep steppin' strong
Late night on the block just kickin' back
Man this marijuana sends blow contacts
But keepin' on the
Pace to pace In the race
Yeah, she's the cool smart girl.

from Damaris
Damaris W.

I was born a child
In disguise
I am now free
To show who I really am
My name is Damaris
Strong and beautiful
Smart and intelligent
Privileged, and proud
I am made to succeed
Never to fail
I am on earth
Independent
Not dependant
I was a child born
With always being told "no"
Now I can hold my head up high
And make my own choices
Be proud of who I am.

Untitled
Charity T.

Me
My life
My time
My rhyme

I feel like I'm stuck in time, back in the 9
trying so hard to move forward
but I keep getting pulled back
and back
further and further
I'm stuck in quick sand
and all I need is a hand.

Falling, I'm falling and I can't get up.
I'm sinking like an anchor sinks to the
bottom.

Me
My life
My time
My rhyme

Take me away from classrooms and notes,
the insanity of hope.
Take me away, away in a boat.

Where I Wanna Go?
Adrienne F.

A place I wanna go,
but I just don't know.
All the people say it ain't so.
Running around trying to find a way to get out of this place.

Growing in a place I thought I would always stay.
Come to find out my place is gone
Now where can I turn?
To the streets is where —it's that now, you know.
Now come of find out there is somewhere to go.
It's not the streets after all you see
Now the poem will end to the rhythm of the beat.

Untitled
Sherrell S.

Sometimes people try to be cool,
put other people down,
and that's not right.
To start a fight,
to make yourself
look and feel good.
Tough.
People always get hurt.
Being popular
isn't always good for you,
you can hurt others feelings
and not even know it.

Untitled
Tennae W.

You can't bring me down,
I'll never turn around and frown.
It's not my fault
you're upside down
and I got my feet
pinned to the ground.

556

You can't hurt my strong
self-esteem.
I know what I want.
I know where I want to be.
I see my dreams.
I dream what I see.

Over and over,
I try to tell you that you don't
have to be my friend.
I don't need you to be with
me to the end.

Untitled
Amanda P.

I think people try to be "cool"
by trying to fit in. If they
feel like they want to hang out
with a group of people that are
popular or whatever, they will
start doing what the group
does, which could be anything.
Stealing, smoking, drinking, etc…
People try to look and
act cool by like, pretending they
like a certain type of music
just because they want to.

Cheesecake
Jonnice C.

Creamy triangle,
white layered sauce.
Taste so sweet, yet a slight bitterness.
Big, red, juicy fireball on the top,
covered with a bloody red, sweet cherry flavor.
Crust so thick and curvy.
Tastes so good
               it melts in your mouth.

Untitled
Dominique G.

To be so cool,
they try to fit in but they can't.

They talk about other people, they
try to fight other people
to see what their friends say,
but at the same time the
people you try to fit in with
are talking about you.
How stupid you are,
"We just using her."
"She a hoe."
But you don't care what they say
because you wanna be popular,
you want people to see you.
At the end you're tired—
You don't wanna be popular no more
'cuz your friends are talking about you.
That's why you should be yourself
and stay yourself.

Mom
Chanel M.

It starts with a phone call from friends anytime
"Chanel, only twenty minutes on the phone."
Sometimes I don't even bother to say anything
"Chanel, take out the trash and no backtalk at home."
"Chanel, do the laundry, wash the dishes, and finally
            GET OFF THE PHONE.
Where's your sister? Do you hear her starting a fight?
Did she do her homework? Take a bath."
"Yes, Mom. I'll be there in a minute. I have to get my might."
The voices and comments are so annoying
I wonder does she do this on purpose?
How much can a teen take?
Is she evil on purpose?

Still I love her and that can never change
She is beautiful in every way like every annoying mom.

Teen Years
Ahna H.

Everyone tells you,
they're the best years of your life.
The thing they don't tell you,
is they are all full of strife.
From a child to a teen,
in less then a year.

It's a lot to deal with,
you have to grow up fast.

As a child you're free,
as a teen you feel locked up.
A child has no worries,
A teen has a lot.

You learn the meaning of love,
you discover broken hearts.
The worries of being accepted,
are the hardest part of all.

What's the "best"
about these years.
When as a teen,
you live in fear.

Chocolate Chip Cookie
Tennae W.

A black man with blackheads on his face.
There is a big black animal burning in the oven.
A tremendous smell in the bakery.
A rumbling in your tummy.
Mrs. Field's specialty,
best with ice cream.
Eat after your meal.

Silver Chain
Kate S.

Thread of metal.
Precious piping.
Strand of Grandmother's hair.
Silver snake.
Metallic veins.
Cherished binding.
Sterling moonbeam.
Shining collar.
Winding river.
Silver vine.

Cherries
Sarah L.

Rudolph's bright red nose.
The rubber bouncy ball.
A big red zit, with a small pit.
A split hairball.
Big bright earrings with the red shine.
The color of crime.
It's my time.
It's the cherries rhyme.

Honey
Shardey W.

Nature glue.
Auntie Mama syrup.
Flavor to chicken.
The spice for tea.
The answer in milk for a cold.
The help in popyeas.
The topping for butter bake biscuits.
The dessert for desire.
The dream for a bear.
The sweetest temptation of life.

from Why Me??????
Kirsten B.

I often think about us and the way it used to be
then I say, "Why me?"
I sit looking at our pictures on my dresser
then I say "Why me?"
Caught up in this love triangle,
"Why me?"
Sitting here loving you, loving me, loving us, loving we.
Then I say "Why me?"
Why was I so foolish?
I can't believe you could pressure me to do this.
Well, I guess time will tell, and love will see
how much, in fact, you really love me.
But, right now that's all too late.

Untitled
Whitney S.

The man is a telescope.
The woman is a star,
lost in space waiting to be found
before her light slowly fades away.
Searching for a way out,
loving escape.
So as he looks around not knowing
that he found his treasure
that will give him
a satisfactory pleasure.

Untitled
Dominique C.

The man is a piece of paper
The woman is a pen
She talks to him
Lets him know what's on her mind
The words of her thoughts
are written all over him.

Their ink sinks into the pores
of his skin
too deep.
Penetrates his soul,
becomes a part of him
that he will never let go.
That's the poison of her love.

Untitled
Loreal S.

The man is a road, dark and smooth.
The woman is a luxury car
who gets to ride on the road.
He is like a smooth rock.
She is the pond that he gets into.

He is the hat
She is the gloves – or even the scarf.
They are made for each other.
You can't have one
without the other.

from They Need to Break Free
Danielle G.

He is the puppet master
and she is his puppet

as he pulls the strings
she follows
does what she's told
says what he's thinking
but what is she thinking?

She keeps her
thoughts to herself
afraid to speak
she might say
something wrong

He's draining her life
the light in her smile
is fading
                stand up on your own two feet.

Like a butterfly
trapped in a cocoon
break free.
Show how beautiful you can be.

Sister
Ahna H., Kendra P., Francesca S. and Carla S.

My sister asking for money
can't pay the last phone bill
gas off, house cold
kids crying, not passing
momma selling
struggling to become successful
life is hard
nothing ever goes your way
It's like…what's the point of even living another day.
Sister, sister, sister, sister.

Something You Would Never Want to Forget
Kai P.

This summer was our summer.
Our summer of fun!
Hanging out on the quad, laying underneath the trees.

Dancing at the Club.
Burping up a storm.
Playing "Never Have I Ever"
Ditching you for other people.
It was all my fault.

Our times in New England
"Help me, I'm stuck"
and in New York—
I'm Moving Out"
also in Rhode Island
"Do you like the Texas accent?"

Our times dining at Gourmet Heaven
You eating your chicken nuggets
Me eating a Panini and my Jones Soda
Anthropology Class
Drinking Red Bull and going to Zoe's café.

from The Pain
Ashley D.

The pain, my heart sank.
I felt like I couldn't move on.
There I was sitting in the front room
teaching my cousin mathematics
while my grandmother lay dead
riding with the paramedics...
So now I'm stuck with the
it will be alrights and it will be OKs
So I stand and say I will see her another day
but it still doesn't take away the anger and
take away the fright
I doesn't make me feel better and I still think about
it all night...

Untitled
Angelica M.

Buffalo soldiers fought every day
they fought for the slaves
made many plans
thought of different things
just to save human beings
never gave up
always put up a fight
just so these people could see the light.

The sight of those people
being treated so bad
makes me want to cry
makes me sad.

Now I am glad to see
these people free
thanks to the soldiers
that fought endlessly.

Birdlike
Angela S.

When I think about birds, I think about you
About your black eyes and your black as dirt body
and the other things that are so dark about you.
As a child you were so dumb and naughty
Now you just remind me of the bottom of my shoe
With gum and dirt in it
Now guess what, I can step all over you?
When I look in your eyes, I see a bit
'Cuz you are burning up inside
You remind me of a old car
Nothing but rust on the outside
Your body reminds me of tar
So dark and black
You remind me of a bird that is black.

Untitled
Dana J.

What people do to think they are cool
is wrong. They should be their own self.
Being somebody you're not is hard because
a lot of people will look at you differently.

Then when they grow up, say about
10 or 15 years, they are not gonna know
who they are. To me I think they
look like fools and clowns. They don't
know what's ahead of them in life
and they will end up being nobodies
if they spend their whole life trying
to fit in.
You shouldn't care.

What We Want to Be
Erica H., Jasmine B., Janita W. and Brandi L.

Sitting here alone thinking about this crew
the career I chose I already knew...

knew what was happening to these people ahead
This group of people I'm helping...my mind is dead
One girl once abused
by her mother who left no clues

The problems I hear are so damn bad
This first day of work is making me mad
mad of love for people who have no hope
helping people with their problems is no joke
coming home from many sessions today
I'm a psychiatrist and this is my career, I say.

Bad Hair Day
Alex M.

Girl came in looking horrified
Man, if I were her, I'd sure cry.
Sat down in my seat and was prepared --
she was ready for me to do her hair.
Washed and blow-dried, pumps 'n curls
Once she walked out first word
I heard was, "damn girl"

Next Vicki, always a major mistake
her hair looked like peach fuzz and a fruit cake.
Gave her a perm with a straw set
Left out sayin' "Get it wet."
Now the grand finale ...it was Noel
All I can say is the girl had been through hell.
Gave her an all-up twist
Boy walked up and she said, "Boy you're dismissed."

Finally, I'm done
I made five hundred and one
Tomorrow is a new day
time for gossip and crazy ways.

My job is crazy, but fun
especially when I graduated with a perfect bun.

The Fun of Art
Angela H.

The fun of art
Never being apart
from what I love to do best
like a bird cooped up in its nest.

Being able to express
feelings through pictures
Putting colors together
Making good mixtures

The room with my computer and drawing board
Drawing houses making them look hot
I can draw it right now
on the spot.

Untitled
Diedre H.

I remember my first love
He was sent from above
Hairy and white all over
I never knew I'd have so much love for you.
You gave me my heart
Like cupid, with a dart.
I miss you to death, my pride and joy
like a child with his favorite toy.

The day you died
a piece of me left with you.
August 7, that day hurts
It seems to me to be the worst.
I love you still even though it hurts,
the best dog ever.

Untitled
Whitney H.

What I would like to remember
is also everything I am bound to forget
all the sleepovers, pillow-fights and good times
will be replaced by…everything else.

The adult life in place of adolescence
worrying about jobs, meetings and interviews
instead of girl talk about boys we loved.

And love?
You'll still never figure it out
no matter how much you try
How many times you're in and out of love

Will I remember you in 20 years?
Will I remember the silly fights and arguments
or the fun times?

The answer is simple:
The things I would like to remember are
the things I'll never forget.

People

Larry O. Dean
2004 Recipient of the *Hands on Stanzas* Gwendolyn Brooks Prize

Pam Osbey
2004 Recipient of the *Hands on Stanzas* Gwendolyn Brooks Prize

Guy Villa
Book Cover Designer

The Poetry Center Staff 2004-2005

Kenneth Clarke
Executive Director

Shirley Stephenson
Development Director

Michelle Taransky
Programs Coordinator

Hands on Stanzas ^{sm}

Program Overview

Schools Receive:

Poets-in-Residence: Each 20-week residency provides weekly instruction for three classes, or approximately 90-100 students, as well as special projects that have a school-wide impact.
Collaboration: *Hands on Stanzas* is designed to fit seamlessly into school curriculum goals.
Books: Each participating school receives a copy of the *Hands on Stanzas Anthology of Poetry*.
Special projects: Examples of school-wide *Hands on Stanzas* projects include: a school poetry magazine, poetry performances, a permanent *Galería de Poesía*, the 'Longest Poem in the World' project, after-school poetry clubs, traveling poetry readings and others.

Students Receive:

Communication tools: Writing for self-expression motivates students to explore how words can work to convey their own thoughts, visions and emotions. Vocabularies grow, imaginations spark, and books are read.
Spotlight: Students share their work on stage in the Ballroom of the School of the Art Institute at annual All Schools Readings. These readings bring together students from around the city.
Access to the arts: "Before *Hands on Stanzas,* I thought poetry was only for rich people and fancy people. Now I think poetry is for all kinds of people." -6th grade *Hands on Stanzas* student
Recognition: Each year, students have the opportunity to be published in the *Hands on Stanzas Anthology of Poetry* and receive one free copy of the book.
Inspiration: "Reading poetry makes me feel like what the writer wrote was so great, I want to do it, too." -6th grade *Hands on Stanzas* student

570

Poets-in-Residence Receive:

Support: Poetry Center staff regularly visit classrooms and assist with arrangements between schools and poets-in-residence.

Professional development: Two intensive workshops conducted by leaders in the field are provided each year, as well as feedback and brainstorming sessions.

Stipends: Chicago poets obtain employment in their field, while making a positive impact on the city's most important resource—its youth.

Resources: Books about creative writing instruction are provided to each Poet in Residence.

Recognition: Each year the *Gwendolyn Brooks Hands on Stanzas Award* provides $1,000 in cash awards to poets-in-residence of distinction.

Hands on Stanzas^{sm} **Sponsorship**

When you give to *Hands on Stanzas,* you're making an investment in the future, helping build stronger, more creative communities in which all members have a voice. The impact of *Hands on Stanzas* extends beyond the reading and writing of poetry to encompass increased student literacy, access to the arts, enthusiasm and academic confidence.

Hands on Stanzas offers Chicago Public School students access to a type of literary instruction they might otherwise never encounter, inspiring their curiosity and providing the tools they need to change the course of their academic—and perhaps even professional—careers.

Become a *Hands on Stanzas*[sm] Sponsor:

- *Make a difference in the lives of Chicago youth*
- *Visit your poet in action in the classroom*
- *Receive invitations to special readings given by students in your classes*

$5,000 funds one 20-week residency in a Chicago Public School

$1,000 funds four weeks of instruction and helps The Poetry Center provide residencies to under-resourced schools

$500 covers the cost of coordinating All School Readings for young poets from around the city

$250 helps fund a portion of the *Hands on Stanzas Anthology of Poetry,* which honors the creative voices of Chicago youth

$50 assists in the purchase of needed resource materials for poetry residencies

The Poetry Center actively fundraises for *Hands on Stanzas.* Any contribution provided by schools allows us to serve more students.

Call 312.899.1229 to make a gift or receive more information.

The Poetry Center is a tax-exempt organization under the laws of the United States. All gifts are tax-deductible.

How to Order Extra Copies:

Extra copies of
The Poetry Center's

Hands on Stanzas ^{sm}

2004-2005 Anthology of Poetry

are available for you to give as gifts to friends and loved ones
or for placing in your library for the benefit of young poets.

To purchase, call 312.899.1229
or send an e-mail to info@poetrycenter.org

Copies are also available at www.amazon.com

$10 each, plus tax and shipping.

VISA and MasterCard accepted.